T0301394

30 Years of Transition in Europe

30 Years of Transition in Europe

Looking Back and Looking Beyond in CESEE Countries

Edited by

Robert Holzmann

Governor, Oesterreichische Nationalbank, Austria

Doris Ritzberger-Grünwald

Director, Oesterreichische Nationalbank, Austria

Helene Schuberth

Head of Division, Oesterreichische Nationalbank, Austria

PUBLISHED IN ASSOCIATION WITH
OESTERREICHISCHE NATIONALBANK, AUSTRIA

 Edward Elgar
PUBLISHING

Cheltenham, UK • Northampton, MA, USA

Published by
Edward Elgar Publishing Limited
The Lypiatts
15 Lansdown Road
Cheltenham
Glos GL50 2JA
UK

Edward Elgar Publishing, Inc.
William Pratt House
9 Dewey Court
Northampton
Massachusetts 01060
USA

A catalogue record for this book
is available from the British Library

Library of Congress Control Number: 2020944682

This book is available electronically in the **Elgar**online
Economics subject collection
http://dx.doi.org/10.4337/9781839109508

ISBN 978 1 83910 949 2 (cased)
ISBN 978 1 83910 950 8 (eBook)

Printed and bound in Great Britain by TJ Books Limited, Padstow, Cornwall

Contents

Contributors

Ada Ámon, Senior Associate, E3G.

Anders Åslund, Senior Fellow, Atlantic Council.

Markus Eller, Principal Economist, Oesterreichische Nationalbank.

Alexia Fürnkranz-Prskawetz, Professor, Technische Universität Wien, Wittgenstein Centre for Demography and Global Human Capital – WIC, Vienna Institute of Demography – VID.

Marina Gruševaja, Professor, RheinMain University of Applied Sciences.

Robert Holzmann, Governor, Oesterreichische Nationalbank.

Mario Holzner, Executive Director, The Vienna Institute for International Economic Studies – wiiw.

Ana Ivković, Vice Governor, National Bank of Serbia.

Michael A. Landesmann, Professor, Johannes Kepler University Linz, Senior Research Associate, The Vienna Institute for International Economic Studies – wiiw.

Anton Pelinka, Professor, Central European University.

Doris Ritzberger-Grünwald, Director, Economic Analysis and Research Department, Oesterreichische Nationalbank.

Jiří Rusnok, Governor, Czech National Bank.

Helene Schuberth, Head, Foreign Research Division, Oesterreichische Nationalbank.

Martin Selmayr, Ambassador of the European Commission to Austria, former Secretary-General, European Commission.

Andrzej Sławiński, Professor, Warsaw School of Economics.

Tomáš Sobotka, Wittgenstein Centre for Demography and Global Human Capital – WIC, Vienna Institute of Demography – VID.

Ágnes Szunomár, Institute of World Economics, Centre for Economic and Regional Studies and Institute of International, Political, and Regional Sciences, Corvinus University of Budapest.

Jorgovanka Tabaković, Governor, National Bank of Serbia.

Philipp Ther, Professor, University of Vienna.

Katja Gattin Turkalj, Director, Publications Department, Croatian National Bank.

Lukas Vashold, Research Associate, Vienna University of Economics and Business.

Boris Vujčić, Governor, Croatian National Bank.

Johannes Wiegand, Division Chief, International Monetary Fund.

Preface

The dramatic events of 1989 starting in Hungary and Poland helped bring down the single most concrete – in every sense of the word – symbol of the division of the European continent: the Berlin Wall. This book pays tribute to this historic event by revisiting the political and economic transformation that has taken place in Central, Eastern and Southeastern Europe (CESEE) over the last 30 years. Even though, in 1989, Francis Fukuyama called the bold victory of economic and political liberalism the 'end of history', he later revised his judgement. Indeed, history has not ended yet, and – in contrast to Fukuyama – others such as Patrick J. Deneen have even stated the failure of liberalism in the meantime. Certainly, the future will have a few more tricks in store. Against this backdrop, this book explores not only driving factors of the successful transition to date but also key challenges that CESEE will be facing in the years and decades ahead.

Part I frames the discussion on three decades of political and economic transformation in CESEE from a historical perspective, mixing praise for the CESEE countries' truly impressive transition and integration achievements with concern. Unfulfilled promises and unrealistic expectations about the speed and ease of transformation contributed to a social, economic and political backlash; a phenomenon unfortunately not unique to the CESEE region. Over time, many people have become disillusioned with the process of transition as economic modernization has failed to produce the expected social outcomes. Yet, at the same time, the anchor of European integration has proven to be able to build the 'best Europe we have ever had', delivering peace, liberty and prosperity. After all, the post-national Europe implied by the 'Jean Monnet Process' was a response to fascism, world wars and holocaust. To reach out to those who feel 'lost in transition', fostering convergence by spurring inclusive economic growth will remain a key factor.

Part II turns the attention to the role of monetary policy during transition as viewed from the perspective of three central bankers in the CESEE region. Following strong currency depreciation and hyperinflation in the 1990s, the Serbian case underlines the importance of restoring confidence in monetary policy and having an adequate fiscal framework in place for inflation targeting to work. Due to a strongly mismanaged economy in Yugoslavia in the late 1980s, Croatia first had to rein in hyperinflation and stabilize the economy in the early 1990s. A decade later, the country faced the challenge of having to manage capital inflows to address resulting imbalances. The Czech experience recalls the early transition phase in which the currency had to undergo a significant devaluation. The subsequent exchange rate peg, adopted with a view to anchoring the economy, worked well initially, yet ultimately proved unsustainable given the impossible trinity of open capital markets, independent monetary policy and a fixed exchange rate. Having abandoned the fixed exchange rate under market pressure, the Czech National Bank then became one of the first central banks to introduce inflation targeting.

The impact of different economic policy approaches on the transition process is the key focus of Part III. History has proved that countries that undertook fast and decisive reforms were most successful in catching up to Western European income levels. Furthermore, in a severe crisis – such as the dismantling of communist rule in CESEE – newly incoming policymakers building on new ideas played an important role in developing and implementing comprehensive reform packages, ideally with adequate and timely international financial support. Crucial factors for successful continued transition include open markets, transparency, good governance, the establishment of property rights and rule of law. Here, the European Union (EU) can assert a positive influence on CESEE countries that are not yet part of the EU. Not least because of the lack of EU accession perspectives, one can observe that Russia's and Ukraine's economic recovery started later and lacked some central reform elements found in other CESEE countries. The main transformation challenges for Russia and Ukraine are the low quality of institutions and the decrease of foreign direct investment (FDI) inflows.

Further lessons from three decades of catching-up are presented in Part IV, which highlights above all the differences in the catching-up process between CESEE and in East Asia. While East Asian countries have built up and successfully managed domestic human capital and research and development (R&D) bases (industrial policy), CESEE economies have largely relied on FDI inflows and suffered from large-scale emigration, especially of the young and well-educated. While East Asia opted for gradual economic opening, CESEE mostly went through a rather fast liberalization of the capital account that led to a dominance of foreign banks in many countries of the region. While in East Asia the state often played a strong role in catching-up, in CESEE catching-up was driven by the EU accession process (the *acquis communautaire*) and (prospective) EU membership. Looking at the relations between CESEE and China, one can observe that CESEE offered China strategic entry points to the EU. CESEE's wish to cooperate with China may partly stem from disappointment from not catching up (more quickly) with advanced EU members.

Part V discusses the challenges for CESEE's near future, focusing on financial and monetary stability. Most CESEE countries experienced strong capital inflows, very dynamic credit growth rates and booming domestic consumption in the years up to 2008, which led to the build-up of macroeconomic imbalances. The unwinding of these imbalances drove several countries into deep recessions when the 2008 crisis hit the region. Hence, effective micro- and macroprudential regulation is a key factor for safeguarding financial stability and avoiding very costly boom–bust cycles. Some of the CESEE countries belong to the relatively small group of countries that had used macroprudential policy tools already prior to the global financial crisis; these tools were indeed effective in containing credit growth and capital inflows in CESEE. However, the implemented macroprudential policies have apparently not yet been effective in dampening the strong recent property price increase in those countries of the region where house price inflation is no longer justified by fundamentals. House price growth might possibly be contained more effectively with borrower-based measures rather than capital-based measures. Turning from financial stability to monetary policy, 30 years after the onset of transition in CESEE, almost every type of monetary and exchange rate regime can be found in the region: from flexible exchange rates and inflation targeting to different types of managed exchange rates, euro area membership and the unilateral use of the euro. Analysing whether this diversity of regimes is a good outcome and how regimes are likely to evolve going forward is worthwhile, especially as regards the prospects, plusses and minuses for non-euro area CESEE countries to adopt the euro.

Finally, Part VI examines the impact of megatrends on the future of CESEE. Thirty years after the fall of the Iron Curtain, one may wonder where Europe stands and where the place of CESEE is in this new constellation, and in the new mandate of the EU institutions. For one, CESEE is strongly represented in the new European Commission which took office in late 2019. And the main topics of the new European Commission are closely related to CESEE. CESEE countries are among the digital forerunners and carbon reduction laggards alike. The search for meaningful action to address the challenges of population ageing, labour migration and brain drain will rely on the solidarity and responsibility of Member States no less than building a green European economy. In this context, however, one may argue that the Iron Curtain as a former East–West divide has now been replaced by a 'Coal Curtain' of Europe. This line on the map marks the divide of the EU, with the share of renewable energy in the CESEE EU countries being much smaller than that in Western EU countries. Another East–West divide is created by rapid population declines in many CESEE countries, versus population increases in Western EU countries. Population decline in the CESEE countries is due to collapsing fertility after 1989 and its slow recovery, lower life expectancy than in the West and strong outmigration. Looking ahead, migration pressures in and migration flows from CESEE – in particular in poorer countries – are expected to stay high, presenting a major future challenge for the CESEE countries. Other challenges to be tackled include the relocation of global power from the West to China, nationalistic tendencies and consequently declining support of European integration.

Summing up, there is no doubt that CESEE will be faced with major challenges when looking 30 years ahead. Yet, when looking back on the past 30 years, there is no doubt, either, that the transformation itself has mostly been a success: per capita income levels have increased impressively, far-reaching reforms have been implemented swiftly and decisively, and macroeconomic and financial stabilization has been reached. The surest path for CESEE's success story of the past decades to continue will be ongoing cooperation in the spirit of the European Union's official motto, 'United in diversity'; a motto that should also be applied to countries beyond EU borders. We thus hope that this volume will not only contribute to the debate on the successes and shortcomings of this historic transformation, but also provide policymakers with insights helping CESEE manage the challenges that lie ahead successfully.

Robert Holzmann
Doris Ritzberger-Grünwald
Helene Schuberth

PART I

A historic transformation: heterogeneity in
CESEE in a changing global context

1. Looking back on 30 years of transition – and looking 30 years ahead

Robert Holzmann[1]

1.1 TRANSITION PARALLELED BY EUROPEAN INTEGRATION

With the fall of the Iron Curtain, a long and difficult, yet unavoidable journey of transition began for the countries of Central, Eastern and Southeastern Europe (CESEE): a transition from centrally planned state socialism to modern democracies, market mechanism and capitalism. Unlike many Asian economies that adopted a more gradual approach, the CESEE countries applied a 'shock therapy' of rapid change. This meant that the initial economic tremor took its toll in the 1990s, in the form of deep recessions, soaring prices, currency depreciations, bank failures and high levels of unemployment (see Holzmann et al. 1995). The CESEE countries' intrinsic strengths came to the fore only later, as privatized industries were restructured, and reforms were implemented. The capital and foreign investment thus attracted propelled productivity and competitiveness, which in turn boosted economic growth.

This unprecedented social, political and economic metamorphosis was paralleled and supported by the process of European reunification. Today, 11 former Eastern bloc countries are united with their former ideological opponents under one European flag, and some of them also under the umbrella of a common currency. While being emancipated and self-confident partners, the European Union (EU) countries share democratic and legal values as well as institutional principles. We must point out that the European Union constitutes a crucial stabilizing anchor and, of course, provides budgetary support even for countries that are not yet members of the European Union.

1.2 SUCCESSFUL REFORMS AND ONGOING INTEGRATION STEPS

Catalyzed in several cases by prospective EU membership, reforms in CESEE eventually started to work. The CESEE economies established a record of significant economic growth and convergence as CESEE became one of the world's fastest-growing regions in the first half of the 2000s. Then, however, with the outbreak of the global financial crisis, the blessing of ever closer trade and financial linkages with Western Europe turned into a major challenge for CESEE. The economic shock quickly spilled over and harshly hit most of the CESEE countries despite their heterogeneity. Countries where the strong – and, in several cases, excessive – pre-crisis expansion had been driven by unsustainable levels of consumption and borrowing were affected the most.

In this context, we should stress the crucial role of the so-called Vienna Initiative, to which Austrian authorities also made significant contributions. At the peak of the crisis, all relevant stakeholders came together to coordinate their actions and thus prevent the imminent risk of a large-scale and chaotic withdrawal of cross-border bank groups from the CESEE region, which could have triggered massive systemic bank crises (see Nowotny et al. 2019).

It goes without saying that the three decades of transition have not been just a walk in the park. Despite great and respectable achievements, the transformation path has been perceived by many as too long, too difficult and too painful. Unfulfilled promises and unrealistic expectations of the transformation process have had various social, economic and political ramifications. While their form and extent vary from country to country, such consequences are reflected to an unforeseen extent in nostalgia and mounting attacks against democratic institutions and liberal values.

1.3   BUILDING BLOCKS AND STUMBLING BLOCKS FOR THE NEXT 30 YEARS

Let us now turn to the major challenges in CESEE when looking ahead. The national populism that has increasingly been taking hold in the CESEE countries resonates particularly well with those who feel 'lost in transition'. While the CESEE countries have caught up impressively toward Western European income levels over the last 30 years, income gaps persist, some of them substantial. Moreover, since economic growth has slackened as a legacy of the global financial crisis, convergence has slowed down. Therefore, it is of the utmost importance for the region to continue fostering convergence by spurring inclusive economic growth. To increase dampened productivity and capital formation, efforts should focus particularly on investments in infrastructure (including digitalization), human capital endowment and innovation, but also on improving the institutional, legal and business environment that supports a dynamic entrepreneurial sector in a Schumpeterian sense.

This is all the more important as potential growth will additionally be strongly limited in the medium to long run by adverse demographic developments, which pose another big challenge for the CESEE countries. In most of the region, the population is shrinking, mainly due to low life expectancy and low birth rates, but also to negative net migration. Whatever the causes, one important answer to future challenges will be to keep older people in the workforce. Fortunately, the trend toward earlier retirement has been reversed over the last decade, but more needs to be done in all countries concerned (see Gal and Radó 2019). Reforms have markedly improved the sustainability of public pension systems, but old-age poverty continues to be a problem in some CESEE countries, particularly for women. Pension reform is, perhaps, a trial and error process, a reminder of the famous quote by Friedrich von Hayek: 'The curious task of economics is to demonstrate to men how little they really know about what they imagine they can design' (von Hayek 1988, p. 76). Indeed, designing a stable pension system without jeopardizing people's confidence requires both science and art.

Whereas CESEE pensioners are staying in their countries, people of working age are emigrating. And even worse, the first to leave are the young and the most skilled, which threatens public health and productivity growth in their home countries. The challenge for CESEE countries with high emigration is to turn this brain drain into a brain gain by attracting people back or recruiting immigrants from third countries. The good news is that economic history provides numerous examples of emigration countries managing to become destinations of re-migration. Since economic development only becomes a pull factor when a certain minimum income threshold is reached, however, good governance and specific policies that improve people's quality of life will be essential to win and keep talents (see European Commission 2018).

Good governance – an elastic concept, admittedly – applies not only to individual countries but also to European institutions. Indeed, European economic integration proceeds between the poles of deepening and enlargement, as we have seen from the recent disagreement about the timing of accession talks with candidate countries before securing the EU's absorption capacity. The Brexit experience suggests that not even the direction of deepening and enlargement can be foreseen with precision. 'Prediction is very difficult, especially about the future' – apparently, this truism of Niels Bohr also applies to the negotiations among the EU Member States about the deepening of Economic and Monetary Union (EMU). A resilient common currency needs integrated markets. Completing the banking union and developing a capital markets union seems less controversial than the creation of a fiscal union. Indeed, the example of the United States (US) – which is not a perfect optimal currency area either – suggests that most of the interregional risk-sharing necessary in a common currency area takes place via financial markets and not via budgetary transfers. Still, the EU budget is dwarfed by the US federal budget. Moreover, fiscal flows lead and facilitate financial flows – not least via safe assets – and thus add a qualitative component to their quantitative contribution to risk-sharing.

Whatever the outcome of this debate, the development and integration of financial markets is the order of the day, both in EMU and in CESEE. Without neglecting the important role of banking in providing finance, particularly to medium-sized businesses, it will be crucial to deepen capital markets.

With the benefit of hindsight, and when drawing lessons from the global financial crisis that then morphed into the so-called sovereign European debt crisis, some missing pieces of the euro area architecture were revealed, such as the lack of a banking union. The establishment of such a union, whose first pillar – the Single Supervisory Mechanism (SSM) – became fully operational in 2014, has probably constituted the most important institutional innovation since the launch of the euro in 1999. For non-euro area EU countries, such as Bulgaria and Croatia, that are preparing to become members of the euro area, this means that they must not only fulfil the Maastricht criteria in a sustainable manner before being able to adopt the euro. Additionally, given that EMU has changed since the crisis, they are also expected to enter into close cooperation with the SSM before introducing the euro (see Backé and Dvorsky 2018). It has long been acknowledged that there is no 'one size fits all' approach to how soon countries should give up their independent monetary policy – a decisive macroeconomic tool – in favour of joining monetary union. Also, public support for such a move differs across CESEE countries, although it has become increasingly favourable.

1.4   CONCLUSIONS

Despite several setbacks and various shortcomings, the CESEE countries deserve our deep respect for their successful transition from dysfunctional command economies to flourishing market economies. However, transition – in the sense of adjustment to a changing and challenging environment – is a permanent process. There are always new challenges ahead; not only in CESEE, but all over Europe and all over the world. We will have to transit to – or through – ageing societies, low carbon economies, digital finance and further economic, financial and monetary integration. Facing all these transitions, it will be key to cooperate in the spirit of the European Union's official motto, 'United in diversity'. Precisely in this vein, we should all collaborate within Europe to be able to better cope with many of the challenges that we will face. We can – to give but one example – help each other to develop financial markets by sharing our experience with products, regulation and supervision, building on the support of international financial institutions, such as the International Monetary Fund and the World Bank. If we all sustain our commitment, we can do our bit in making sure that the success story of the past decades in CESEE will continue for many years to come.

NOTE

1.   Andreas Breitenfellner and Tomáš Slačík, of the Oesterreichische Nationalbank's staff, contributed to this chapter.

REFERENCES

Backé, P. and S. Dvorsky (2018), 'Enlargement of the Euro Area toward CESEE: Progress and Perspectives', Focus on European Economic Integration Q3/18, 43–56.

European Commission (2018), 'Addressing Brain Drain: The Local and Regional Dimension', Report by the European Committee of Regions, available at https://cor .europa.eu/en/engage/studies/Documents/addressing-brain-drain/addressing-brain -drain.pdf (accessed on 31 January 2020).

Gal, R.I. and M. Radó (2019), 'Labor Market Participation and Postponed Retirement in Central and Eastern Europe', in R. Holzmann, E. Palmer, R. Palacios and S. Sacchi (eds), *Progress and Challenges of Nonfinancial Defined Contribution Pension Schemes: Addressing Marginalization, Polarization, and the Labor Market (Volume 1)*, Washington, DC: World Bank Group, 371–398.

Holzmann, R., J. Gács and G. Winckler (1995), *Output Decline in Eastern Europe: Unavoidable, External Influence or Homemade?*, Dordrecht: Kluwer Academic Publishers.

Nowotny E., D. Ritzberger-Grünwald and H. Schuberth (2019), *How to Finance Cohesion in Europe?*, Cheltenham, UK and Northampton, MA, USA: Edward Elgar Publishing.

von Hayek, F.A. (1988), *The Fatal Conceit: The Errors of Socialism*, London: University of Chicago Press.

2. 1989: the year of the great ambivalence

Anton Pelinka

2.1 RE-NATIONALIZATION AND EUROPEANIZATION

1989 was the year of the most dramatic transformation in Europe since 1945. The Cold War ended, the barbed wire between Hungary and Austria was lifted and the Berlin Wall came down. This transformation consisted of an 'Epitaph for World Communism' and of 'Redrawing the map of Europe' (see Service 2015, pp. 390, 427). As Agnes Heller (2012, p. 55) put it: 'The collapse of the communist regime was the last great turning point in the history of the twentieth century'.

Before those dramatic changes became possible, the transformation started in the very centre of Communist Europe: Mikhail Gorbachev declared the end of the Brezhnev Doctrine (see Taubman 2017, p. 481) – the end of the geostrategic principle which allowed the Union of Soviet Socialist Republics (USSR) to intervene in the internal affairs of its Eastern European allies (if necessary using the might of the Red Army) and stabilize the Marxist–Leninist one-party rule. In June 1989, free elections in Poland were the starting point for the domino process which would, within a very short time, bring an end to the Communist one-party dictatorship in Central and Eastern Europe. All former Communist countries in Europe started the transformation from a Marxist–Leninist one-party system to pluralistic democracies: toward a competitive multi-party system with free elections, with checks and balances in the form of media pluralism and an independent judiciary. With the exception of Russia and Belorussia (and, at least for a certain period, Moldova and Serbia), all former European Communist states opted for a 'Western' orientation. That included the North Atlantic Treaty Organization (NATO) as well as European Union (EU) membership.

The events of 1989 changed the European balance of power; that is, of military and political and economic power. 'For a short while, it seemed as if the world would be left with only two dominating powers: the United States, and the slowly emerging and expanding European Union' (see Heller 2012, p. 65). Both the United States and the EU were built upon identical principles: liberal democracy and liberal economy; on pluralistic, competitive political and as well economic systems. The 'East' had used its newly won freedom to opt to become like the West. This was an assumption dominating the thinking in Eastern Europe during the first years of transformation.

Some aspects of this 'Westernization' included one specific aspect which may have been overlooked in 1989 and the coming years. Becoming a member in the EU implied the necessity to shift power from the nation state to the Union, especially concerning the Single Market architecture and the acceptance of the supremacy of European law. This necessity contradicted a specific interpretation of the collapse of the USSR's dominance as enshrined in the Brezhnev Doctrine. Soon two perspectives were seen as a contradiction: did the democratic freedom, won in 1989, include the freedom to build a sovereign nation state, a freedom defined as the 'return of the past'? Or was the democratic freedom a window of opportunity to join the European Union, a democratic federation in the making?

For Central and Eastern Europe, the year 1989 was seen as the renaissance of national sovereignty. But 1989 was also the year of the beginning of a policy leading to the reduction of national sovereignty within the European Union. In the dominant feeling of 'national liberation', that second aspect of Europeanization had been more or less ignored. The European Union was perceived as an instrument to guarantee prosperity and individual freedom; but not as a transnational, a supranational institution limiting Czech or Latvian sovereignty in the same way as the EU limits French or German sovereignty.

The transformation of former Communist Europe seemed to be the triumph of national liberation. But by turning toward the West, the transformation process followed two different textbooks: the renaissance of the nation state based on a Westphalian understanding of national sovereignty; and the adaption to the standards of political and economic design, which – following Robert Schuman and Jean Monnet – was focused on a post-national Europe. Monnet especially 'envisaged a democratic supranational federation that would take shape gradually, incrementally, and over a lengthy period of time through a process of continuous reform' (see Kershaw 2018, p. 156).

In Western Europe, the process of European integration was designed and implemented with the clear intention to reduce national sovereignty. The 'Jean Monnet Process', starting in 1951 with the foundation of the European Coal and Steel Community, tried to control, to contain and to limit nationalism. But in Central and Eastern Europe, 'Westernization' starting in 1989 was perceived as the triumph of national sovereignty and, in that respect, the return of history. This is one of the contradicting perceptions which overshadow the ongoing integration today.

2.2   THE CONTRADICTION OF NARRATIVES: NATIONAL HEROISM OR THE DEFEAT OF THE 'SECOND WORLD'?

The transformation processes in Poland and Hungary, in Czechoslovakia and Romania and in the German Democratic Republic (GDR) were the result of different national developments, which can be characterized as 'national liberation' and 'national democratization'. But first and foremost, transformation was the result of the more or less peaceful surrender of the 'Second World's' centre: of Moscow, of the USSR, of Marxism–Leninism, of a military–political–economic system which dominated by raw power the eastern half of Europe since 1945.

Concerning the transformation in Central and Eastern Europe, the two narratives seem to contradict each other: the narrative of national heroism, and the narrative of geopolitical unavoidability. Both narratives are correct, both tell correct stories. The question is not about 'right' or 'wrong', the question is which narrative tells the decisive story: decisive for the outcome of the year 1989. The 'Children of the Revolution' of 1989 (see Shore 2013, p. 273) – the generation which formed its own political and social understanding after the downfall of communism – have been formed by the contradiction between the national (and tentatively nationalistic) and the European (and tentatively cosmopolitan) narrative: was the end of Communist dictatorship in Lithuania or Poland, in Hungary or Romania first and foremost the result of Lithuanian (Polish, Hungarian, Romanian) heroism, or was the national resistance against dictatorship one piece of the puzzle of an all-European, even of a global, megatrend?

Beginning with 1945, the Soviet Union started to rule over the Baltic States and Poland, Czechoslovakia and Hungary, Romania and Bulgaria and East Germany. It was obvious that the Soviet rule was based on one factor first and foremost: on military power, on military occupation. From the start of its rule, the USSR was confronted with opposition: political opposition, such as the Hungarian 'Small Landowner Party', which won the first and only democratic elections until 1989; military opposition, such as the resistance of the Polish Home Army; and civilian resistance, such as the demonstrations in East Berlin in 1953, in Hungary in 1956, in Czechoslovakia in 1968, and in Poland in 1980.

If we compare East Berlin in the summer of 1953 with East Berlin in the autumn of 1989, Prague in the summer of 1968 with Prague in the autumn of 1989, as well as Budapest in the autumn of 1956 with Budapest in 1989, there is no doubt that the failures of 1953 in East Berlin, those of Prague in 1968, and those of Budapest in 1956, were not the result of a lack of national heroism. Poles and Czechs, Slovaks and Hungarians, East Germans and Romanians who tried to transform the existing dictatorship into democracy, acted heroically before 1989. Yet, they did not succeed. They were unable to succeed due to the intervention of Soviet tanks, due to the policy represented by the post-Stalinist warlords in Moscow who were interested in securing their European zone of interest; in other words, their share of Europe that the Red Army had liberated and conquered in its war against the armed forces of the 'Greater German Empire'.

The difference between the failures of transformation attempts before 1989 and the successes of 1989 was defined by the transformation in the very centre of the bloc itself, in Moscow. Transformation in the periphery of the bloc could not be successful so long as the bloc's centre was unwilling to accept transformation in the USSR. The history of the demise of the European Communist systems started in 1985, when the small ageing and ailing elitist leadership of the Soviet Communist Party transferred the power to the generation of Gorbachev and Yeltsin.

Gorbachev realized that the 'peaceful competition' between West and East had resulted in the defeat of the world shaped by Lenin and Stalin. Economically, technologically, psychologically, the post-Stalinist leadership had lost. It needed decades before this basic fact was recognized by the disciples of Marxism–Leninism. Not only was the 'socialist camp' unable to overtake the West, as Khrushchev had promised and as Brezhnev had still claimed to believe, but also Soviet communism was bankrupt: economically and technologically, morally and intellectually.

There was heroism on the streets in East Berlin in 1953 as well as in 1989; there was heroism in Budapest in 1956 and in 1989; there was heroism in Prague in 1968 and in 1989. But what we have to accept is that the heroism of the people who fought against the Marxist–Leninist dictatorship, who fought for freedom from the orders coming from Moscow – that heroism did not fail because of a lack of dedication and courage before 1989; and that heroism did not succeed because of any significant increase in Polish or Czechoslovakian, in East German or Hungarian dedication and courage in 1989 compared with the preceding decades. The difference was that in Moscow, a new leadership had accepted defeat in its competition with the West. The consequence was that Mikhail Gorbachev cancelled the Brezhnev Doctrine. The decisive factor which made the transformation in 1989 a success was not the renaissance of nationalism. The decisive factor was the strength of liberal, of Western, democracy.

2.3   RETURN TO GOOD (OR NOT SO GOOD) OLD EUROPE, OR JOINING A COMPLETELY NEW EUROPE?

Looking back today, what has been the decisive outcome of the last three decades? Was it – is it – the return of a Europe as it was shaped after World War I, by Brest-Litovsk, Versailles, Trianon? How different is post-1989 Europe from the Europe which failed after 1918, 1919, 1920?

Let me rephrase the question: how safe and how democratic was Poland between the rebirth of the Polish state and the invasion of German and Soviet troops in September 1939? How free was the newly established state of Slovakia as a Nazi satellite? What was the impact of the authoritarian Horthy regime on the daily liberty of Hungarians? How stable was Romania between authoritarianism, military dictatorship and the pressure from different sides: from Nazi-Germany and from the USSR? How successful was Yugoslavia in convincing its nationalities that the new state of Serbs, Croats and Slovenes was more than Greater Serbia?

How was it – starting already in 1922 – that Italy became a model of a political system, globally soon known as 'fascism'? Spanish democracy did not survive this period, and neither did democracy in Portugal. Is this Europe of failing democracies the Europe that post-Communist countries were eager to return to in 1989?

How can we explain the hidden agenda of the nostalgia for the last century's first half, for the decades of world wars and the holocaust? Nostalgia for Mussolini's Italy, for Horthy's Hungary, for Tiso's Slovakia, for Antonescu's Romania, or for the united Germany of Hitler? Why are populist movements on the rise; movements, most of which are defined by a simplistic nationalist understanding of 'Us' versus 'Them'? Of course, there is a multiplicity of explanations; there are many scholarly written articles and books trying to explain the renaissance of nationalism. Let me just give you one rather abstract interpretation, which is that the success and the visibility of neo-nationalistic populism all over Europe is an attempt to escape the complexities of globalization: globalization, the contemporary face of modernization; globalization, which is not the result of a conspiracy but the result of the logics of economic and cultural modernization. Populism is the promise of return to a catastrophic but nevertheless romanticized past. But why is this promise appealing to significant segments of society?

Disappointment is one of the explanations. Looking back, it was naïve to hope for an easy linear transition to pluralistic democracies and to Western prosperity. 'During the democratic awakening, many East Europeans had dreamt of political freedom to participate in politics, material prosperity to enjoy consumption, individualism to enjoy consumption, individualism to realize different life styles' (see Jarausch 2015, p. 695). Despite the end of the old, the Communist authoritarian rule, pluralistic democracy did not mean the rule of 'the people' but the rule of a more or less representative, more or less democratically legitimized elite. Democracy was more complex than many had expected. And prosperity did increase, but not for all and not at the same speed.

This disappointment explains the return of old-fashioned nationalism which had dominated Europe in general and Central Europe in particular. It is a 'reframed' nationalism (see Brubaker 2007), a nationalism in new clothes, but in its substance still the old nationalism, as it is based on the old understanding of politics as a conflict between 'Us' and 'Them'. The revival of nationalism is an opening of a Pandora's box, including the possibilities of border disputes. The reframing of nationalism is the 'rebirth of history', as Misha Glenny (1992, p. 38) has seen it in the case of the former Yugoslavia: nationalism put different states 'on a collision course that would result in war'.

Ivan Krastev has highlighted the answer in the migration 'crisis' of 2015. Refugees and migrants, coming from the Middle East or from Africa, were not perceived as 'Us'. They were seen as 'Them'. And especially in Central and Eastern Europe, the 'crisis' brought out into the open the 'historically rooted suspicion of anything cosmopolitan' (see Krastev 2017, p. 57); a suspicion which strengthened the rise of populist parties all over Europe.

There exists an answer to the challenges of globalization: the integration of nation states into a common European Union. This integration has proven to be able to build the best Europe we have ever had: a Europe of peace, a Europe of liberty, a Europe of prosperity. Of course, it is not a perfect Europe. But it is a Europe that we are invited to improve. It is a Europe which follows the principle: 'We are all different – we are all equal'. This Europe – developed from a West European Economic Community into an all-European Union – is an unfinished federation. This Europe is not dictated by a centre, like pan-European empires from the past, from the Roman Empire to the Empire of Charlemagne, from Napoleon's Empire to the empire which signalled through its ruby-red stars shining from the Kremlin's towers its intention to build a 'New World'. All those empires imploded.

The Europe of the Union is not an empire; it has no centre, as Rome or Paris or Berlin, Vienna or Constantinople or St Petersburg (later, Moscow) were centres of empires of the past. It is an association that any democratic European state has been and still is invited to join. This Europe has become the biggest economic player worldwide, ahead of the United States (US) and of China. But it is still lacking the political instruments that it would need to create a stabilizing balance between the US and Asia. But for the first time in its history, Europe is not defined by intra-European warfare. For the first time, Europe could speak with one voice; and sometimes Europe acts beyond Germany and France, Poland and Bulgaria. Sometimes, Europe is already one.

Europe needs 'deepening'. The European Union has to become an 'ever closer Union' (see Dinan 1999) to fully develop its economic potentials. As long as the EU is a concert in which Germany and France and Poland and Italy are performing without a conductor, without much of a federal authority, Europe is lagging behind the US and China. Europe has to become more of a global actor, and less of a loose confederation in which nation states follow their specific national interests.

2.4   THE END OF HISTORY, OR THE RETURN OF HISTORY?

The process of European integration has not yet reached the point of no return. The future of a still not fully united Europe is open. The integration which started as the unification of Western Europe after 1945 can still go on, by transforming the Union into a federation not so different from the United States of Europe as envisaged by Jean Monnet. But the Union can also be dismantled, the European integration replaced by the return of the Europe of the past: Europe as an extremely diverse continent, deeply divided by the contradicting interests of different nation states.

To put the focus on Europe's future, three scenarios of a realistic outlook can be discussed. These scenarios contradict but they do not exclude each other. The future of Europe will not be defined by an 'Either–Or', but by a 'More or Less'. By a 'More or Less' between two extremes: between the 'End of History' and the 'Return of History'. All three scenarios are based on tendencies and probabilities, and must not be misunderstood as prophecies.

Scenario 1: Democracy – defined as political pluralism, free and fair elections, checks and balances, an independent judiciary – has never been so undisputed in Europe. There is an ongoing debate about 'liberal democracy', about the minimum standard of democracy. But there is no serious debate about the necessity of political liberty, about the need for an independent judiciary, about the positive role a free media has to play. Before 1945, in most parts of Europe, democracy did not exist, and before 1939, many observers believed that democracy had been declared at its end, declared a victim of global megatrends. For many, democracy was a dirty word, as we can read in Josef Goebbels' diaries; and for Josef Stalin, before 1939 and also after 1945, liberal democracy was just the window dressing of the bourgeoisie's rule, one pretext in the class war. Since 1989, beginning with the Central and Eastern European domino process – the first domino fell with the Polish elections in June 1989 – Communist dictatorship came to an end, as fascist dictatorship had been defeated decades ago. Democracy in Europe today has its deficits, but the principles of liberal, of pluralistic democracy are widely accepted.

Scenario 2: Behind the façade of democracy, authoritarian tendencies are rising: populist movements and populist parties reflect a deep-seated resentment against representative democracy. Democracy as majority rule is seen as being in contradiction to minority rights, and 'the people' as being in opposition against representative government. The difference between 'Us' and 'Them' – whoever that might be – is overemphasized or even invented. Complex rules, developed over the years and enshrined in constitutions, guaranteed by supreme courts, are denounced as elitist constructions. The very concept of enlightenment, of rationalism, seems to be on the defensive. Thomas Hobbes's view of politics as permanent warfare mobilizes a significant part of political energy. This energy becomes manifest in the frustration of those who see themselves as being on the losing side, despite the political freedom they have all been invited to enjoy since 1989. It is a frustration used and organized by populist movements and populist parties. In such an atmosphere of a politics of exclusion, of excluding all who are defined as 'others', democracy can be lost; and with the loss of democracy, the process of European integration could turn into a process of disintegration.

Scenario 3: As all countries within the EU are profiting economically from the Union's Single Market, an end to European integration as started after 1945 in the western part of the continent is possible, but not probable. The situation the United Kingdom finds itself in after the Brexit referendum in 2016 will prevent further attempts by other members to leave the Union. The Union will survive for the foreseeable future; as an unfinished federation, with an unfinished democratic structure, consisting of democratic Member States with some democratic deficits. In the short run, Europe's future will be defined by 'muddling through', or 'soldiering on'. The alternatives to European democracy as we observe it today are too dreadful. A return to pre-1914 and to pre-1939 Europe is an option nobody wishes for. Europe will survive: less democratic than it could be; less unified than possible; not strong enough to be able to play in the same political league which will be dominated by the United States of America and the People's Republic of China.

Politically, Europe can be proud of its successes, of the successes made possible by the events of 1989. But mentally, Europe must not get lost in nostalgia, which tends to make us forget the self-destructive energy the Europe of the past was characterized by.

REFERENCES

Brubaker, R. (2007), *Nationalism Reframed: Nationhood and the National Question in the New Europe*, Cambridge: Cambridge University Press.

Dinan, D. (1999), *Ever Closer Union: An Introduction to European Integration* (European Union series), London: Palgrave Macmillan.

Glenny, M. (1992), *The Fall of Yugoslavia: The Third Balkan War*, New York: Penguin Books.

Heller, A. (2012), 'Twenty Years After 1989', in V. Tismaneanu and B.C. Iacob (eds), *The End and the Beginning: The Revolutions of 1989 and the Resurgence of History*, Budapest: CEU Press, 55–67.

Jarausch, K.H. (2015), *Out of Ashes: A New History of Europe in the Twentieth Century*, Woodstock, UK and Princeton, NJ, USA: Princeton University Press.

Kershaw, I. (2018), *The Global Age: Europe 1950–2017* (The Penguin History of Europe series), New York: Viking.

Krastev, I. (2017), *After Europe*, Philadelphia, PA: University of Pennsylvania Press.

Service, R. (2015), *The End of the Cold War: 1985–1991*, London: Macmillan.

Shore, M. (2013), *The Taste of Ashes: The Afterlife of Totalitarianism in Eastern Europe*, New York: Broadway Books.

Taubman, W. (2017), *Gorbachev: His Life and Times*, New York: W.W. Norton & Company.

3. The price of unity: the transformation of Germany and Eastern Europe after 1989

Philipp Ther

Anniversaries of historic events make us look at history from a perspective shaped all the more by the present. In 2009, and even in 2014, reviews of transformation and of the 'shock therapies' of the 1990s were still mostly or overwhelmingly positive. The global crisis of 2008–2009 and the recent electoral successes of right-wing populists and nationalists have called into question neoliberal narratives of economic success and even the (in Hannah Arendt's words) liberal revolutions of 1989.[1] In 2009, the German government organized a huge Festival of Freedom in front of the Brandenburg Gate in Berlin to celebrate the twentieth anniversary of the presumed *annus mirabilis*. On this occasion, artists were invited to design plastic replicas of pieces of the Berlin Wall, which were lined up and then made to collapse, creating a staged domino effect that symbolized the end of communism. What it rather looked like, however, was an involuntary reference to the global financial crisis. In the end, a domino effect of the bankruptcy of Lehman Brothers on other banks has been prevented, as has the collapse of entire economies in Central, Eastern and Southeastern Europe (CESEE) after the end of communism. Although another depression like the one in the 1930s was averted, the financial crisis and the subsequent euro crisis delegitimized the order created in 1989. Eastern and Southern Europe were hit particularly hard, which called into question European integration; a project that may, in a way, be considered globalization on a smaller scale. Against this background, the 2014 review of European transformation was – yet again – surprisingly positive. Harvard economist Andrei Shleifer and Californian political scientist Daniel Treisman chose 'Normal Countries' as the title of their 2014 review of the transformation process (see Shleifer and Treisman 2014).

Anyone who experienced the 'normalization' era in Czechoslovakia that followed the suppression of the Prague Spring would have severe doubts about the term 'normal'. What is considered 'normal' always depends on the prevailing social and political order. Shleifer and Treisman (2014) referred to the synchronous development of former communist countries into free market economies and liberal democracies, confirming Francis Fukuyama's thesis of the end of history (Fukuyama 1989). Thanks to comprehensive modernization, the authors argued in the journal *Foreign Affairs* (see Shleifer and Treisman 2014), the post-communist countries had become normal countries; and in some ways, better than normal. Shleifer and Treisman (2014) praised radical reforms – and not gradual reforms – as the best variant of transformation.

The present chapter discusses a case of post-communist transformation that was mostly omitted from the English-language literature on CESEE but which, nonetheless, can be regarded as another testing ground for shock therapies: the former German Democratic Republic (GDR). The example of the GDR is particularly interesting because it shows that transformation did not stop at Europe's former East–West divide, but that the underlying economic principles and the economic policies they informed had strong repercussions on the West. In the following, this type of feedback will be referred to as 'cotransformation', a phenomenon that had a particularly heavy impact on Germany because of unification. In this sense, Germany is a special case, all the more deserving of closer examination.

Germany was rather swift in overcoming the financial and economic crisis of 2008–09 and has since been perceived internationally as a model of economic success. A look back to the late 1990s, however, shows how quickly an upswing can turn into a decline, and vice versa. In 1999, *The Economist* referred to Germany as 'the sick man of the euro' (see *The Economist* 1999). At that time, Germany seemed to be caught in a vicious circle of low growth, rising unemployment and government debt (see Ther 2016a).

Germany's crisis at the time was not least a result of economic policy decisions taken in 1990. In the subsequent decade, the bankrupt GDR and the Socialist Unity Party of Germany (SED) were repeatedly blamed for the economic problems in eastern Germany. What is often ignored, however, is that the main actors of German transformation came from the West. This had to do with the course of German unification, which entailed an extensive exchange of elites in eastern Germany. The electoral success of the Alternative for Germany (AfD) in eastern Germany and, most recently, Bochum historian Marcus Böick's 2018 history of the East German privatization agency, Treuhandanstalt, have triggered a long overdue debate about the reform policies of the early 1990s and, particularly, privatization. Especially as a historian, one should be wary about the wisdom of hindsight; yet, one also needs to be very critical of the Thatcherite slogan stating that 'there is no alternative'.

The economic reforms in the five 'new *Länder*' – which is what they were called in 1990 in a slightly paternalistic manner – aimed at a swift alignment with the West. Not only the Federal Republic of Germany but the entire Western world saw the outcome of the Cold War as a confirmation of the superiority of their political and economic system. Socialism has lost, capitalism has won; this is how renowned economist Robert Heilbroner put it in the *New Yorker* magazine in early 1989 (see Heilbroner 1989, p. 98). Not much later, the International Monetary Fund (IMF), the World Bank and the United States Department of the Treasury adopted the Washington Consensus. This economic standard prescription for crisis countries – arranged as a decalogue very much like the Ten Commandments – was first intended for debt-ridden Latin American countries but was then applied, above all, to post-communist Europe. It starts out with the objective of macroeconomic stabilization – in fact, this always meant austerity programmes – and leads on to the triad of liberalization, deregulation and privatization. By way of conclusion, the Washington Consensus makes a case for foreign direct investment (FDI) and global financial capitalism (for details on the Washington Consensus, see Ther 2016b).

3.1   THE YEAR 1989 FROM A GLOBAL PERSPECTIVE

The Washington Consensus was part of the global transformation that took place in 1989, as was the democratization of Chile. Chile is important in this context because advisers associated with the Chicago School of Economics were active there. International observers therefore attributed Chile's long recovery following the 1982 Latin American debt crisis mostly to radical privatization, internal and external liberalization and deregulation (only the profitable copper mines remained in state ownership). Chile marks the beginning of the neoliberal 'success stories' that later had a strong impact on post-communist Europe. On closer examination, it is questionable whether Chile's upswing, which lasted until the Asian financial crisis of 1998, can be attributed to the neoliberal economic policy stance under Augusto Pinochet, or rather to the Christian and social democrats' economic policy after 1989, which strove for 'social equilibrium'[2] by actively fighting poverty and increasing purchasing power.

   The ideas of the Washington Consensus were taken up in Europe faster than its authors could have anticipated. In June 1989, Solidarność won a landslide victory in the first free elections in post-war Poland, and the communists were happy to let the opposition take over the government so that it would be blamed for the economic malaise (which is exactly what happened in the 1993 parliamentary elections). In the summer and autumn of 1989, the country's first post-communist finance minister, Leszek Balcerowicz, developed a reform plan which was soon to be named after him. What came first in the Balcerowicz Plan was macroeconomic stabilization, as Poland was suffering from high inflation that began to show signs of expanding into hyperinflation, unsustainable external debt (more than 70 per cent of gross domestic product, with repayment being impossible, given the country's trade deficit alone) and other consequences of its dysfunctional planned economy.

As the Polish version of *perestroika* – the Wilczek reforms – had failed, prominent experts had already begun to turn toward radical reforms at the end of 1988. As early as in 1988, the weekly paper *Polityka* reported on the growing influence of 'Eastern Thatcherites' (see Borkowski 1988, pp. 1, 4). Much like the Washington Consensus, the Balcerowicz Plan aimed at comprehensive privatization and swift internal and external liberalization. Although it was clear that the reforms would lead to massive social cutbacks and dismissals, and that they would be accompanied by a wage limitation law, the majority of the left wing of Solidarność and the followers of Catholic social teaching approved. We can thus speak of a 'Warsaw Consensus', which was – like its role model – arranged as a decalogue.[3]

The effects of the reforms were mixed. Inflation was indeed brought under control, but gross domestic product (GDP) went down by a total of 18 per cent in 1990 and 1991. Industrial production declined by almost one-third, and wage limitations dampened demand over a sustained period. Another effect was the huge numbers of unemployed: in 1992, 2.3 million people in Poland were without employment, 13.5 per cent of the labour force.[4] Critics such as Grzegorz Kołodko, later post-communist finance minister, therefore spoke of a 'shock without a therapy'.[5] While some international experts would have approved of an even more radical course, Balcerowicz made certain concessions: for instance, he reduced the speed at which large enterprises were privatized; so all in all, he acted in a rather pragmatic way. In 1992, the economy started to pick up again, and Poland was the first of the former Eastern bloc countries to recover from the deep recession of 1989–91. Thus, the shock therapy was internationally perceived to be a success. At the political level, it was not: the parties that had evolved from Solidarność lost the 1993 elections against the post-communists. These, however, did not take back the reforms as previously promised, but only mitigated them.

Turning to Germany, Theo Waigel, West German finance minister in 1989, and Wolfgang Schäuble, one of the main authors of the Unification Treaty, were neither among the followers of the neoliberal Chicago School of Economics nor in favour of a 'shock therapy'. Both ministers of the centre-right government were Christian Democrats and adherents of ordoliberalism and the German model of a 'social market economy'. But apart from social cushioning, stronger government regulation and a system of collective wage agreements, the neoliberal and ordoliberal reform concepts were largely congruent. In Czechoslovakia, the Chicago School had direct influence; Nobel Memorial Prize winner Milton Friedman, for instance, toured East Central Europe in 1990 and found a particularly enthusiastic supporter in Václav

Klaus, then minister of finance in Czechoslovakia.[6] The latter's model of voucher privatization was, in turn, taken up in Russia. It did not work there, however. Rather, it led to the emergence of oligarchs, who bought up most of the vouchers, distorted privatization through insider deals, and have dominated the Russian economy ever since.

3.2   THE GERMAN SHOCK THERAPY

Radical economic reforms can be pushed through most easily if the economies concerned are on the brink of collapse. This was the case, without doubt, in the last year of the GDR. The exchange rate of the East German mark (DDM) to the Deutsche mark (DEM) declined to 7:1 in the autumn of 1989, and went even lower at times in the winter that followed. This meant that East Germany's high foreign debt could no longer be serviced. The asymmetry of power between West and East was reflected, *inter alia*, in the type of reunification that was chosen: German reunification was executed as an 'accession' of the five 'new *Länder*' pursuant to Article 23 Basic Law; and not pursuant to Article 146, which was actually intended for such a scenario. This means that what we are dealing with here was in fact an enlargement of West Germany and not a unification of two equal states.

The sharp fall of the East German mark mirrored the economic problems of the GDR and the gloomy expectations of its future. However, depreciation had already started much earlier. While in the 1980s the GDR insisted on the parity of the East German mark – both officially and in the compulsory exchange of currency for West Germans – the GDR's foreign trade bank halved the internal clearing rate to the Deutsche mark (like the other currencies of the communist countries, the East German mark was not convertible). In 1988, the foreign trade bank's internal exchange rate, which was kept strictly secret, came to no more than DDM 4.40 to DEM 1, because the GDR was not able to sell its goods at a higher exchange rate.

Illegal moneychangers in the backyards of East Berlin or Leipzig paid roughly the same rate; the black market thus reflected the economic situation more accurately than the official exchange rates. When the East German mark depreciated after the fall of the Berlin Wall, wages and salaries in the GDR, which were low at any rate, depreciated even further. Like in Poland or Czechoslovakia, a tank of fuel or a broken washing machine often were enough to strain a household's budget. This economic crash, together with the general uncertainty, explains why the call 'We are one people' grew louder and louder in the autumn and winter of 1989–1990.

By the spring of 1990, a new slogan had taken hold: '*Kommt die D-Mark, bleiben wir, kommt sie nicht, geh'n wir zu ihr!*' ('If we get the Deutsche mark, we'll stay; if we don't, we'll come get it'.) The last part of the slogan referred to the threat of mass emigration from the GDR, to escape economic misery. In the East German election campaigns of 1990, the Christian Democratic Union (CDU) offered an obvious way forward: quick reunification and, *en route*, economic and monetary union with West Germany. The CDU kept this electoral promise: on 1 July 1990, the Deutsche mark – symbol of prosperity – became the official currency of East Germany, prompting celebrations in Berlin, Leipzig and other cities. But how come a 1:1 exchange rate was applied, given the rapid depreciation of the East German mark after the fall of the Berlin Wall?

The Deutsche Bundesbank cautioned against the economic risk of too-strong appreciation, arguing the case for a 2:1 exchange rate. Representatives of the State Bank of the GDR even called for a 7:1 exchange rate, as this would have corresponded to the country's economic power and would thus have enabled eastern German companies to compete with western German industry.[7] In the end, however, the West German government under Federal Chancellor Helmut Kohl took a political decision and opted for the 1:1 exchange rate (the only exception being large savings deposits and company debts, to which a rate of 1:2 or 1:3 applied, respectively). This move helped the Christian Democrats to win the first elections in unified Germany in the autumn of 1990. A key argument used in public debates was that it served to prevent another wave of mass migration from eastern to western Germany. The freedom of movement indeed distinguished the situation in Germany from that of the other post-communist countries.

3.3   GERMANY'S SPECIAL PATH

Given their focus on national unity and traditional orientation toward the West, the western German elites turned a blind eye on what was happening in their immediate neighbourhood. The Czechoslovak koruna (CSK), the currency of Czechoslovakia, which was almost as wealthy as the GDR, also dropped dramatically in the winter of 1989–1990. Its exchange rate declined to a three-times lower black market rate, that is, to around CSK 15 to DEM 1. Unlike the West German government, the Czechoslovak government accepted this depreciation. Following the example of Poland and Hungary, Minister of Finance Václav Klaus intended to keep the national currency cheap in order to boost exports; save the large, formerly socialist enterprises; and keep unemployment down. This strategy worked rather well until the Czech banking crisis of 1996. While the currency depreciation made Czechoslovak exports cheaper by a factor of around 3 (that is, when taking the official exchange rate in 1989 as a point of reference), German monetary union meant a fourfold price increase for East German exports compared with the 1988 clearing rate. This automatically meant that eastern German products – a Wartburg car, to name a typical example – would never be able to compete with a Škoda or any other Czech product, and that production shifts in industry would most likely pass eastern Germany by.

Monetary union was followed by a second shock to the eastern German economy: the quick liberalization of foreign trade. When East Germany joined the Federal Republic of Germany and, by doing so, the European Community, all trade barriers fell; a step that is laid down, in principle, in the Washington Consensus. The eastern German economy was not able to cope with this competition. From this perspective, joining the European Union (EU) not before 2004 was an advantage for the other post-communist countries. But still, the conditions for integration into the European single market and the world market were a lot less protective than in the three decades after 1945, when Western Europe was reconstructed and West Germany experienced its *Wirtschaftswunder*.

The third particularity of German transformation was radical privatization, which disregarded a basic market mechanism. There were times when Treuhandanstalt, the German government agency responsible for privatization, was in charge of 12 534 enterprises with more than 4 million employees. More than 10 000 enterprises were sold by the end of 1992 alone; that is, in a period of only two years (for details, also on data provided in the following, see Böick 2018). If such huge numbers of enterprises are put onto the market, it is clear that their sales prices will drop dramatically. And indeed, instead of the expected profit of around DEM 600 billion, Treuhandanstalt recorded losses in the amount of DEM 270 billion; that is, more than DEM 15 000 per (former) GDR citizen. At the end of 1994, Germany's federal government proudly announced the dissolution of Treuhandanstalt, stating that privatization had been completed. But with most privatized enterprises, production was simply discontinued. In the enterprises sold by Treuhandanstalt, only every fourth job was preserved according to Böick's (2018) calculations. To this day, many mostly medium-sized towns whose prosperity had depended on a small number of large factories have not been able to cope with this structural break.

These critical remarks on Germany's shock therapy – which, unlike Poland's, never became known by that name – prompt the question of whether there would have been any alternatives. In the early 1990s, this was of course denied: 'there is no alternative' was the prevailing attitude toward the reforms. Maintaining a realistic exchange rate during monetary union would have disappointed many voters in eastern Germany and created an even wider pay and pensions gap. Would this have been enough for even more people to move from eastern Germany to western Germany, as had been feared? This question cannot be answered *ex post*. It is a fact, however, that despite the cushioning of the reforms and despite high transfer payments from western Germany to eastern Germany, 1.4 million people moved from the eastern to the western

German *Länder* in only four years (on East–West migration, see Martens 2010). In this respect, the wider objective of monetary union, namely to keep the people in eastern Germany, was not achieved.

When we look beyond Germany, we see that there were indeed alternatives to quick privatization. In Poland, the Czech Republic and in particular in Slovakia, for instance, large enterprises of strategic importance continued to be run under state management and were sold only at the end of the 1990s. This did not mean that these enterprises continued to make losses like they did before 1989; they had to work for profit, which some of them actually succeeded at.

A measure to which there most likely was 'no alternative' was the liberalization of foreign trade and the opening of the eastern German market. Slowing down these processes would probably have been possible only within a special customs area, with different import restrictions or within a special economic zone. The People's Republic of China applied such measures in a number of regions; in the EU, however, these would have been difficult to enforce. Moreover, a special economic zone in eastern Germany or in parts of the East German *Länder* would have entailed stronger economic competition for western German producers; something neither politicians nor enterprises in western Germany had any interest in. Tough competition from the West also hit those former GDR citizens who had started their own businesses. Compared with other professional groups and with new entrepreneurs in Poland and the Czech Republic, they fared worse. Often, the self-employed experienced a social decline; in the worst case, their businesses went bankrupt (see Diewald and Mach 2006, p. 261). The professional group that suffered the least were civil servants; unless they lost their positions because they had secretly collaborated with the State Security Service (Stasi) or held a prominent position in the SED. Through monetary union and the expansion of collective wage agreements to include the five 'new *Länder*', eastern German civil servants saw their salaries climb substantially. This was all the more true for the many western German civil servants who were sent to work in eastern Germany. They even received special bonus payments (colloquially called *Buschzulage*) for working in eastern Germany. However, the German federal government lacked further visions about which social classes and elites, apart from imported civil servants, were to carry eastern Germany forward.

The price for this mixture of national self-centredness, neoliberalism and lack of vision for society was an unprecedented economic downturn. By the mid-1990s, industrial production in eastern Germany had dropped to 27 per cent of its 1988 level. No other post-communist country in Europe, not even war-torn Bosnia and Herzegovina, saw a comparably dramatic decline (see Norkus 2012, p. 80). As a result, 1.4 million people from the 'new *Länder*' left their homes in the period up to 1994, as already mentioned. This number corresponded almost exactly to that of newly established businesses in Czechoslovakia: the Czechoslovak Socialist Republic (CSSR) had almost as many inhabitants as the GDR, which allows for comparisons of the two countries. In Poland and in Hungary, too, many people started their own businesses. Altogether, around 4 million businesses were newly established in the Visegrád countries in the first five years after 1989.[8] In the GDR, the number of newly founded businesses was significantly lower.

The collapse of the eastern German economy strained the government budget and, in particular, social security funds which, directly or indirectly, had to provide for the millions of unemployed. The government issued early retirement programmes, the cost of which was mostly imposed on pension funds, and health insurance providers had to make high transfer payments as well. But pacifying the eastern German 'losers of transformation' by social benefits could not be financed in the long run (for details on the crisis of the German welfare state, see Ritter 2006). The continuous rise of social security contributions, taxes and government debt continued in the 1990s, at the expense of economic growth throughout Germany. The united Germany had reached a dead end. Federal Chancellor Helmut Kohl lost the 1998 federal elections, and Gerhard Schröder won; not least, by promising reforms.

3.4   SECOND-STAGE REFORMS AND COTRANSFORMATION

Schröder's centre-left coalition government, formed by the Social Democratic Party of Germany (SPD) and Alliance 90/The Greens, then took a series of measures that had already been implemented in East Central Europe at an earlier stage. These included the partial privatization of pension funds and labour market liberalization. For some time, Germany saw lively discussions about introducing a flat tax[9] on wages and income and an otherwise strongly simplified tax system, as well as about collecting healthcare contributions instead of income-related health insurance contributions. With regard to post-communist Europe, we may speak of a cotransformation that originated in the problems of running eastern Germany and eventually impacted on the former West Germany. Of course, reforms and policy models in the West were also a point of reference, especially the social reforms enacted by United Kingdom prime minister Tony Blair's New Labour.

What was new about the red–green labour market and social reforms was that they hit people in western Germany as hard as people in eastern Germany, although the latter were affected more by the cutbacks because of the high level of long-term unemployment. Moreover, lower wage growth (below the level of inflation in some years) caused 'internal depreciation'. This situation, however, had rather resulted from the negotiations between employers and trade unions under the *Bündnis für Arbeit* (Alliance for Work), which was in place from 1998 to 2002, than from the reforms. Even before that time, compromises were frequently made at the enterprise level, in line with the slogan 'preserving jobs through pay restraints'. This was the contribution that corporatist Germany, though much condemned at the time, made to ensuring that German industry could later regain competitiveness.

Most mainstream economists have lauded the long-term effect of the Hartz reforms. But the reforms had a negative effect on social and regional disparities. Social inequality in Germany rose from its original level, which almost matched levels observed in Scandinavia, to levels comparable with those recorded in other post-communist countries such as Hungary or Poland. Germany's Gini coefficient, the international standard measure of income inequality, went up from 0.25 in 1999 to 0.29 in the 2009 crisis year.[10] While these developments cannot be traced to one single factor such as Hartz IV, it is indisputable that the social and labour market reforms increased fears of social decline. This was, in fact, the intention: the threat of poverty was to motivate people to take on jobs that were badly paid and for which they had to commute much further.

This negative mobilization, which took on an even greater dimension in the poorer post-communist countries, may have contributed to the subsequent 'German job miracle', but at the same time it caused uncertainty among broad segments of society. This is where we find the underlying reasons for the high numbers of votes for the right-wing populist party Alternative for Germany (AfD) in eastern Germany: in Saxony, the AfD even came in strongest in the 2017 parliamentary elections, beating the CDU by a narrow margin. For Germany, this was a political shock; which, however, comes as less of a surprise when comparing the former GDR with Poland, the Czech Republic or Slovakia. Both here and there, it was not only the 'transformation losers' who voted for populist parties, but also middle-class voters who were now better off than before, but who remembered former unemployment and social decline and were afraid – not least on account of the so-called refugee crisis and its instrumentalization by right-wing populists – that things might change and they might have to face social cutbacks yet again.[11]

The fundamental problem here, as with the EU as a whole, is that the current economic order is beneficial particularly to those countries, regions and social groups that are already well positioned. Other parts of Europe and its societies, by contrast, are falling behind and have poor economic prospects.

In some ways, Hartz IV meant a reversal of the 1990 strategy. While monetary union aimed for a swift Westernization, Hartz IV and, above all, the newly introduced low-wage sector (for example '*Ein-Euro-Jobs*', which implied an hourly rate of €1) led to an adjustment of labour costs to wages that were common in Poland and the Czech Republic at the time. This is yet another example of how the united Germany was cotransformed. The very concept of a low-wage sector, however, was developed by Chicago School economists and tested in the 1980s in the 'Rust Belt' states of the United States. Later, the experiment was discarded because it did not yield the desired results.

The Hartz reforms, however, did little to ease the predicament of the five 'new *Länder*'. This was due, among other things, to the fact that labour market activation (the unemployed were now called 'job seekers') did not help much in regions where there were no or hardly any jobs. There, the government had no other option than to support the unemployed, send them into early retirement or occupy them through job creation measures. This continued to be costly; in total, net transfer payments from western to eastern Germany in the 25 years from 1989 to 2014 came to €1.6 trillion (in this case, 'net' means that return flows from eastern to western Germany and transfers to the federal budget, for example through taxes collected from eastern Germans, are taken into account).[12] In record years, net transfer payments amounted to up to €100 billion, which were spent on modernizing infrastructure, privatization and, above all, social benefits.

Despite these flows of funds, the 'new *Länder*' only generated roughly two-thirds of western German GDP per capita in 2015 (these figures are based on collated economic data for the five 'new *Länder*'; for details, see the extended new edition of Ther 2016a).[13] The Czech Republic, which had to cope without the support of a 'big brother' in the West, reached almost the same GDP per capita (purchasing power parity) without these transfer payments.

3.5   SUMMARY AND CONCLUSIONS

Germany's history since the fall of the Berlin Wall gives rise to critical questions on various topics: the neoliberal reform concepts of the early 1990s and the early 2000s on the one hand, and the effectiveness of government spending programmes on the other. Moreover, any critical examination should also deal with the long-term consequences of the massive uncertainty that was created within society by mass unemployment, the high rates of East–West migration and the way the German public has dealt with these issues since 1990. This applies not only to the former GDR, but to all new EU Member States where economic reforms – irrespective of their economic assessment – came at a price, both politically and socially. Obviously, not enough people have profited from the reforms (see Milanovic 2013). One consequence of these disparities has been a drastic increase in labour migration from East to West.

It would be too simple, however, to trace any later successes or problems to the shock therapy Germany went through. Moreover, countries that hesitated to implement reforms in the early 1990s (such as Romania, Bulgaria and

Ukraine) did not fare any better. Still, the argument by Shleifer and Treisman (2014) that there was a direct causal link between the radical reforms and subsequent economic growth – in terms of cause and effect – cannot be upheld. There were other factors that also played a decisive role in the course of economic transformation, such as timing: the forerunners of reform had an enormous initial advantage, as had those countries that had already permitted private businesses to a greater extent in the 1980s. Another equally important factor was the geographical proximity to Western European markets: production was moved to post-communist countries located closer to Western Europe rather than to countries farther off. Irrespective of these factors, educational levels were comparably high across all post-communist countries (a fact that was woefully ignored during the time of transformation), experts were well trained and wage levels were low. This is not to say that good or bad economic policies did not play a role. But the argument that the shock therapy was at the root of all subsequent economic success does not hold, as the examples of eastern Germany and Poland show.

Moreover, if we only told a success story, we would disregard the problems that occur when building democracies, as exemplified in the populist revolt that took place in the 2001 and 2005 elections in Poland, or in the protest votes for the post-communist Party of Democratic Socialism (PDS) in eastern Germany. The global financial crisis of 2009 and the euro crisis of 2011 called into question the *teloi* of transformation: the pure doctrine of market economy, liberal democracy and the desired convergence with the West. With the *annus horribilis* of 2016 (a majority of pro-Brexit votes in the British EU referendum, Donald Trump elected President of the United States, defeat of the reformatory left in the Italian constitutional referendum), we have entered a new era. Since then, 'the West' as a relatively homogeneous community of values that had been in place since the end of World War II has ceased to exist. In this respect, transformation – which after 1989 had been understood to be teleologically designed – has come to an end. The core countries of liberal capitalism – England and the United States – have become increasingly protectionist; parliamentary democracy and the rule of law have been weakened; European integration has almost come to a standstill or is being scaled back; and even the word 'reform' has widely fallen into disrepute. All this is happening in an economic context that is actually characterized by a generally buoyant global economy. We do not know what might happen politically if there were a recession or a strong rise in interest rates. But as we have seen from the 1989 experience, each change also holds an opportunity.

NOTES

1. Of course, Arendt had not yet discussed the events of 1989 in her book *On Revolution* (Arendt 1963), but they fit in with her pattern of constitutional or liberal revolutions laid down therein.
2. The phrase was coined by Alejandro Foxley, Chile's first post-dictatorial finance minister, whose views were influenced by Catholic social teaching. For details on his reform concepts, see various documents that can be found in the World Bank archive's files on Chile; in this context, in particular, an 11-page manifest from 1988 and the records of conversations on the occasion of Foxley's at the World Bank in 1989 stored in the World Bank archive, World Bank File 16435 (Chile – Lending, Economy and Program (LEAP) – General – Volume 2), the annex to the World Bank report of 18 October 1988, and World Bank File 16436 (Chile – Lending, Economy and Program (LEAP) – General – Volume 3), and the report of 30 October 1989 (all World Bank files quoted here are without pagination). On Chile's economic policy and the historical changes of 1989, see also Ffrench-Davis (2010).
3. For details on the contemporary rationale behind the reforms, see Balcerowicz (1992). In this book, Balcerowicz uses the word 'shock', which he had prudently avoided in 1989. For details on the American consultants' view of the design of these radical reforms, see Lipton and Sachs (1990, pp. 47–66).
4. See the figures in wiiw (2012), table II/1.7. In December 1989, Balcerowicz had expected a slight decrease in demand and a limited rise in unemployment (see Balcerowicz 1989, pp. 1, 5, in particular column 2 on p. 1).
5. For details, see also Kołodko (2000). For the positive narrative of the shock therapy, against which he was arguing and polemicizing, see Balcerowicz (1992).
6. See also the television documentary called *Free to Choose*, which Friedman produced in 1990 for the Public Broadcasting Service (PBS), a United States public television broadcaster. In episode 4 on *Freedom and Prosperity*, Friedman travelled to CESEE. The episode also features Václav Klaus, who readily confirms Friedman's teachings. The programme is accessible online at www.youtube.com/watch?v=l2h5OR1QX3Y (retrieved on 11 November 2018). Klaus appears at minute 20.
7. For details on the calculation of the exchange rate, see Sinn and Sinn (1992). For details on the proposal by the State Bank of the GDR, see an interview by Deutschlandfunk of 28 February 2015, with the bank's vice president Edgar Most, accessible online at www.deutschlandfunk.de/25-jahre-treuhandanstalt -eine-einzige-schweinerei.694.de.html?dram:article_id=312882 (retrieved on 20 February 2019).
8. See the figures on enterprises provided in Berend (2009, p. 61). It should be added, though, that many of these newly self-employed persons took this step because they had lost their jobs. Many of these one-person businesses in trade and retail went out of business when Western supermarkets began to spread.
9. After the turn of the millennium, the flat tax was introduced in all the other post-communist countries (see Appel and Orenstein 2018, pp. 90–116; on pension reforms at the global level, see Orenstein 2009); however, in the aftermath of the 2009 crisis, it was discontinued in many countries.
10. The data quoted here for Scandinavia and CESEE are accessible at www.gini -research.org/articles/cr. The respective country reports also provide information

on the type of data collection. For details on the social impacts of the Hartz reforms, see *inter alia* Dörre et al. (2013) and Butterwegge (2015).

11. For details, see one of the most perceptive books published recently among the many contributions on populism: Manow (2018, p. 94).
12. The figure of €1.6 trillion is quoted from Kühl (2014). The problem with these estimations is that the German federal government has not collected exact statistical data on transfer payments since 1999. Transfer payments also comprise reconstruction aid (which, in some cases, could also be applied for in western Germany) and special benefits, for example special economic promotion programmes. A comprehensive calculation of all individual types of payments and return flows can be found in Blum et al. (2009).
13. The calculations provided in Ther (2016a), in turn, are based on data on the so-called NUTS2 regions, which are available from Eurostat at ec.europa.eu/eurostat/tgm/table.do?tab=table&init=1&language=en&pcode=tgs00006&plugin=1 (retrieved on 11 November 2018). Eurostat data are updated regularly; the last census in Germany, for example, entailed adjustments as population figures were corrected downward and thus GDP per capita had to be corrected upward. There is also the problem that due to the unification of East and West Berlin, the data on the former capital of East Germany are not included here, while Prague is of course included in the data of the Czech Republic and pulls the GDP of the entire country upward. Hence, one could argue about the comparability of these data. Nevertheless, the tendency is clear enough, like before 1989, when the Czech part of Czechoslovakia trailed the GDR quite closely; nowadays the Czech Republic is not far behind the Eastern *Länder* of Germany. Of course, there are other economic data that are more comprehensive than GDP data, such as the Human Development Index (HDI); but only GDP data have been collected regularly also at the regional and local level (according to NUTS3 regions, *inter alia*) since 1989; this is why Ther (2016a) and this chapter refer mostly to GDP data.

REFERENCES

Appel, H. and M. Orenstein (2018), *From Triumph to Crisis: Neoliberal Economic Reform in Postcommunist Countries*, Cambridge: Cambridge University Press.

Arendt, H. (1963), *On Revolution*, New York: Viking Press.

Balcerowicz, L. (1989), 'Albo szybko, albo wcale', in *Polityka* 33 (48), 2 December, 1 and 5.

Balcerowicz, L. (1992), *800 Dni Szok Kontrolowany*, Warsaw: Polska Oficyna Wydawnicza.

Berend, I.T. (2009), *From the Soviet Bloc to the European Union*, Cambridge: Cambridge University Press.

Blum, U., J. Ragnitz, S. Freye, S. Scharfe and L. Schneider (2009), 'Regionalisierung öffentlicher Ausgaben und Einnahmen – Eine Untersuchung am Beispiel der Neuen Länder', IWH special issue 4, Halle: Institute for Economic Research.

Böick, M. (2018), *Die Treuhand. Idee – Praxis – Erfahrung 1990–1994*, Göttingen: Wallstein.

Borkowski, M. (1988), 'Sprzedać, oddać, wydzierżawić', *Polityka* 32 (49), 3 December, 1 and 4.

Butterwegge, C. (2015), *Hartz IV und die Folgen. Auf dem Weg in eine andere Republik?*, Weinheim/Basel: Beltz Juventa.

Diewald, M. and B. Mach (2006), 'Comparing Paths of Transition: Employment
    Opportunities and Earnings in East Germany and Poland During the First Ten Years
    of the Transformation Process', in M. Diewald, A. Goedicke and K. U. Mayer (eds),
    After the Fall of the Wall. Life Courses in the Transformation of East Germany,
    Stanford: Stanford University Press, 237–268.
Dörre, K., K. Scherschel, M. Booth, T. Haubner, K. Marquardsen and K. Schierhorn
    (2013), *Bewährungsproben für die Unterschicht? Soziale Folgen aktivierender
    Arbeitsmarktpolitik*, Frankfurt: Campus.
The Economist (1999), 'The Sick Man of the Euro', 3 June, www.economist.com/node/
    209559 (retrieved on 5 May 2014).
Ffrench-Davis, R. (2010), *Economic Reforms in Chile: From Dictatorship to
    Democracy*, London: Palgrave Macmillan.
Fukuyama, F. (1989), 'The End of History?', *National Interest* 16, Summer, 3–18.
Heilbroner, R. (1989), 'The Triumph of Capitalism', *New Yorker*, 23 January.
Kołodko, G. (2000), *From Shock to Therapy: The Political Economy of Postsocialist
    Transformation*, Oxford: Oxford University Press.
Kühl, J. (2014), '25 Jahre deutsche Einheit: Annäherungen und verbliebene
    Unterschiede zwischen West und Ost', 4 July, www.bpb.de/politik/innenpolitik/
    arbeitsmarktpolitik/55390/25-jahre-deutsche-einheit?p=all   (retrieved   on   20
    February 2019).
Lipton, D. and J.D. Sachs (1990), 'Poland's Economic Reform', *Foreign Affairs* 3 (69),
    47–66.
Manow, P. (2018), *Die politische Ökonomie des Populismus*, Berlin: Suhrkamp.
Martens, B. (2010), 'Zug nach Westen – Anhaltende Abwanderung', 30 March, www
    .bpb.de/geschichte/deutsche-einheit/lange-wege-der-deutschen-einheit/47253/zug
    -nach-westen?p=all (retrieved on 20 February 2019).
Milanovic, B. (2013), 'Reform and Inequality in the Transition: An Analysis Using
    Panel Household Survey', in G. Roland (ed.), *Economies in Transition: The Long
    Run View*, London: Palgrave Macmillan, 84–108.
Norkus, Z. (2012), *On Baltic Slovenia and Adriatic Lithuania: A Qualitative
    Comparative Analysis of Patterns in Post-Communist Transformation*, Budapest:
    CEU Press.
Orenstein, M. (2009), *Privatizing Pensions: The Transnational Campaign for Social
    Security Reform*, Princeton, NJ: Princeton University Press.
Ritter, G.A. (2006), *Der Preis der deutschen Einheit. Die Wiedervereinigung und die
    Krise des Sozialstaates*, Munich: C.H. Beck.
Shleifer, A. and D. Treisman (2014), 'Normal Countries: The East 25 Years after
    Communism', *Foreign Affairs* 93 (6), www.foreignaffairs.com/articles/142200/
    andrei-shleifer-and-daniel-treisman/normal-countries (retrieved on 17 May 2019).
Sinn, G. and H.-W. Sinn (1992), *Kaltstart. Volkswirtschaftliche Aspekte der deutschen
    Vereinigung*, Tübingen: dtv.
Ther, P. (2016a), *Die neue Ordnung auf dem alten Kontinent. Eine Geschichte des
    neoliberalen Europa*, Berlin: Suhrkamp.
Ther, P. (2016b), 'Neoliberalismus, Version: 1.0', *Docupedia-Zeitgeschichte*,
    docupedia.de/zg/ther_neoliberalismus_v1_de_2016 (retrieved on 2 February 2019).
wiiw (2012), *wiiw Handbook 2012*, Vienna: wiiw.

PART II

A central banker's view on monetary policy
during transition

4. Monetary policy challenges during transition: the case of Serbia

Jorgovanka Tabaković and Ana Ivković

During the period of transition to market economies, the economies of former socialist countries underwent major changes. As regards monetary policy, for example, central banks changed monetary policy goals, regimes and instruments. Although almost all of the countries concerned differed in terms of their starting point and monetary policy implementation, their central banks all focused on low and stable inflation in the transition agenda. Yet, bringing inflation down from high or moderate levels to low levels is a long and costly process, even in advanced economies.

The Serbian case can be used as a good example of a small and open economy with deep roots of euroization and hyperinflation back in the 1990s. It took Serbia years to find the right path; since 2012, however, policymakers have made a turnaround. Imbalances have been reduced, growth structures changed, structural reforms implemented, and prices as well as exchange markets stabilized. Moreover, from 2012 onward, the country's inflation targeting regime switched to a consistent approach to and full coordination of its policies, with full commitment to stability.

4.1 LEGACY FROM THE PAST: SERBIA'S TRANSITION PATH

The period after the fall of the Berlin Wall was marked by transition challenges for many countries, including Serbia. It was a time when there were no instructions on how to guarantee successful transition. There were only the standard policy recommendations of the so-called Washington Consensus (see Williamson 1990), which primarily reflected the views of the majority of experts in academia and international institutions. Transition implied a broad range of changes, such as privatization, new institutional infrastructure, deregulation, price liberalization, tax reforms and a newly created business environment. Yet, the interpretation and implementation of these changes varied from one country to another.

In general, the economies of former socialist countries underwent major changes during the transition period. They were faced with specificities that were rather complex and full of challenges. During transition, central banks, too, had to offer solutions and adjust their monetary policy toolkit. This was not an easy task, especially due to the lack of adequate theories or models that could be applied to countries in transition, but most of all, due to the lack of success stories. This is exactly where the case of Serbia comes in, serving as an example of what a difference the right policy toolkit can make.

Serbia went through several different stages during transition, with each of them involving specific problems. Although beginning formally in the late 1980s, it was only ten years later that the transition process in Serbia began technically. During the 1990s, a gross domestic product (GDP) gap opened up, even though the starting position of Serbia was better compared to that of many other transition economies as well as other former Yugoslav republics. This is why, despite accelerated progress since mid-2012, Serbia now has to catch up much more as it lost much more compared to other countries, due to reasons given in the next section.

The Late 1980s and the 1990s

Despite problems during the period of the former Yugoslavia, such as high inflation and external debt, Serbia had better macroeconomic and infrastructure preconditions than many other socialist countries at that time. However, due to several events, the country had to bear huge losses. The break-up of Yugoslavia first reduced, and then halted payment and trade transactions between former republics altogether. Moreover, irreparable human and material losses were caused by the wars, the bombing of Serbia, the economic embargo, the deindustrialization, the grey economy and the devastating effects of one of the worst hyperinflation episodes in the world. Yet, the loss of people was the biggest loss the Serbian economy experienced. The economic policy pursued, including privatization without appropriate institutional infrastructure, called into question the prospects of a market economy. Due to this combination of events, Serbia saw a dramatic fall in economic activity, employment and wages instead of growth and development. Money printing, the collapse of the domestic currency and unsustainably rising public and external debt put a further drag on the country's economy.

Attempts to Stabilize the Economy in 2000–2012

In the early 2000s, the state of the Serbian economy was quite challenging: a wrecked economy, hyperinflation, huge external debt, loss of the Yugoslav market, lack of foreign exchange reserves. All of this called for macroeconomic stabilization and numerous reforms. At the start of the stabilization process, the authorities chose the exchange rate as a nominal anchor for curbing inflation. Indeed, inflation was brought down from around 110 per cent at end-2000 to around 15 per cent at end-2002, but it was still above the price stability level. Subsequently, the monetary policy strategy was changed first to real exchange rate targeting (in 2003), and then to inflation targeting (implicit from August 2006, explicit from 2009 onward). Yet, on average, inflation was still over 10 per cent (11.5 per cent in 2003–2008).

At the time, Serbia's economic growth was such that attempts were made to compensate for the large gap of the 1990s. Despite being relatively high (around 6 per cent annually from 2001 to 2008), economic growth largely relied on the rise in services (with reduced shares of industry and agriculture) on the production side. On the expenditure side, it strongly relied on final consumption (see Figure 4.1). As domestic demand grew much faster than GDP, the difference was made up by imports (mostly of consumer goods), which was financed by privatization receipts, cross-border borrowing of the private sector and domestic loans. At this point, it is worth mentioning the specifics of credit expansion both in Serbia and in other countries of the region at the beginning of the 21st century. Starting from low levels, high lending activity growth rates resulted from dynamic consumption-driven economic growth and the process of real income convergence toward the EU. One of the reasons behind this

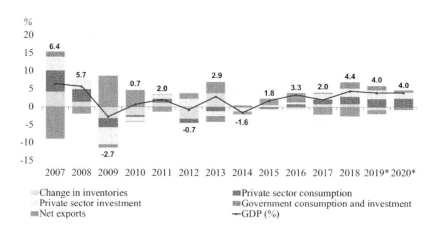

Note: * Forecast.
Sources: Statistical Office of the Republic of Serbia and National Bank of Serbia calculations.

Figure 4.1   Real GDP growth and components

pre-crisis growth in credit activity was the privatization of the financial sector, which led, in particular, to the arrival of foreign banks which aimed at increasing their market shares. Back then, banks based their assessment of credit risk and collateral on less conservative models than they do today.

In 2008, the developments described above culminated in record high external trade and current account deficits (see Figure 4.2). As this process was gaining momentum, the volume of credit expansion entered the territory where it spurred inflationary pressures, which necessitated the implementation of measures to limit lending to the household sector. The rise in the required reserve ratio and the introduction of a limit on loans to households in relation to core capital caused credit expansion to be lower than if these measures had not been implemented. Nevertheless, expansion continued at high rates.

Then, the global economic crisis emerged and further aggravated the unfavourable trends in the Serbian economy. At the time, both internal and external imbalances were posing huge challenges for monetary and economic policies in general. Inflows of foreign direct investment (FDI) contracted sharply, while foreign banks started deleveraging toward their parent banks. It became obvious that consumption-driven economic growth was no longer sustainable in the long run and that Serbia had to shift to a growth model based on investments and exports. Major balance-of-payments adjustments took place in 2009; yet, they were not led by exports but rather by a drop in domestic demand and economic contraction.

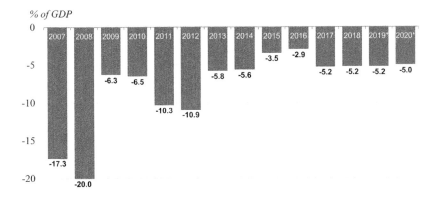

Note: * Forecast.
Source: National Bank of Serbia.

Figure 4.2   Current account balance

Economic recovery over the following four years (2009–2012) was relatively slow, with two of the four years recording negative growth rates. The positive effects of more expansive fiscal policies on economic activity did not materialize as most fiscal stimuli spilled over to imports, which influenced the gradual, but cumulatively significant, deepening of external and fiscal imbalances (see Figures 4.2 and 4.3). In such conditions, public debt soared, the country's rating deteriorated, and risk premiums increased.

In such a macroeconomic environment, monetary policy was also facing strong challenges. Monetary policy easing in Serbia during the first years following the crisis could not be applied to a greater extent due to persistent and relatively strong external shocks, volatile capital flows toward emerging economies, prevailing inflationary pressures and accumulated internal and external imbalances. The first effects of the crisis – reduced foreign capital inflows and withdrawals of foreign currency deposits from the banking system – caused the dinar to depreciate despite significant interventions. This put an additional upward pressure on the already high inflation expectations.

Responding to the crisis, the National Bank of Serbia (NBS) introduced a number of changes to regulations in early 2009, this time with a view to stimulating credit activity and enabling more favourable credit repayment terms. In this context, the Vienna Initiative played a major role.

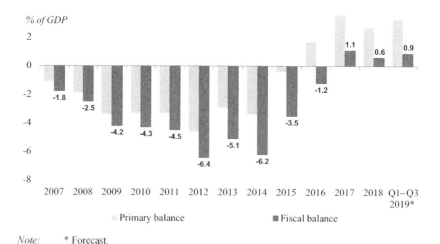

Note: * Forecast.
Source: Ministry of Finance.

Figure 4.3   Fiscal balance

The three years that followed saw alternate periods of monetary policy easing and tightening. Monetary conditions became quite volatile, which was not conducive to business. A vigorous rise in the prices of primary agricultural commodities, which spilled over to food prices and inflation expectations, in combination with depreciation pressures led to a relatively strong increase in year-on-year inflation (see Figure 4.4) and to calls for monetary policy tightening in 2010 and 2012. In general, inflation was volatile in that period, mainly reflecting volatile food prices with a relatively high share in the consumer price index, but also the volatile exchange rate of the dinar at the time.

Real Transformation of the Serbian Economy from mid-2012 to 2019

The Serbian economy[1] started to fundamentally transform into a stable and viable economy from 2012 onward when investments and exports took over from consumption the dominant role in GDP formation. It was the time when the Serbian economy was placed on a sustainable growth trajectory, with the NBS contributing significantly to such a fundamental transformation.

The lack of results as regards the stabilization of inflation in the period 2009–2012 did not call into question the implementation of the inflation targeting regime; rather, it imposed the need to re-examine the approach applied, partly because of the (post-)crisis environment. It was necessary to restore the credibility of monetary policy, as Serbia was faced with hyperinflation back in the 1990s, high euroization and a consequently high exchange rate

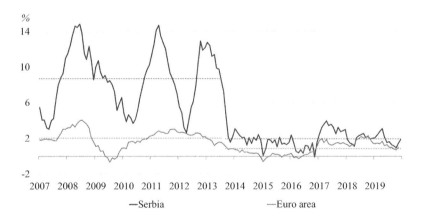

Sources: Statistical Office of the Republic of Serbia and Eurostat.

Figure 4.4   Year-on-year inflation rate

pass-through to prices which affected the monetary policy transmission mechanism and dented trust in monetary policy.

By combining regular instruments – that is the key policy rate, required reserves, foreign exchange market interventions and standing facilities – the NBS has succeeded in delivering stability and supporting growth since the second half of 2012. From a monetary policy perspective, it was the combination of rules and flexibility that brought stability and supported growth, coupled with coherent policies, including successful fiscal consolidation, central bank independence and communication as the fifth transmission channel of monetary policy. All of that was rounded off with a proactive approach. Thus, it was not just the framework that played an important role; it was also the approach. With the same instruments, quite different results have been achieved, and stability has been cemented.

Many monetary policy challenges were successfully dealt with in this period. First, Serbia managed to bring down inflation from double-digit rates to levels comparable with those of other European countries within one year. Afterwards, inflation was kept at a low and stable rate of around 2 per cent on average annually. Low inflationary pressures resulted from both international and domestic factors, with the latter including the relative stability of the exchange rate, restrictive fiscal policies and anchored inflation expectations. Low cost pressures were attributable, albeit not exclusively, to a drop in the prices of oil and other primary commodities. This was apparent from the fact that countries which did not reduce their imbalances recorded high inflation rates in the same period. In these countries, this was mainly due to the depreciation of their national currency amid geopolitical tensions, macroeconomic imbalances and higher volatility of capital flows. In Serbia, the impact of import prices on inflation and the impact of the exchange rate on prices played an important role as well. Analyses carried out by the NBS suggest that changes in import prices spilled over to domestic prices with a one-quarter lag on average. In the period before 2012, the effect of a shock in global primary commodity prices on domestic inflation was amplified by the effects of a significant depreciation of the dinar (see Figure 4.5).

However, the relative stability of the dinar exchange rate in the period after 2012 diminished the volatility of imported inflation and its impact on domestic inflation and inflation expectations (see NBS 2018). Thus, in the case of Serbia, relative stability in the foreign exchange market was one of the factors causing inflation to decline from double-digit rates to 2 per cent and to remain at low levels thereafter. Other important factors were good coordination of policies, regained credibility and improved communication.

Second, Serbia recognized the urgent need to anchor inflation expectations of the financial and corporate sectors as they were above 10 per cent most of the time and oscillated significantly (see Figure 4.6).

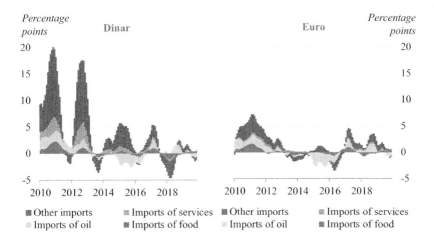

Sources: Destatis, FAO, Bloomberg, Eurostat, Statistical Office of the Republic of Serbia and National Bank of Serbia calculations.

Figure 4.5   *Contribution of individual components to year-on-year import price growth*

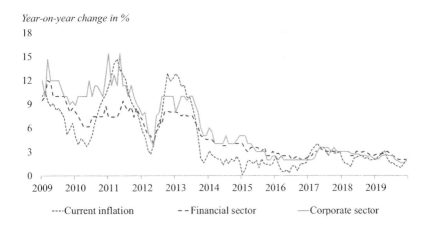

Sources: Gallup, Ninamedia, Ipsos and Statistical Office of the Republic of Serbia.

Figure 4.6   *Current inflation and short-term inflation expectations*

The results on the inflation front, boosted by transparent and intensive communication with the general public, brought inflation expectations within central bank target bands from 2013 onward. The anchoring of expectations had a positive feedback effect, given that stable and anchored inflation expectations helped, in turn, to maintain inflation at a low and stable level. It was the turning point for regaining much-needed monetary policy credibility and greater resilience to potential negative effects resulting from international developments. After that, inflation expectations of the financial and corporate sectors fluctuated between 2 per cent and 3 per cent for an extended period of time, which led, among other things, to the lowering of the inflation target to 3 per cent ±1.5 percentage points from 2017 onward (see Figure 4.7).

Third, monetary policymakers faced the huge challenge of addressing the lack of trust in the domestic currency, which was reflected in the high share of foreign exchange loans and deposits. By creating a stable environment in terms of inflation and relative exchange rate stability, dinar savings started to rise. Seven years later, in 2019, dinar savings were 4.5 times higher than in 2012, with 10 per cent of dinar savings being deposited for more than two years. At the same time, the share of public debt in dinars increased from 19 per cent in 2012 to 28 per cent in 2019. In December 2018, Serbia's updated dinarization strategy was signed (the original strategy dates back to 2012) to acknowledge what had already been done and to focus on what remains to be done (see NBS and Government of the Republic of Serbia 2018).

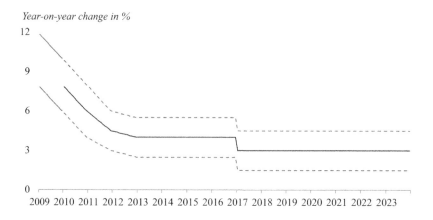

Source: National Bank of Serbia.

Figure 4.7   *Inflation target and corridor in Serbia from 2009 onward*

Fourth, Serbia addressed the high level of non-performing loans (NPLs) which also had a constraining effect on the monetary policy transmission mechanism. The burden of NPLs, a problem inherited from the past, was resolved systematically in coordination with all relevant stakeholders. In parallel, key macroeconomic assumptions for the sustainable reduction of NPLs were created or revised, contributing to a more favourable and predictable investment environment. As a result, the regulatory framework, together with stability and recovering lending activity, brought the share of NPLs down by 18 percentage points and their stock by around 80 per cent (see Figure 4.8) compared to the period when the NPL resolution strategy was adopted.

Fifth, another challenge that had to be tackled was the high interest rate environment which hindered not only the greater use of the dinar, but also investment activity. In line with inflation results, a monetary policy easing cycle was initiated back in May 2013 (see Figure 4.9), and is still ongoing. In 2019, interest rates on dinar-denominated loans to households were more than two times lower than in 2013, while those on corporate loans were four times lower.

As the Serbian financial system is in a structural liquidity surplus, reserve requirements and repo operations are used to mop up liquidity. Year-end 2012 saw a shift to liquidity-absorbing repo operations at variable interest rates, stimulating banks to use a greater part of their excess liquidity for lending activity. With these measures, an additional mechanism for addressing tempo-

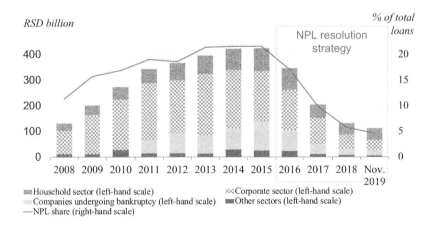

Source: National Bank of Serbia.

Figure 4.8 *Breakdown of NPLs by sectors*

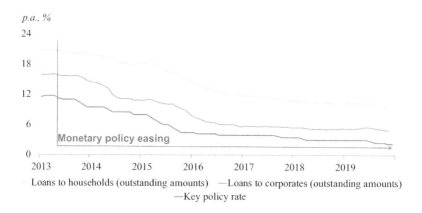

Source: National Bank of Serbia.

Figure 4.9   Interest rates on dinar-denominated loans to the
             non-financial sector

rary shocks was introduced, giving monetary policy greater flexibility in times
of more volatile capital flows. In other words, the introduction of these measures was a sort of a turning point in the dinar money market. Together with
monetary policy easing, they fed through to lower interest rates in the money
market due to higher competition, translating via this channel into lower
lending rates. This, in turn, increased the disposable income of households
and corporates, and stimulated lending as well as investment activities. From
2015 onward, investment loans in Serbia have had almost the same 'power' as
FDI inflows. In parallel, with the stability achieved and the demand for dinars
rising, the real tradable yield curve in Serbia with a ten-year tenor was created,
which will be extended to 12 years in 2020.

The narrowing of internal and external imbalances and the implementation
of a number of structural reforms (including labour market, investment, construction, bankruptcy proceedings and tax reforms) considerably improved
the overall investment climate. As a result, Serbia improved its position on
international competitiveness lists, and saw its country risk premium lowered
by close to 400 basis points compared to 2012 (see Figure 4.10). Moreover, the
country's credit rating was upgraded by one notch to investment grade.

Amid an improved investment environment, the investment cycle started
in 2015, with investments speeding up and growing by more than 15 per cent
on average in 2018–2019. This is why, in their latest December 2019 report,
Standard & Poor's assessed that the credit rating upgrade reflected Serbia's

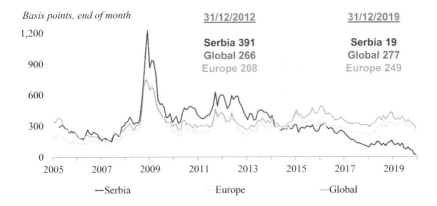

Source: JP Morgan.

Figure 4.10   Emerging Market Bond Index (EMBI) Serbia, Global and Europe

resilient exports and investment-driven economic growth despite the challenging external environment:

> Serbia's remarkable departure from its previous track-record of weak and volatile growth has been accompanied by the reduction in macroeconomic imbalances: net public debt has gone down; net FDI has exceeded current account deficits supporting external deleveraging; and price and financial stability has been enhanced . . . Our ratings on Serbia are supported by its educated workforce, the favorable prospects for FDI, the government's strong fiscal performance, moderate public debt, and credible monetary policy framework. (Standard & Poor's 2019)

4.2   MONETARY POLICY AND EXCHANGE RATE REGIMES

As outlined above, the state of the Serbian economy was quite challenging in the early 2000s, calling for macroeconomic stabilization and numerous reforms. From a monetary policy perspective, the 21st century saw several evolutionary stages of our monetary policy regime, until the right one – inflation targeting – was chosen.

Monetary Aggregate Targeting Supported by a Managed Floating Exchange Rate (Closer to a Peg) in 2001–2003

With the start of price liberalization from 2001 onward and the foreign exchange market unification,[2] the exchange rate served as a nominal anchor for fending off high inflation rates. The exchange rate, together with monetary aggregate targeting defined by Serbia's economic programme with the International Monetary Fund (IMF), formed the backbone of the monetary policy programme of that period. Even though inflation was lowered significantly, the surge in foreign capital inflows remained a huge challenge for monetary policy. Conditions characterized by an unstable money demand function undermined efforts to achieve the targeted monetary aggregate growth rate. All these factors taken together dented the credibility of monetary policy and its effectiveness in curbing inflation expectations.

De Jure Monetary Aggregate Targeting Supported by *De Facto* Real Exchange Rate Targeting in 2003–2006

Starting in 2003, the focus shifted to the problem of huge external imbalances which posed a challenge to monetary policy. The NBS tried to deal with external imbalances by containing real appreciation, thus allowing greater exchange rate flexibility and nominal depreciation of the dinar. However, due to a high level of euroization and the consequently high pass-through of nominal depreciation to inflation,[3] inflation was once again in double digits in 2004. The problem of external imbalances was not solved; on the contrary, it was aggravated further. This confirmed yet again that the exchange rate could not be used as the only tool to reduce the high current account deficit, and that structural competitiveness needed to be strengthened.

Implicit Inflation Targeting in 2006–2009

It was quite obvious at the time that other monetary policy responses were needed. Consequently, preparations were being made to switch to implicit (informal) inflation targeting which was introduced in September 2006. The following transition period from end-2006 to end-2008 was used to make the necessary changes to the monetary policy framework and to prepare for the core principles of inflation targeting. Based on the results achieved, we may conclude that monetary policy was only partly effective, not only due to the then loose fiscal policy that significantly hindered the stabilization of inflation at low levels, but also due to the high daily volatility of the dinar exchange rate.

Formal Inflation Targeting Supported by a Managed Floating Exchange Rate Regime from 2009 Onward

The initial years of inflation targeting (2009–2012) were marked by high and volatile inflation resulting not only from shocks in the international commodity markets, primarily in the global prices of oil and food, but also – and even more so – from the pronounced depreciation of the dinar and highly expansionary fiscal policy. Inflation came to 10 per cent on average, with inflation expectations following the same pattern. In April 2011, inflation reached 14.7 per cent, before falling sharply to around 2 per cent in 2013 and remaining at that level for the following six years (see Figure 4.4).

While international factors (low global prices of oil and food) contributed to low and stable inflation over these six years, domestic factors did so even more. They included full coordination of monetary and fiscal policies, relative exchange rate stability (see Figure 4.11) and anchored inflation expectations.

The road to achieving price stability required adequate and timely monetary policy measures. The easing cycle, which kicked off in May 2013, and the fiscal consolidation programme, which was adopted and consistently implemented as of end-2014, allowed for continued monetary policy accommodation, taking into account risks emanating from the international environment. The cuts in the key policy rate fully translated into lower interest rates for the private sector (see Figure 4.9). Lower interest rates, in turn, increased the dis-

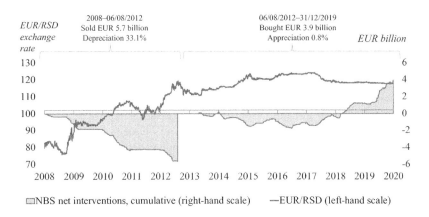

Source: National Bank of Serbia.

Figure 4.11   Exchange rate movements and NBS interventions in the foreign exchange market

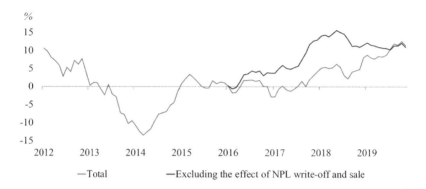

Source: National Bank of Serbia calculations.

Figure 4.12   Real year-on-year growth rates of corporate loans

posable income of corporates and households, and supported lending to corporates (see Figure 4.12), economic growth (see Figure 4.1), higher investment, employment and a favourable outlook.

Amid conditions characterized by a relatively high exchange rate pass-through to inflation and concurrent turbulences in the international financial market, the relative stability of the exchange rate in 2013–2019 was one of the factors that lowered inflation expectations in the long run (see Figure 4.6), anchoring them within the NBS target tolerance band. Relative exchange rate stability was also important for financial stability, given a relatively high share of foreign exchange-indexed loans in total loans. Moreover, it boosted business confidence, and gave an impetus for a strong investment cycle.

The exchange rate of the Serbian dinar was assessed as appropriate by many institutions, one of them being the IMF. In its report following Article IV consultations published in July 2019, the IMF assessed Serbia's external position according to the External Balance Assessment Lite methodology as 'broadly consistent with fundamentals and desirable policy settings'. Also, according to the current account approach, Serbia's current account norm was estimated at –4.6 per cent of GDP, 'suggesting an exchange rate broadly consistent with fundamentals' (IMF 2019).

In parallel, in their report published in December 2019, Standard & Poor's explained why they upgraded Serbia's credit rating by one notch to investment grade as follows:

The National Bank of Serbia (NBS) has proved its operational independence, earning credibility over the past six years. Effective actions under the inflation-targeting regime has [*sic*] allowed the NBS to anchor inflation expectations – despite a historically high euroization and past episodes of macroeconomic instability – and deliver low-single-digit inflation since late 2013 … Serbia's exchange rate regime is relatively flexible to allow the economy to adjust to evolving external conditions, while simultaneously avoiding sharp swings in the real effective exchange rate. Due to the still-extensive euroization of the economy, the NBS intervenes occasionally in the foreign exchange market to smooth short-term exchange rate volatility … Foreign exchange interventions have helped the NBS maintain both price and financial stability, as well as boost its international reserves to a record-high €13.5 billion. (Standard & Poor's 2019)

In late December 2019, JP Morgan published its report on expected macroeconomic and financial developments in emerging economies for 2020 (see Oganes and Goulden 2019). In its report, JP Morgan underscored that the Serbian dinar is realistically – that is, correctly – valued. Out of 25 analysed currencies of emerging markets from around the world, the Serbian dinar was one of two currencies singled out as realistically valued. According to the composite measure of all analysed currencies, 21 out of 25 emerging markets currencies are 'overvalued' or 'undervalued'. In its analysis, JP Morgan used various indicators, such as:

- the real effective exchange rate;
- relative productivity (GDP to employment);
- trade conditions (import to export prices);
- differences in interest rates (relative to the currency with which national currencies of each of the countries are compared);
- external balance (external debt to GDP); and
- fiscal (budgetary) balance.

The factors behind JP Morgan's assessment that the Serbian dinar is neither 'overvalued' nor 'undervalued', but correctly valued, are rising productivity and the share of investment in GDP, including a robust FDI inflow, which, along with domestic investment in infrastructure, contribute to future growth in productivity and exports. Moreover, JP Morgan's assessment was also based on the strong reduction of the share of external debt in GDP and the positive results achieved on the fiscal front.

4.3   CONCLUSIONS

During the last 30 years, a lot has changed in both developing and developed economies. Not only transition, but also modern developments have led to quite a different approach to policy implementation. The Phillips curve has flattened, structural characteristics of economies have changed, and global value chains have emerged. The crisis has stimulated a growing focus on the

Table 4.1   Stabilization of the Serbian economy and investment cycle

• **Predictability of business conditions and favourable terms of funding** • **Fiscal consolidation** • **Structural reforms** **Improved macroeconomic indicators** • Serbia's progress in rankings on competitiveness and relative ease of starting business • Credit rating upgrades **More favourable business and investment environment**	– **Monetary policy relaxation** by the NBS facilitates a strong reduction in interest rates on dinar-denominated loans, which increases the disposable income of the corporate and household sectors and supports economic growth, higher investment, employment and a favourable outlook. – **By preserving financial stability**, reducing the level of NPLs by around 80 per cent and by undertaking other measures, the NBS contributes to strengthening banks' credit potential. – **In December 2019, Standard & Poor's increased Serbia's rating by one notch to investment grade. In their report, they highlighted the NBS' credibility and operational independence** (see NBS 2019), as well as the adequacy of monetary policy decisions within the inflation targeting regime which have resulted in years-long preservation of low and stable inflation and anchored inflation expectations. Standard & Poor's also emphasized that the exchange rate regime and the preserved relative stability of the exchange rate – in addition to mitigating excessive short-term volatility – increased Serbia's resilience to potential shocks from the international environment, while facilitating, at the same time, the development of the domestic financial market.

Investment growth: During the new investment cycle (2015–2019), gross fixed investments increased by around 50 per cent in cumulative terms, with a strong rise in private investments (around 40 per cent) and government investment (around 90 per cent), bringing the share of investments in real GDP to around 24 per cent (from 17.5 per cent). Well-managed public finance enabled Serbia's government to support the growth outlook by increasing investment in infrastructure, which will also be in the focus of the 2020–2025 Growth Agenda.

Economic growth led by export and investment in tradable sectors: In 2015–2019, investment growth of around 10 per cent on average per year accounted for two-thirds of growth in that period. At the same time, this resulted in the modernization of production capacities.

Growth in competitiveness and exports: With the economy having become more advanced in technological terms and more cost-efficient, the value of goods and services exports increased by 65 per cent in 2015–2019, while the share of exports in GDP rose by more than 10 percentage points to around 50 per cent in 2019 (balance-of-payments methodology).

Microeconomic growth sustainability: In 2015–2018, the financial result of corporates improved by around RSD 630 billion. Interest expenses decreased by close to 50 per cent and exchange rate gains and losses by around 80 per cent. Corporates used their savings to increase investment, contributing, with this positive synergy, to making the medium-term growth outlook brighter.

Rise in the standard of living: In 2015–2019 (Q3), unemployment declined from 17 per cent to 9.5 per cent. At the same time, owing to increased employment and wages primarily in the private sector, household consumption was up by more than 6 per cent in real terms. Structural indicators, such as the youth and women unemployment rate, also improved substantially.

Serbia's sustainable growth model entails a more favourable growth outlook. It is opening up additional possibilities to accelerate growth and ensure a rise in living standards, investment and competitiveness as well as further transformation.

macroprudential framework at the global level. Digitalization has won more and more proponents. Central banks have introduced the fifth channel of monetary policy transmission, becoming more transparent and implementing formal or informal forms of forward guidance. In a nutshell, we have all learned a lot.

In Serbia, the real transformation of the economy and policy setting started back in 2012. From a monetary policy perspective, we have learned some important lessons from a decade of inflation targeting. These lessons stemmed, on the one hand, from conditions brought about by the crisis and, on the other hand, from the country's openness and readiness to introduce new solutions that fitted the domestic environment and helped overcome the external challenges as well as achieve our prime objectives. Such an approach was adopted during the second period of regime implementation and the results achieved proved that it had been justified. Since mid-2012, the Serbian economy has transformed fundamentally into an economy with low and stable inflation at around 2 per cent, anchored inflation expectations, a relatively stable currency, record-high foreign exchange reserves and NPLs that went down by 80 per cent. Furthermore, the country's economy has recorded a solid fiscal position, decreasing public debt, strong exports and a halved current account deficit. The period that was used for stabilization was followed by a period marked by a strong investment cycle (see Table 4.1 for detailed results). Since then, unemployment has more than halved, investments have been rising at two-digit rates and employment and wages in the private sector have been on a dynamically rising path. Serbia's growth composition has changed, with the share of consumption declining and the share of investment rising. The country's credit rating is rising, while its risk premium is at a record low. We may again quote Standard & Poor's, which noted that 'Serbia's remarkable departure from its previous track record of weak and volatile growth has been accompanied by the reduction in macroeconomic imbalances'.

NOTES

1. For more information on the state of the Serbian economy, the measures taken and the results achieved, see Tabaković (2017, 2018, 2019) as well as Tabaković and Ivković (2019).
2. Prior to the foreign exchange market unification, there was an official – *de jure* – foreign exchange market, and a so-called black – *de facto* – foreign exchange market.
3. The pass-through from exchange rate to inflation was estimated to have been nearly full after one year.

REFERENCES

International Monetary Fund (IMF) (2019), 'Republic of Serbia: Staff Report for the 2019 Article IV Consultation and Second Review under the Policy Coordination Instrument-Press Release; Staff Report; Information Annex; Staff Statement; and Statement by the Executive Director for Republic of Serbia', Country Report No. 19/238, July.

National Bank of Serbia (NBS) (2018), Inflation Report, February.

National Bank of Serbia (NBS) (2019), 'Serbia Upgraded To "BB+" on Resilient Macroeconomic Fundamentals; Outlook Positive', available at https://www.nbs .rs/internet/latinica/18/18_3/18_3_2/izvestaji/SP_20191213.pdf (accessed on 13 December 2019).

National Bank of Serbia (NBS) and Government of the Republic of Serbia (2018), 'Memorandum on the Dinarisation Strategy', available at https://www.nbs.rs/ internet/english/30/Memorandum_Dinarisation_Strategy_2018.pdf (accessed on 19 December 2018).

Oganes, L. and J. Goulden (2019), 'Emerging Markets Outlook and Strategy for 2020: Better for Growth but Not for Returns', JP Morgan, available at https://www.jpmm .com/research/content/GPS-3194562-0 (accessed on 10 December 2019).

Standard & Poor's (2019), 'Serbia Upgraded To "BB+" On Resilient Macroeconomic Fundamentals; Outlook Positive', available at https://www.mfin.gov.rs/wp-content/ uploads/2019/12/Research-Update_Serbia_Dec-13-2019.pdf (accessed on 13 December 2019).

Tabaković, J. (2017), 'Central Bank Policy After the Crisis: Example of Serbia', *Ekonomika preduzeća* 65 (1–2), 83–102.

Tabaković, J. (2018), 'Resolution of Non-Performing Loans in Serbia: Stability as an Imperative', *Ekonomika preduzeća* 66 (1–2), 91–105.

Tabaković, J. (2019), 'A Decade of Full-Fledged Inflation Targeting in Serbia', *Ekonomika preduzeća* 67 (1–2), 83–100.

Tabaković, J. and A. Ivković (2019), *Monetary Policy – No Final Victories*, Belgrade: HERAedu.

Williamson, J. (1990), 'What Washington Means by Policy Reform', in J. Williamson (ed.), *Latin American Adjustment: How Much Has Happened?*, Washington, DC: Institute for International Economics.

5. Monetary milestones of the past 30 years: the Czech National Bank's view

Jiří Rusnok

The November 1989 Velvet Revolution ushered in a transformation of the economic order in what was then Czechoslovakia. Central planning rapidly gave way to market forces, initially in a monetary framework based on a fixed exchange rate (supplemented with money targeting). This provided the economy with its only nominal anchor. Everything else – the legal framework, property rights, institutions, and so on – was in flux.

This chapter describes the monetary milestones in the history of Czechoslovakia and subsequently the Czech Republic over the past 30 years, and draws lessons from them. The episodes covered include the adoption of the fixed exchange rate regime (within the framework of wider economic transformation measures), the separation of the Czechoslovak currency in 1993, the exit from the exchange rate peg in 1997, the adoption of inflation targeting in 1998, the creation of a special privatization account in 2001, the 2002 and 2008 appreciation bubbles, and the introduction of an exchange rate floor in 2013. I conclude with some thoughts on the pros and cons of potentially replacing the Czech koruna with the euro as the currency of the Czech Republic in the future.

The experiences of the last 30 years described below provide an opportunity to formulate some key conclusions regarding the benefits, costs and risks associated with having your own currency and relatively independent monetary policy. For most of these conclusions, parallels can be found in the other countries of Central and Eastern Europe. The Czech Republic's disorderly exit from its fixed exchange rate system was a textbook case of what happens when policymakers ignore common economic wisdom. The main finding here is that having your own currency is beneficial and useful in certain situations, but its custodians really need to know how to treat it correctly. If they underestimate what is needed to maintain it, an independent currency will become – as they say of fire – a good servant but a bad master. The past three decades have taught us that while the koruna has at times been a shock absorber and has thereby stabilized the Czech economy, at several other times it has been a source of exchange rate shocks and has thus harmed the economy. The first type of experience implies that it would be good to keep the koruna in the future, whereas the second type of experience argues in favour of introducing the euro. This is the core framework for my thoughts on potential future adoption of the single currency.

5.1   1991: ADOPTION OF THE FIXED EXCHANGE RATE REGIME

The first monetary milestone after the revolution was the publication of a blueprint for economic transformation in September 1990. The transformation consisted of four pillars: (1) the creation of a stable macroeconomic framework (restrictive monetary and fiscal policy); (2) a fundamental change in ownership (restitution and privatization); (3) price liberalization and the introduction of a competitive environment; and (4) the introduction of internal convertibility of the koruna. The 'fathers of the transformation' opted for quite a fast transition ('shock therapy'), in contrast to the more gradual approach advocated by the former communist reformers.

During 1990, devaluation expectations led to speculative accumulation of foreign currency by firms and a fall in the central bank's foreign exchange (FX) reserves. This hastened the devaluation process. The koruna was devalued by 114 per cent in cumulative terms in the course of the year (by 2.1 per cent on 1 January 1990, 16.3 per cent on 8 January, 55.2 per cent on 15 October, and 15.9 per cent on 28 December). The various exchange rates that had existed under the old system had meanwhile been gradually unified. The aim was to reasonably 'overshoot' the rate of devaluation and to prevent an exchange rate–price–wage spiral, all while maintaining balance-of-payments equilibrium (FX reserves amounted to just one month's worth of imports at the start of 1990).

The most important monetary measures were taken in 1991. Some 85 per cent of prices were liberalized on 1 January. Foreign trade was also deregulated and a 20 per cent import surcharge introduced. 'Internal convertibility' of the koruna was also established, implying a full FX supply obligation for exporters. The hard currency conversion limit applying to households (for tourist purposes) was increased in a series of steps (to 2000 korunas in 1990, 5000 korunas in 1991, 7500 korunas in 1992 and 1993, 12,000 korunas in 1994, and 100,000 korunas in 1995). This process culminated with the introduction of full external convertibility of the koruna (current account liberalization) on 1 October 1995, when the country became a member of the Organisation for Economic Co-operation and Development (OECD).

The adoption of the fixed exchange regime was a key element of the economic transformation process. At a time of dramatic change, it provided the economy with a nominal anchor for prices and wages in the gradually forming macroeconomic framework. Thanks to the fixed exchange rate, the initial price shock caused in early 1991 by price liberalization weakened fairly quickly, so that inflation in the former Czechoslovakia amounted to 'only' 56.6 per cent for the year as a whole. This scandalously high inflation from today's perspective, however, was the lowest in the region at the time, as prices in other transforming economies were rising at rates of hundreds or even thousands of per cent.

The fixed exchange rate worked very well in the early years of the transformation, as it delivered exactly what was expected of it: it helped to anchor inflation expectations (and inflation) at approximately 10 per cent (until 1998) and became the cornerstone for long-term real appreciation of the koruna against the stable convertible currencies. The wage level catch-up process thus went on primarily in an environment of faster growth in domestic wages and a stable nominal exchange rate. This mechanism later changed (with the switch to a floating rate), but it proved entirely appropriate for the first few years of the transformation process.

5.2 FEBRUARY 1993: SPLIT OF THE CZECHOSLOVAK CURRENCY

The next landmark was the break-up of the former Czechoslovakia on 1 January 1993. Although the Czech and Slovak economies were rather similar in many respects, it is very likely that the federal state was not an optimal currency area. A disproportionately high number of exporters were based in Czech territory. In addition, the Slovak economy was hit by an asymmetric shock – the collapse of the country's defence industry – when Eastern markets broke down during the initial transformation crisis.

The currency separation is a good example of how great a role expectations play in certain phases of economic development. Following the division of the state at the start of the year, savings began to pour from Slovak to Czech banks. These flows were motivated by expectations that the Slovak government would endeavour as soon as possible to implement an independent economic policy that would be more expansionary than the one appropriate for the Czech economy. An even more important stimulus for the flows of savings was the expectation that the Czech koruna would gain in value against the Slovak koruna following the creation of the two successor currencies. This speculative behaviour hastened the course of events.

The currency was separated cleanly and smoothly on 8 February 1993. The conversion rate between the Czech and Slovak currencies was derived from

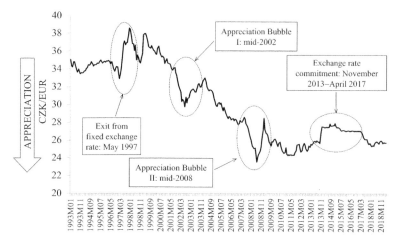

Note: CZK/EUR; January 1993–April 2019.
Source: Eurostat.

Figure 5.1   Key exchange rate events since January 1993

their exchange rates against the German mark and other currencies. A customs union was created to mitigate the decline in mutual trade. A special clearing system was set up in which payments up to a certain amount were settled in the domestic currency. The difference in the relative performance of the two economies was reflected in the exchange rate between their currencies: the Slovak koruna later depreciated by about 20 per cent against the Czech koruna. Before the currency separation, the level of uncertainty had been high and quickly mounting; but after the split, it quickly faded and the situation surprisingly soon settled down. With the benefit of hindsight, the currency separation was the neatest and cheapest economic solution to a politically driven decision. The whole process went smoothly thanks to flawless preparation.

The overall lesson from the currency separation is that a monetary union will not last long if the member economies are not similar enough and/or if consistent economic policies are not pursued. The rapid implementation of the currency separation (around 40 days after the political division of the former Czechoslovakia) very likely averted potentially large imbalances and disruptive speculative flows. It would be exaggerating only a little to say that speed is all that matters. The architects of the currency separation deserve praise for acting decisively. Figure 5.1 uses the exchange rate of the Czech koruna against the euro to illustrate other monetary milestones since the establishment of the independent Czech koruna.

All the exchange rate swings were caused by massive capital flows. As we will see below, the Czech National Bank (CNB) faced them with a variety of policies and instruments, with varying degrees of success.

5.3   MAY 1997: EXIT FROM THE PEG

If the separation of the former Czechoslovak koruna was an example of how to treat a monetary union and an exchange rate peg correctly, the process of exiting the fixed exchange rate in the Czech Republic should be a warning for every policymaker and student of economic history. As mentioned above, between 1991 and 1997, Czechoslovakia – and later the Czech Republic – had a fixed exchange rate.[1] Changes occurred in many areas as the economic transformation progressed. One such change was the gradual dismantlement of the state's foreign exchange monopoly through liberalization of the capital account. This took place not only officially, but also spontaneously as the whole of economic life was steadily liberalized. The liberalization of capital flows was commenced in 1995, when the country became the first in the region to join the OECD.

The speed with which capital flows were liberalized, coupled with adherence to the fixed exchange rate (which had helped to establish a stable macroeconomic framework at the start of the transformation process), sowed the seeds of future economic problems. The co-existence of free capital flows, a fixed exchange rate and independent monetary policy – a textbook example of the 'Impossible Trinity' – caused the monetary framework to become progressively undermined. The CNB was aware that the framework was inconsistent, so on 28 February 1996 it widened the koruna's fluctuation band to ±7.5 percentage points from parity in order to weaken the motive for capital inflows. This measure proved insufficient and the inflow of capital stimulated by the high interest rate differential between koruna assets and foreign currency assets continued. The CNB found it increasingly difficult to counter this inflow. In the course of 1996, and especially at the start of 1997, there were mounting expectations that the fixed exchange rate would sooner or later be abandoned. The uncertainty about the sustainability of the peg increased further when it became apparent that the overheating economy faced an unprecedented current account deficit. After the government's efforts to repair the broken macroeconomic and monetary framework proved ineffective (in April 1997, it introduced a package of stabilization measures signalling that it was insufficiently aware of the depth of the problem), the markets became convinced that the fixed exchange rate was unsustainable.

A speculative attack was launched on the Czech currency in May 1997. The CNB made massive interventions to defend the weak koruna, losing one-third of its FX reserves in just a few days. On 27 May, it exited the peg and the koruna then weakened. Interest rates were raised significantly to prevent capital outflows and halt the depreciation. Inflation accelerated and uncertainty soared. The economy was hit by a purely home-grown twin crisis of recession and bank failures.

The lesson of the belated and very costly exit from the peg is clear: if you liberalize your capital account, it is high time to start thinking about floating your exchange rate. A fixed exchange rate that proved its stabilization ability at the start of the transformation process can turn into the main source of instability at a more advanced stage. Having a consistent monetary and exchange rate framework is everything.

5.4   1998: INTRODUCTION OF INFLATION TARGETING

In January 1998, the Czech Republic became the first country in Central and Eastern Europe to adopt inflation targeting (IT). The initial IT framework which emerged from the ashes of the broken monetary framework was rudimentary and underdeveloped, primitive even. Since then, it has undergone a host of refinements.

The inflation target was initially set in the form of a gradually descending band for net inflation. In 2002, this was changed to headline inflation; and in 2006, the target range was replaced with a point target and the objective was changed from disinflation to stable inflation, in line with the advanced economies.

The CNB's analytical tools have also evolved enormously over time. To begin with, the central bank produced short-term forecasts based primarily on simple expert judgement. In mid-2002, it put its Quarterly Projection Model (QPM) into service; this involved switching from an assumption of constant interest rates to one of endogenous interest rates and an endogenous exchange rate. The QPM was succeeded by the g3 dynamic stochastic general equilibrium (DSGE) model in 2008 and the more detailed g3+ in 2019.

Under IT, the CNB has steadily increased its openness to the point where it is now rated the most transparent central bank in the world according to the composite index of Dincer et al. (2019). The CNB also enjoys a high degree of credibility (although that diminished after it adopted its exchange rate commitment in 2013; see below). As a result, inflation expectations in the Czech Republic are now firmly anchored to the inflation target. IT also proved its worth during the financial crisis, as it allowed the CNB to deploy unconventional monetary policy tools (see the section on the exchange rate commitment below).

To sum up, IT proved successful in steering the Czech economy from disinflation (1998–2010) to price stability (after 2010). It provides a consistent, credible, transparent and flexible (and therefore highly useful) policy framework. This process took time, but was well worth the effort.

5.5   2001: CREATION OF A SPECIAL PRIVATIZATION ACCOUNT

In 2000, the government decided to sell off large state-owned firms (utilities and others). Concerned about the risk of excessive appreciation of the koruna if the privatization proceeds flowed through the market, the CNB (in close cooperation with the government) set up a special scheme whereby the government's foreign currency income was converted off the FX market. As a consequence, the privatization revenue led to a big increase in the CNB's FX reserves.

Overall, the privatization account did its job: the privatization of large companies had no impact on the koruna whatsoever. This capital flow management measure was employed successfully in a specific period of the transition to a market economy, a period of major changes in ownership. Monetary policy thus aided the economic transition.

5.6   MID-2002: APPRECIATION BUBBLE I

The koruna started to appreciate in late 2001 after the European Central Bank (ECB) began to lower its interest rates and the CNB failed to react immediately. Between January and April 2002, the interest rate differential between the koruna and the euro stood at a relatively high 1.5 percentage points. In both April and July, the Czech currency was a full 13 per cent stronger than a year earlier. The stronger koruna passed through to low inflation (0.1 per cent in 2003), which led in turn to higher real wages, faster growth in household consumption and disturbances to the business cycle.

The CNB responded by rapidly cutting interest rates (even doing so outside its regular monetary policy meetings, on a Monday rather than a Thursday) and by intervening against the koruna in the foreign exchange market. The bubble burst in July 2002 and the koruna depreciated.

This episode teaches us that monetary policy autonomy has its limits: a large interest rate differential can imply sizeable capital flows even in the absence of a currency peg. Fortunately, the existence of a consistent monetary framework under IT meant that policies or measures outside the traditional toolbox were not required.

5.7   MID-2008: APPRECIATION BUBBLE II

A second appreciation bubble occurred in July 2008, when the koruna appreciated by 17 per cent year on year (based on monthly averages) to its strongest ever nominal level (briefly below CZK23 to the euro). There was no clear reason for the appreciation, but it was probably due to improved sentiment about the koruna on financial markets.

This time the CNB responded with verbal interventions by Governor Zdeněk Tůma. This action proved to be well-timed and sufficient. The koruna soon started to weaken and follow a depreciation trend (due, in part, to the subsequent financial crisis). The episode had no major impacts on the economy.

The lesson here is that even in good times and with a consistent monetary policy framework in place, capital flows can become a source of exchange rate shocks with no obvious causes. Other things being equal, such an erratic exchange rate path may justify thoughts of potentially adopting the euro.

5.8   NOVEMBER 2013–APRIL 2017: EXCHANGE RATE COMMITMENT

In November 2013, the CNB – faced with strong disinflationary pressures and having reached the zero lower bound (ZLB) on interest rates – introduced a commitment to stop the koruna strengthening below CZK27 to the euro. On the weaker side of this exchange rate floor, the koruna was allowed to float freely. The bank declared that it was prepared to make unlimited FX interventions to maintain the floor.

The stated aims of this unconventional monetary policy measure – which was roughly equivalent to cutting interest rates by one percentage point – were to further ease monetary conditions at the ZLB, to tackle the disinflation/deflation pressures and to revive the economy and achieve the inflation target more quickly.

The weakening of the koruna fostered an economic recovery and a gradual rise in inflation in 2014. The recovery was also aided by growth in external demand and the end of restrictive domestic fiscal policy. In mid-2015, the CNB started intervening to defend the floor. The CNB prolonged the commitment five times due to strong and longer-lasting (mainly external) disinflationary pressures and more (and longer-lasting) accommodative ECB monetary policy. In late 2016/early 2017, however, the commitment ceased to be necessary for sustainable fulfilment of the CNB's primary objective of maintaining price stability, and it was discontinued on 6 April 2017. This was the first step toward normalizing monetary policy; that is, using interest rates as the main monetary policy instrument again.

In terms of subsequent exchange rate volatility, the exit was rather smooth; smoother than expected, in fact. However, the consequences of the commitment included an unprecedented inflow of speculative capital. As a result, the CNB's FX reserves ultimately tripled as a percentage of nominal gross domestic product (GDP). In the absence of any counterparty, the koruna became 'overbought' and weakened modestly. This implied faster subsequent normalization of interest rates. Since mid-2017, the CNB has raised its main policy rate eight times to a level of 2.00 per cent as of January 2020.

Despite heavy criticism from sections of the Czech public, the FX commitment delivered what the CNB had expected of it. Model-based and empirical analyses confirm that it had positive effects on inflation and the real economy (see Brůha and Tonner 2017). However, it diminished the bank's credibility in the eyes of the public.

The most important lesson to be drawn from the time of the CNB's exchange rate commitment is that the IT framework proved to be so flexible that it allowed the exchange rate to be used as an unconventional monetary policy instrument. Using the exchange rate seemed the best option for the Czech economy given the large weight that exchange rate changes have in inflation (exchange rate pass-through). It is gratifying that the recovery of the Czech economy following the exit from the commitment was so robust that it allowed the CNB to return interest rates toward their usual levels (that is, to normalize monetary policy). It should be noted that, although the euro area discontinued the use of unconventional instruments in the form of quantitative easing for some time, it recently returned to it. The Czech Republic's most important trading partners – Germany, Slovakia, France, Italy and Spain – thus have far more accommodative monetary conditions than the Czech economy. This fact alone argues against adopting the euro at the moment.

5.9   GOING FORWARD: THOUGHTS ON ADOPTING THE EURO

Adopting the euro has its pros and cons. The biggest long-term benefit is growth in foreign trade. Its average contribution to long-term GDP growth is generally estimated at several tenths of a percentage point a year. This mounts up appreciably over the years.

However, there are several arguments against introducing the euro. The euro area is not an optimal currency zone; one size does not fit all. In addition, its institutional architecture is still not complete. The balance of the costs and benefits of the euro is not guaranteed, and may change. The political nature of the euro area can lead the authorities to implement suboptimal solutions to economic problems. Finally, converging economies face a risk of overheating due to a low real interest rate.

The CNB and the Czech Ministry of Finance conduct regular assessments of the Czech Republic's preparedness to adopt the euro. They have yet to recommend that the government adopts the single European currency. In their most recent report (see Ministry of Finance of the Czech Republic and Czech National Bank 2018), they concluded that the Czech Republic was compliant with all the Maastricht convergence criteria except that on participation in the exchange rate mechanism. The preparedness of the Czech Republic itself to adopt the euro had improved further compared to previous years, although some shortcomings – especially the incomplete process of real economic convergence – persisted. The economic situation in the euro area had stabilized, but the level of economic development in euro area countries remained uneven and convergence was ongoing in only some of the new Member States. Moreover, unresolved debt and structural issues persisted in a number of countries. Other issues mentioned in the report included the fiscal indiscipline of some members and the ongoing discussions about the future institutional set-up of the European Union and the euro area.

The euro is sometimes credited with almost supernatural powers. This diverts attention from more important problems, such as the quality of domestic policy. A country can thrive and falter inside and outside the euro area. The euro is not, and can never be, the solution to bad domestic economic policy.

5.10   CONCLUSIONS

Over the past 30 years, the koruna has gone from being a central-planning accounting unit to a fully fledged national currency backed by an independent, transparent and credible central bank. The currency has had multiple roles over the years. Between 1991 and 1997, it acted as a nominal anchor, one of the few available at the time. On three occasions, it became a source of exchange rate shocks (in 1997, 2002 and 2008). On the other hand, it cushioned the economy from the negative external demand shock of the 2009 financial crisis. And from 2013 to 2017 (by which time low and relatively stable inflation, and well-anchored inflation expectations, had taken over as the nominal anchor), it was used as an unconventional monetary policy tool at the ZLB.

The exchange rate regime preordained the specific form of real appreciation of the Czech currency. Under the fixed exchange rate in 1991–1997, inflation fluctuated roughly in the range of 9 per cent to 11 per cent. In the low-inflation environment since 1998, the exchange rate has mostly been appreciating or stable.

The general lesson of the Czech experience is that under exchange rate pegs, expectations can have a decisive effect on how events unfold. In 1990, devaluation expectations accelerated the devaluation steps taken by the central bank. In 1993, the expected split of the Czechoslovak koruna hastened that separation. In 1997, expectations of the demise of the currency peg prompted a speculative attack on the koruna and brought forward the exit from the peg. And in 2017, the expected discontinuation of the CNB's exchange rate commitment stimulated huge speculative capital inflows and caused the central bank's currency reserves to skyrocket (but did not hasten the exit from the commitment). Speculative flows such as these can be damaging to the economy when the monetary framework is inconsistent. Heightened uncertainty and massive capital flows are early warning signals that a peg is becoming unsustainable. Timing the exit right is everything.

To sum up, having your own currency is great as long as you treat it correctly, which the Czech Republic has not always done over the past 30 years. The overall balance of the benefits and costs of keeping the Czech koruna seems quite favourable.

NOTE

1. The composition of the currency basket was changed several times over the course of the economic transformation. A currency basket comprising the German mark (65 per cent) and the United States dollar (35 per cent) was introduced on 3 May 1993.

REFERENCES

Brůha, J. and J. Tonner (2017), 'An Exchange Rate Floor as an Instrument of Monetary Policy: An Ex-post Assessment of the Czech Experience', CNB Working Papers No. 2017/04.

Dincer, N., B. Eichengreen and P. Geraats (2019), 'Transparency of Monetary Policy in the Postcrisis World', in D.G. Mayes, P.L. Siklos and J.-E. Sturm (eds), *The Oxford Handbook of the Economics of Central Banking*, New York: Oxford University Press, 287–333.

Ministry of Finance of the Czech Republic and Czech National Bank (2018), 'Assessment of the Fulfilment of the Maastricht Convergence Criteria and the Degree of Economic Alignment of the Czech Republic with the Euro Area', December.

6. Croatia: from hyperinflation to the road to the euro area

Boris Vujčić and Katja Gattin Turkalj

At the beginning of the 30-year transitional period spanning from 1990 to 2020, Croatia was battling high inflation. To be precise, in 1989, inflation stood at 2500 per cent year on year (Figure 6.1), only to drop to 130 per cent in the subsequent year and to 250 per cent in the year after that (in 1991). Prior to the implementation of the stabilization programme in October 1993, inflation was hovering around 30 per cent per month, not exploding, but not subsiding either.

There is almost nothing more detrimental to a society than high inflation. It distorts relative prices, destroys business incentives and shortens investment horizons by effectively blocking the whole economy. In spring 1993, the

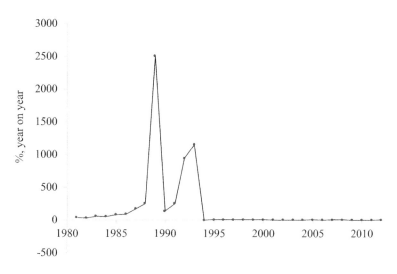

Source: National Statistical Institute.

Figure 6.1   *Year-on-year changes in the consumer price index (CPI)*

balance of payments was in surplus, no pressure was coming from excess demand, nor was there excess money supply. In such conditions, there should not have been fundamental pressures for price growth, yet inflation was raging, pointing to the crucial role of inflation expectations (see Anušić et al. 1994) which was ultimately used to 'break the back' of high inflation. A devastated financial system, inflation inertia, long-term irreversibility of currency substitution and, more importantly, an environment in which one has never experienced, nor even believed in, the possibility of low inflation – that was the reality only 30 years ago. From the current perspective, where 'bringing inflation up' to target and negative interest rates dominate the narrative, it is difficult to recall that time. Nevertheless, one of the important legacies of the past 30 years is that we now look at high inflation episodes in the 'rear view mirror'.

After successfully taming hyperinflation, the liberalization of the capital account and the opening of the financial system took place in the following decade. State-owned banks were privatized, and the new entrants were mostly foreigners, setting the stage for high capital inflows in the early 2000s. Capital inflows were channelled through the banking sector and fuelled excessive credit growth, while exacerbating external imbalances. The Croatian National Bank (CNB) slowed down the growth of external indebtedness by implementing a complex set of measures that made external financing more expensive. Restrictive measures were predominantly curbing external borrowing, but other areas were targeted as well. It was a game of 'cat and mouse' where various reserve requirements were introduced, only for banks to try to circumvent them, then the CNB would broaden the measures, until the next round. Instruments included various types of marginal reserve requirements, higher weights for exchange rate-induced risks and the like, all the way up to the outright credit growth ceiling.

From today's perspective, it may look self-evident to introduce macroprudential measures, but at the time, the word 'macroprudential' did not even exist. The CNB implemented the measures in spite of differing views or reservations from international financial institutions and the domestic environment, as everyone expected growth to continue forever. The dominant narrative was the one of inflation targeting against the background of capital account liberalization, and only market-based measures were considered to be legitimate parts of a central banker's toolbox. Administrative measures were not looked upon with approval.

Today, macroprudential and financial stability measures are firmly established in the central banks' toolkit, with systemic risks being widely analysed. More importantly, the narrative on capital flows and appropriate responses to excessive capital surges became more nuanced. There is a wide debate on spillover effects of the monetary policy stance from advanced economies, mostly through capital movements. Better and more granular risk management, and a systemic view on financial stability and macroprudential risks, are among the most important lessons drawn from the above-mentioned transitional period.

The financial crisis and how the CNB responded to mitigate the crisis and to enable external liquidity in an environment characterized by a 'sudden stop' in capital flows was yet another challenge the CNB had to overcome in the transitional period. The CNB abolished the marginal reserve requirement and reduced the reserve requirement, lowered minimal foreign currency claims and intervened in the foreign exchange market. The net liquidity input by the CNB and foreign banks corresponded to around 14 per cent of gross domestic product (GDP). Foreign banks stood by their local subsidiaries during the onset of the crisis and supported them by injecting liquidity. These measures resulted in ample liquidity in the banking sector, leading to credit growth in all domestic sectors. One-third of these funds was directly or indirectly used by the government to repay domestic and foreign debt.

Subsequently, the situation in the monetary sphere normalized gradually. With the benefit of hindsight, swift and decisive responses to the crisis and successful maintenance of external and internal liquidity as well as financial sector stability were among the toughest trials that monetary policy had to face in the last 30 years.

During the last decade, the Croatian economy consolidated external and internal imbalances, but with much lower average GDP growth than in the pre-crisis period. External and internal balances were restored, and from 2017 onward we have been running twin (budget and current account) surpluses instead of pre-crisis twin deficits. In retrospect, we can conclude that the CNB was conducting a restrictive countercyclical monetary policy during the years preceding the crisis. Consequently, the CNB was able to inject significant liquidity into the system when the crisis hit. This, in turn, then allowed the central bank to make a sharp 'U-turn' toward adopting an expansionary countercyclical monetary stance (see Figure 6.2).

Policy frameworks today are much more robust compared with the pre-crisis era, especially in the financial stability area. European integration and financial infrastructure have come a long way in the last decades, as is evidenced by the launch of the banking union as well as the establishment of the European Stability Mechanism (ESM), the European Financial Stability Facility (EFSF), the European Systemic Risk Board (ESRB) and the Single Resolution Mechanism (SRM). This is not to say, however, that the union is complete. Finally, monetary policy space today is more limited than a decade ago, both for the European Central Bank (ECB) and for the central banks in the transition countries that place more weight on cyclical, and especially structural policy, measures to effectively address the next downturn.

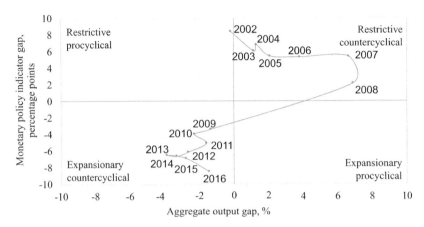

Notes: The gap in the monetary policy indicator is the spread to the average value. The
monetary policy indicator is the share of credit institutions' assets that is held in total assets
of credit institutions for regulatory purposes. The credit institutions' assets held for regulatory
purposes (reduced by the liquidity surplus) include the calculated kuna reserve requirement, the
allocated foreign currency reserve requirement, the marginal reserve requirement, CNB bills and
the minimum required foreign currency claims.
Source: CNB calculations.

Figure 6.2   *Cyclicality of Croatia's monetary policy*

The next challenge for the CNB is joining the Exchange Rate Mechanism II
(ERM II) and adopting the euro. The euro is Croatia's strategic goal, but it is
much more difficult to enter the euro area today than it was 15 years ago. The
obligation to introduce the euro was incorporated in the Croatian European
Union (EU) accession treaty; however, earlier adoption was hampered,
given large macroeconomic imbalances. Today, macroeconomic fundamentals
provide Croatia with a good foundation for participating in the ERM II and for
meeting the criteria for introducing the euro. Croatia has attained a significant
level of real and nominal convergence. The long-standing price and exchange
rate stability and progress in fiscal adjustment indicate Croatia's readiness to
meet the convergence criteria soon after joining the ERM II. Decisive policy
reform implementation and pursuing a prudent fiscal policy are necessary
regardless of whether or not the euro is introduced.

The steps toward euro adoption had already been taken when the government passed its Strategy for the Euro Adoption in 2018, which was accepted
after a broad public debate. After that, Croatia sent a letter to the ECB requesting to enter into close cooperation, and in July 2019, Croatia announced its
intention to participate in the ERM II. The letter of intent was sent to the euro

area Member States, Denmark and relevant EU institutions. The Eurogroup, after having received Croatia's letter, welcomed the country's fulfilment of policy commitments outlined in the Action Plan which encompasses 19 measures in six areas:

- preparations for establishing close cooperation with the ECB;
- strengthening macroprudential powers and the toolkit of the central bank;
- reinforcing the capacity of the national statistical office;
- continuing the anti-money laundering and anti-terrorism financing activities; and
- upgrading the country's business climate and improving business conditions by further trimming para-fiscal charges.

Croatia plans to deliver on all measures by mid-2020 and to apply for entry into the ERM II in the course of 2020.

Beyond these technical and procedural steps, Croatia is a small and open as well as highly euroized economy which is strongly integrated into euro area trade and financial flows. According to the optimal currency area theory, Croatia would benefit from participating in the currency area (see Šabić and Brkić 2018). Joining the euro would have long-lasting positive macroeconomic and financial effects, with limited one-off or short-term costs.

Benefits would include the reduction (almost the elimination) of foreign currency risk in the private and public sectors, and significant contributions to financial stability. Foreign currency risk would be eliminated from the economy, which would permanently increase its resilience. Investing in Croatia would be easier, and regulatory burdens on the financial sector would be reduced.

Furthermore, interest rates would converge closer to the core euro area countries, and currency risk would be eliminated, resulting in favourable effects on the country's risk premium and in a substantial reduction in regulatory costs for banks. All of this, in turn, would have a positive effect on interest rate levels. Financing costs for Croatian households and companies would be lower than if the country remained outside the euro area. As a result of eliminating the costs of currency exchange transactions, Croatia would be able to increase its competitiveness, which would lead to positive effects on foreign trade and investment, and boost both the economy and the standard of living.

The biggest negative effect would be the loss of autonomous monetary policy, but Croatia has so far only been able to a limited extent to pursue an autonomous monetary policy, due to the exchange rate regime and other county-specific reasons, such as the high level of euroization.

Research undertaken also proves that Croatian business cycles are synchronized with euro area cycles. Beyond the coherence of business cycles,

Croatia and euro area core countries also show similar reactions to supply and demand shocks. Hence, not only are the coherence of business cycles and the correlation of supply and demand shocks between Croatia and euro area core countries relatively high, but the symmetric (common) shocks also explain, for the most part, the dynamics in domestic GDP. The contribution of asymmetric (idiosyncratic) shocks is significantly smaller (see Kotarac et al. 2017). Consequently, the monetary policy of the ECB will suit the needs of the Croatian economy. For idiosyncratic shocks, there are macroprudential tools that are still largely within the national domains (see Kunovac et al. 2018).

Finally, public opinion polls conducted so far have shown that the public welcomes the adoption of the euro. To strengthen the public's support, the effects of the euro on prices should be explained in great detail to dispel widespread and unfounded stories that prices in countries that adopted the euro rose significantly thereafter.

For a country that, not so long ago, was battling high inflation, capital surges and financial crisis spillovers, joining the ERM II simultaneously with entering into close cooperation with the Single Supervisory Mechanism (SSM) and the SRM seems like a less demanding choice. However, there are new challenges ahead. Monetary policy today operates in uncharted territory. The low interest rate environment turns out to be a long-lasting phenomenon, and 'the new normal' reduces the room for manoeuvre for traditional policies, especially in the accommodative direction. Beyond monetary policy, challenges also arise from unfavourable demographic trends, tight labour markets, cryptocurrency disruption and automatization coupled with an artificial intelligence revolution. All of this necessitates additional efforts to search for policies that will sustain inclusive growth and promote real convergence and living standards. Going forward, the CNB will tackle these issues within the common European framework of a new and stronger Europe ready to face challenges in an uncertain world.

REFERENCES

Anušić, Z., Ž. Rohatinski, V. Šonje, R. Martić, A. Mervar, Ž. Miljenović and M. Škreb (1994), *Road to Low Inflation*, Government of Republic of Croatia.

Kotarac, K., D. Kunovac and R. Ravnik (2017), 'Coherence of Business Cycles and Economic Shocks between Croatia and Euro Area Member States', CNB Working Papers No. 53.

Kunovac, D., M. Mandler and M. Scharnagl (2018), 'Financial Cycles in Euro Area Economies: A Cross-Country Perspective', Deutsche Bundesbank Working Paper No. 4.

Šabić, A. and M. Brkić (2018), 'Is the Euro the Optimum Currency for Croatia: An Assessment Using the Optimum Currency Area Theory', CNB Surveys No. 30.

PART III

Modes of transition: the impact of different economic policy approaches

7. Ten lessons from 30 years of post-communist economic transformation

Anders Åslund

Thirty years of post-communist transformation allow us to draw broad lessons.[1] In 1989, the old communist order broke down in Eastern Europe, and two years later the Soviet Union collapsed. This was a truly liberal revolution akin to 1848, a time of optimism and liberalism. In Eastern Europe, the two leading slogans were: 'we want a normal society' and 'we want to return to Europe'. What was meant by a normal society was not further specified, but people aspired to a liberal democracy and a free market economy based on private ownership of the means of production and the rule of law. The return to Europe implied an aspiration to join the European Union (EU) (see Dahrendorf 1990).

Looking at the post-communist world today, the outcomes of the transformation have been strikingly different for the countries involved. Out of the 21 countries of the former Soviet Bloc in Europe and the Soviet Union, 18 are market economies,[2] but only nine are full democracies by the standards of Freedom House (2019). Moreover, the countries' economic achievements vary greatly (for a discussion of their aspirations and varied outcomes see, for example, Åslund 2013).

The intellectually dominant radical reform programme for post-communist countries closely followed the Washington Consensus prescriptions. However, the original radical reform programme, the Balcerowicz Plan, was published before the Washington Consensus in September 1989 (see Williamson 1990). It was more radical than the Washington Consensus, as its prescriptions were adjusted to the economic conditions in Poland at the time.

The Balcerowicz Plan became the standard for a radical, comprehensive reform as its prescriptions also applied to other countries in similar predicaments. It was lucid, and its main objectives were easy to summarize: macroeconomic stabilization, deregulation, privatization and a reinforced social safety net. While the plan's prescriptions for macroeconomic stabilization and deregulation were highly radical, the plan was rather vague on how to carry out privatization. Innovative ideas included measures such as making the currency convertible on the current account, completely liberalizing imports and permitting full domestic liberalization instantaneously (see Lipton and Sachs 1990; Sachs 1990; Balcerowicz 1992). To mitigate social costs, the Balcerowicz Plan prescribed generous pension and unemployment benefits.

7.1   TEN LESSONS FROM POLITICAL ECONOMY

The political economy of policy reform is a fine art. A comprehensive overview on the political conditions necessary to sustain meaningful economic reform can be found in the edited volume *The Political Economy of Policy Reform* by Williamson (1994). The summary below contains ten principles, partly economic, partly political.[3]

First, an enlightened elite and the broad public need to understand that the old system is finished. Several years of severe economic decline are not sufficient; rather, there needs to be public understanding that the old economic system is no longer viable. This was the case in the Soviet Union from 1985 onward, after the Soviet economy had stagnated since 1979. Such awareness, however, can only develop if a certain intellectual freedom is permitted.

Second, no major economic reforms can take place unless a political breakthrough occurs. In the early transition period, this means democratization. Later on, it may imply a regime change or simply a major change of government through elections. Poland illustrated how great the limitations on reforms were until the Soviet Union eased its military control in December 1988. In Russia, the failed August 1991 coup marked the democratic breakthrough, facilitated by the democratic Russian presidential election of Boris Yeltsin on 12 June 1991. In Georgia, the peaceful Rose Revolution of 2003 brought about new reforms (see Saakashvili and Bendukidze 2014). In Slovakia, the 2002 parliamentary election victory of Mikuláš Dzurinda heralded a term of highly successful economic reforms that have not been reversed, while Dzurinda could do little in his first four-year term with a much broader coalition.

Third, successful reforms require new leaders. You cannot teach an old dog new tricks. In the absence of established institutions, leaders form the rules, and incumbent leaders tend to insist on the old ways. Moreover, incumbent leaders usually appoint other members of the old establishment. New leaders, however, are honest and want to serve their country rather than enrich themselves and their families. The best example of this is Estonia. In 1992, Lennart Meri, a 63-year old independent writer, became president; and Mart Laar, a 32-year old historian, became prime minister. With a score of serious reformers, who all turned out to be honest, they laid the foundation for the most successful post-communist transformation. However, in all too many countries, promising reform leaders turned out to enrich themselves rather than to serve their nation, and the results suffered accordingly.

Fourth, new leading economic policymakers need to come in. Typically, these are young, well-educated outsiders who, after having lived and studied abroad, return home with new insights, while still knowing their old society well enough to understand it. According to Williamson (1994), reforms taking place in Latin America in the 1980s were carried out by young Latin Americans who had earned their PhD in economics from excellent US universities. In Eastern Europe, reforms were brought about by a similar group of outsiders, mostly economists. Outstanding examples include Leszek Balcerowicz, Václav Klaus, Mart Laar, Yegor Gaidar and Anatoly Chubais. None of them obtained their degree from a Western university, as hardly any Eastern Europeans were allowed to study abroad. Balcerowicz (2014, p. 29) stated, 'I cannot emphasize enough the importance of a cohesive economic team with clear and determined leadership'. Even honest reformers can waste a lot of time on internal squabbles.

Fifth, the newly appointed policymakers need to swiftly develop a comprehensive reform programme. Having entered the government in times of severe crisis and with limited administrative capacity, they need to focus on key concerns, ignoring side issues. Moreover, their reform programme should be short and simple, containing essential policies and clear principles. As a case in point, Balcerowicz presented his programme within one month of the formation of a new government in September 1989. He emphasized that, in a systemic transition, information and statistics are exceedingly poor, underscoring that statistics cannot be trusted for decision-making in the early transition period (see Balcerowicz 1992). A dominant feature of statistical distortions was that the output decline was greatly exaggerated, which led to calls for a change in strategy. According to Balcerowicz (2014, p. 28), his government's greatest mistake was to double pension expenditures as a share of gross domestic product (GDP) because some members of the government feared that pensioners would suffer too much. Klaus provided the clearest focus on ten major reform issues in his programme, but his mistake was that he stuck to his limited number of concerns for too long, not paying attention to other matters as the capacity of his government expanded.

Sixth, a democratic and well-functioning parliament is essential to pass the necessary reform laws. In his 1990 article on the virtues of parliamentarism, Linz laid out the classical argument for parliamentary rule. Remington et al. (1998) subsequently presented his elaborations as a strong argument for parliamentarism. A sharp dividing line runs between Central and Eastern Europe and the former Soviet Union, with Central and Eastern Europe having adopted the parliamentary system because of the inner workings of democracy, peer inspiration and EU integration. While the EU does not demand a parliamentary system, interactions with the EU and its decision-making systems make such a system the natural choice. In the former Soviet Union, by contrast, presidential systems dominate, and all of the seven purely presidential regimes are authoritarian (that is, Azerbaijan, Belarus, Kazakhstan, Russia, Tajikistan, Turkmenistan and Uzbekistan). The five semi-democratic countries in the former Soviet Union (that is, Armenia, Georgia, Kyrgyzstan, Moldova and Ukraine) have mixed presidential–parliamentary systems that change frequently and tend to be dysfunctional with poor economic results.

A parliamentary system is preferable for many reasons. To begin with, it requires and offers far more transparency than a presidential regime. Furthermore, in order to achieve decent quality, draft laws need to be discussed and amended, and cannot be steamrollered through parliament. In a democratic parliament, draft laws are discussed at length in parliamentary committees, and the interests of all relevant constituencies can be heard. As a result, new laws enjoy the support of the constituencies that have elaborated them. A quickly drafted and adopted presidential decree, by contrast, enjoys no authority. In 1994, Kazakhstan's president, Nursultan Nazarbayev, adopted several major economic codes as decrees. Although their content was sensible, they did not gain credibility among the public because of their rapid adoption without discussion or debate. Finally, parliaments have the right to monitor the implementation of laws, while presidential administrations, usually sitting in the building of the former Central Committee of the Communist Party, easily lapse back into the Soviet practice of informal telephone calls, leaving no paper trail.

Seventh, sufficient and timely international financial support is vital. People usually underestimate the pivotal importance of international financial assistance, which often determines whether a country opts for serious reforms. The question is not how much financial support a country receives in absolute terms or in relation to its GDP, but whether it obtains an adequate amount of financial assistance conditioned on appropriate policies at the right time. And the right time is usually very early. Today, Central Europeans often claim that their culture and inheritance were the key to success, rendering international assistance superfluous. Such assistance, however, did play a vital role. Indeed, the Central European countries and the Baltics did succeed, but a crucial condition for their success was the necessary aid which they received in time. The post-Soviet nations, by contrast, initially failed because they did not obtain vital financing. At the time, many complained about Western 'Russia first' policies, meaning that the West focused too much on Russia, ignoring the other post-Soviet states. In the former Soviet Union (excluding the three Baltic states), however, all of the leaders looked at Moscow. Yet, if not even Russia received sufficient funding to succeed, how could the remaining post-Soviet countries have possibly got enough support? The leaders of these countries were painfully aware of the fact that they were less prepared than Russia to implement market economic reforms.

Eighth, a swift implementation of reforms is vital to their success in a crisis. As the leading Estonian reformer Mart Laar (2002, p. 10) observed, 'The only thing we knew was that there was no time to lose'. He also coined the expression, 'To wait is to fail'. In other words, when a house is on fire, the fire brigade should not wait; rather, it should rush to help as fast as possible. The same holds true for tackling a severe financial crisis. At the time of a political breakthrough, the new regime experiences a brief honeymoon period even if the economy is collapsing. The old ruling elite, on the contrary, is demoralized, out of balance and disorganized. Yet, the old elite will recover more quickly than anticipated, offering unexpectedly strong resistance. For Boris Yeltsin, for example, the honeymoon – or the period of 'extraordinary politics', as Balcerowicz called it – lasted for no more than five months. The importance of fast and comprehensible reforms was clear to the early radical reformers, notably to Balcerowicz, Klaus and Laar. Klaus (2014, p. 56) argued, 'We considered radical reform as the only way to avoid chaos, instability, and political turmoil and to obtain at least the basic support of our fellow citizens'. The names of those who did not understand the need for rapid action have faded from history.

Ninth, public understanding of reforms is vital. People need to understand the reform proposals in order to support them. Unfortunately, almost all reformers failed when it came to educating the public. The exception was Klaus, who spent his Saturdays talking to ordinary people in small towns about the need for radical economic reform. As he put it himself, 'We knew that successful transformation must fulfill three basic preconditions: (a) present a simple, clearly formulated positive vision of where to go; (b) demonstrate our knowledge of how to get there; and (c) prove our ability to sell both to the public' (Klaus 2014, p. 56). Unsurprisingly, he was politically the most successful reformer, serving two terms as prime minister and two terms as president of the Czech Republic. Most reformers, however, saw themselves as technocrats, initially leaving politics to politicians. Belatedly, they realized that they had better become politicians as well. Williamson (1994, p. 26) noted that reformers needed 'the will and ability to appeal directly to the public and bypass vested interests'.

Tenth, in a severe crisis when radical new thinking is required, no consensus is possible. Radical reforms are inevitably controversial, as their purpose is to break the power and privileges of the old elites who are thus bound to oppose reforms. The vested interests of the old elites are the root of the problem. On behalf of their interests, the old elites will mobilize the media against any reforms that may harm their privileges. Initially, reformers had feared strikes among workers or protests against austerity measures and price increases, but neither materialized for many years. As Hellman (1998) points out, it is not the ordinary people who are the greatest obstacle to successful market reforms, but the elites. Therefore, democracy is not an obstacle to reforms; rather, it is the best means to beat the recalcitrant old elites. Moreover, as is shown in Diamond (1995) and Åslund (2013, p. 246), the correlation between democracy and reforms is strong. At the same time, as Sachs (1994, p. 505) pointed out, 'In deep crises, there simply is no consensus to build upon, only confusion, anxiety and a cacophony of conflicting opinions'.

These insights gained by analysing the political economy of crisis resolution are hardly original; yet, they are all too often overlooked. Ultimately, policy reform is about restoring confidence in the state, which requires fast, firm and consistent action. People understand if mistakes are made during policy reforms as long as the reform efforts themselves are honest and based on principles. However, they will not understand, and will be unforgiving of, corruption.

7.2   PROPERTY RIGHTS, DEMOCRACY AND DEVELOPMENT

In 2019, almost all of the post-communist countries managed to resolve their main economic policy problems. With the exception of Belarus, Turkmenistan and Uzbekistan, all of the post-communist countries are market economies, meaning that goods and services are exchanged on markets rather than being allocated by a centralized state. In each country, inflation is moderate, and budget deficits and public expenditures are no longer major concerns. Conservative fiscal and monetary policies prevail. Public debt is under control, and so are current accounts. The virtues of sound macroeconomic policies have been understood surprisingly well. The gospel of the International Monetary Fund (IMF) has not only been understood, but even appreciated.

The post-communist countries have gone through three distinct periods of economic growth, each lasting approximately one decade. From the end of communism to 1999, output fell sharply, and recovery was limited. Central Europe did far better than the former Soviet Union. From 2000 to 2008, the entire region went through a tremendous commodity and credit boom, with growth rates in the former Soviet Union averaging 9 per cent a year. Growth rates were lower in Central Europe. After the global financial crisis, growth rates were much lower, with Central Europe doing best, while growth rates in Eastern Europe (that is Belarus, Russia and Ukraine) remained almost stagnant.

The region is not converging economically. A few countries, notably Estonia and Poland, have gone through great economic development, almost tripling their GDP per capita measured in purchasing power parities (PPP).

By contrast, according to the IMF (2019), the current GDP per capita level in PPP of several post-Soviet countries (that is, Kyrgyzstan, Moldova, Tajikistan and Ukraine) is almost as low as the level recorded in the early 1990s. Post-communist countries tend to converge with their neighbouring countries outside of the former communist bloc rather than with one another. The Baltic states, on the contrary, converge with their Scandinavian neighbours, while Tajikistan converges with its neighbour Afghanistan, as Treisman (2014) observed.

Furthermore, the post-communist world has coalesced into three opposing blocs. The first bloc consists of 11 formerly communist countries, now members of the European Union, that have two important characteristics in common: (1) they are all classified as free or democratic by Freedom House (2019), with the exception of Hungary under Prime Minister Viktor Orbán, with reasonably good governance; and (2) they have brought corruption under reasonable control according to Transparency International (2018), ranking from 18 (Estonia) to 77 (Bulgaria) among 180 countries on the organization's Corruption Perceptions Index.

The second bloc includes seven of the 12 post-Soviet countries that are authoritarian and pervasively corrupt. They are best described as authoritarian kleptocracies that serve their ruling elites rather than the respective country as a whole. They have ended up in a bad equilibrium, with high corruption and severe repression, resulting from the extraordinary rent seeking that has prevailed from the outset of transition. In the 2000s, the bloc's economies grew rapidly thanks to the commodity boom, but since it has receded, their growth rates have fallen sharply. There is no reason to expect that the countries' economic growth will accelerate significantly in the future.

The third bloc consists of five former Soviet countries (that is, Armenia, Georgia, Kyrgyzstan, Moldova and Ukraine) which form an intermediary group between the first two blocs. Freedom House (2019) labels these countries as semi-free; Transparency International (2018) ranks them as less corrupt than other post-Soviet countries, with the exception of Belarus. What is interesting about these five countries is that they are not in equilibrium, and that it is not obvious which road they will take. They are seen as oligarchic, and tend to be politically unstable, which has slowed down their growth so far but may lead to higher growth in the future. With its peculiar mixture of pervasive corruption but great freedom, Ukraine seems to be at the battlefront between the forces of East and West, where the West stands for democracy with rule of law, while the East represents authoritarianism with pervasive corruption (Åslund 2017).

The fundamental problem that all post-Soviet countries apart from Georgia are facing is the weakness of their property rights. In the countries under authoritarian rule, the president controls the courts, which naturally reach judgments to the president's benefit. Moreover, the presidential families are greatly involved in business. These developments have led to the former oligarchies becoming increasingly centralized and authoritarian. State capture, or kleptocracy, and authoritarian rule go together. As a consequence of the absence of real property rights, the ruler as well as those ruled move their cash abroad.[4] This means that most of these countries save much more than they invest, with the low investment ratio resulting in chronically low economic growth. The unwillingness of private businessmen, local or foreign, to invest leads to rising state dominance and renationalization, which is particularly noticeable in Russia.

To sum up, we know how to build a market economy, and radical economic reform programmes have worked out well as far as they went. A big problem that has yet to be resolved is how to guarantee private property rights; a problem that seems to require the establishment of a democracy. To a considerable degree, economists have done their job, even if new problems arise and even if it is always desirable to reach a higher level. By and large, however, the baton has now been passed to political scientists to design democratic systems, and to lawyers to establish the rule of law, as successfully as economists have built market economies. So far, acceding to the European Union has proven to be the best tool available to achieve these objectives. Hopefully, the Eastern Partnership will evolve to play a similar role in the Western Balkans and Eastern Europe.

NOTES

1. This chapter is an update of my article on a quarter of a century of post-communist transformation (see Åslund 2018).
2. Except for Belarus, Turkmenistan and Uzbekistan.
3. The summary draws on Åslund (2013, pp. 248–252).
4. For a discussion of this conundrum in Russia, see Åslund (2019).

REFERENCES

Åslund, A. (2013), *How Capitalism Was Built: The Transformation of Central and Eastern Europe, Russia, the Caucasus, and Central Asia*, Second Edition, New York: Cambridge University Press.
Åslund, A. (2017), 'The Three Regions of the Former Soviet Bloc', *Journal of Democracy*, 28 (1), 89–101.
Åslund, A. (2018), 'Ten Lessons from a Quarter of a Century of Post-communist Economic Transformation', *Economics of Transition*, 26 (4), 851–862.
Åslund, A. (2019), *Russia's Crony Capitalism: The Path from Market Economy to Kleptocracy*, New Haven, CT, USA and London, UK: Yale University Press.
Balcerowicz, L. (1992), *800 dni skontrolowanego szoku* (800 Days of Controlled Shock), Warsaw: Polska Oficyna Wydawnicza 'BGW'.

Balcerowicz, L. (2014), 'Poland: Stabilization and Reforms under Extraordinary and Normal Policies', in A. Åslund and S. Djankov (eds), *The Great Rebirth: Lessons from the Victory of Capitalism over Communism*, Washington, DC: Peterson Institute for International Economics, 17–38.

Dahrendorf, R. (1990), *Reflections on the Revolution in Europe*, London: Chatto & Windus.

Diamond, L. (1995), 'Democracy and Economic Reform: Tensions, Compatibilities, and Strategies for Reconciliation', in E.P. Lazear (ed.), *Economic Transition in Eastern Europe and Russia*, Stanford, CA: Hoover Institution Press, 107–158.

Freedom House (2019), *Freedom in the World 2019*, available at www.freedomhouse .org (accessed on 14 December 2019).

Hellman, J.S. (1998), 'Winners Take All: The Politics of Partial Reform in Postcommunist Transitions', *World Politics* 50 (2), 203–234.

International Monetary Fund (IMF) (2019), *World Economic Output*, database available at www.imf.org (accessed on 14 December 2019).

Klaus, V. (2014), 'Czechoslovakia and the Czech Republic: The Spirit and Main Contours of the Postcommunist Transformation', in A. Åslund and S. Djankov (eds), *The Great Rebirth: Lessons from the Victory of Capitalism over Communism*, Washington, DC: Peterson Institute for International Economics, 53–72.

Laar, M. (2002), *Little Country That Could*, London: Centre for Research into Post-Communist Economies.

Linz, J. (1990), 'Presidents vs. Parliaments: The Virtues of Parliamentarianism', *Journal of Democracy* 1 (4), 84–91.

Lipton, D. and J.D. Sachs (1990), 'Creating a Market in Eastern Europe: The Case of Poland', *Brookings Papers on Economic Activity* 20 (1), 75–147.

Remington, T.F., S.S. Smith and M. Haspel (1998), 'Decrees, Laws, and Inter-Branch Relations in the Russian Federation', *Post-Soviet Affairs* 14 (4), 287–322.

Saakashvili, M. and K. Bendukidze (2014), 'Georgia: The Most Radical Catch-Up Reform', in A. Åslund and S. Djankov (eds), *The Great Rebirth: Lessons from the Victory of Capitalism over Communism*, Washington, DC: Peterson Institute for International Economics, 149–164.

Sachs, J.D. (1990), 'What Is to Be Done?', *The Economist*, 13 January, 19–24.

Sachs, J.D. (1994), 'Life in the Economic Emergency Room', in J. Williamson (ed.), *The Political Economy of Policy Reform*, Washington, DC: Institute for International Economics, 501–523.

Transparency International (2018), *Corruption Perceptions Index 2018*, available at https://www.transparency.org/cpi2018#results (accessed on 14 December 2019).

Treisman, D. (2014), 'The Political Economy of Change after Communism', in A. Åslund and S. Djankov (eds), *The Great Rebirth: Lessons from the Victory of Capitalism over Communism*, Washington, DC: Peterson Institute for International Economics, 273–296.

Williamson, J. (1990), *Latin American Adjustment: How Much Has Happened?*, Washington, DC: Institute for International Economics.

Williamson, J. (1994), *The Political Economy of Policy Reform*, Washington, DC: Institute for International Economics.

8. The impact of different transition patterns and approaches on economic development in EU-CEE11, Russia and Ukraine

Marina Gruševaja

Transition in Central and Eastern European countries started rather unexpectedly. No country was prepared to undertake the challenge of simultaneous changes in the economic, political and social arenas. The declaration of the end of the socialistic era followed a long period of trial and error. In hindsight, an analysis of the experiences of different transitional countries in the past 30 years is important to understand the transitional process in order to identify certain general patterns as well as similarities and dissimilarities of the economic development outcomes of different transition countries.

Before discussing the similarities and dissimilarities, it is worthwhile to examine the prevailing theoretical foundation of the transitional process. Some ideas were derived from the experiences of other developing countries that aimed to build market-enhancing governmental capacities and/or establish efficient markets. Other theories were proposed through the evaluation of the ongoing transitional process. The greatest differences in outcomes were observed between 11 European Union (EU) Member States in Central and Eastern Europe (EU-CEE11) and non-EU Member States, such as Russia and Ukraine, both of which are geographically close to the non-EU Member States.

8.1 THEORETICAL OVERVIEW

Thirty years ago with the sudden collapse of the Eastern Bloc of communist countries, the main focus was directed toward economic transition from centrally planned to market-oriented economies. In an attempt to create efficient markets within the shortest time span, the transition countries mainly followed the path of radical liberalization stipulated by the Washington Consensus, a reform agenda developed and approved by the International Monetary Fund (IMF) and the World Bank for Latin America in 1989 (see Williamson 1994, 2004).[1] The original Washington Consensus, an approach for economic

Table 8.1   The Washington Consensus

Original Washington Consensus	'Augmented' Washington Consensus Previous ten items plus:
Fiscal discipline	Corporate governance
Reorientation of public expenditures	Anti-corruption
Tax reform	Flexible labour market
Financial liberalization	World Trade Organization (WTO) agreements
Unified and competitive exchange rates	Financial codes and standards
Trade liberalization	'Prudent' capital-account opening
Openness to foreign direct investment (FDI)	Non-intermediate exchange rate regimes
Privatization	Independent central banks/inflation targeting
Deregulation	Social safety nets
Secure property rights	Targeted poverty reduction

Source: Rodrik (2002).

transition, specified ten main characteristics of liberal market economies, and the policy prescriptions for developing countries were drawn from them. In terms of implementation, two strategies were suggested. The first strategy was 'shock therapy', a rapid and almost simultaneous reform process in all ten areas prescribed by the Washington Consensus. The second was Gradualism, a sequencing of reforms according to political/economic feasibility and their slow and gradual implementation without a specific prescribed order. Shock therapy was more appealing as it offered the promise of managing the transition within a short time span, while avoiding the emergence of vested interests.

As shock therapy did not fulfil the expectations of a very rapid transition to market economies, the focus shifted to institutional transformation and institutional reforms. The original Washington Consensus was also augmented into a more comprehensive form. It emphasized the crucial role of secure property rights (see Acemoglu and Johnson 2005) along with the importance of further institutional provisions (Rodrik 2002; see Table 8.1).

The prescribed economic reforms (rapid privatization, liberalization and stabilization) did not deliver the expected results as they were rarely supported by the rules that structure social interactions. The new legally enforced formal institutions, such as those governing deregulation, market and price liberalization and secure property rights, had to be supported by informal institutions. Informal institutions have self-enforcing and reinforcing attitudes toward, *inter alia*, the rule of law, corruption and regulations. Informal institutions change slowly and require a certain period of learning and re-learning on both sides: by those enforcing them as well as by those affected by the new formal rules. A slow change in the informal institutions might support the transition process. It might also cause a slowdown and path dependence of economic development, even creating lock-ins at times (see North 1990). As the transition process continued for a much longer time than expected, increasing institutional discrepancy was identified as the cause of the unintended, inefficient or time-lagged outcomes of economic reforms (see Gruševaja 2005). Notably, institutional complementarities – or in other words, successful adjustments in changes for both formal and informal institutions – support a transitional process (see Aoki 2001). Subsequently, the institutional transition approach assumed a more prominent role in the transition literature.

The 'varieties of capitalism', the latest concept or approach, refers to both theoretical findings mentioned above and is based on the assumption that different countries with market economies gain comparative advantages or suffer from disadvantages by developing and maintaining economic and institutional coherence. Originally, Hall and Soskice (2001) identified two types of economies: liberal market economies (LMEs) and coordinated market economies (CMEs). The LMEs rely on the market to coordinate the activities of the different actors (such as firms, investors and employers), while the CMEs also use non-market coordination mechanisms (such as trade unions, collaboration between firms and income redistribution). This new framework improved the understanding of the similarities and differences among developed economies, and the role of institutions and their influence on and coherence with market-related economic activities. Applying this framework to the transition countries of Central and Eastern Europe (CEE) and to the countries of the former Soviet Union, the third concept, dependent market economies (DMEs), was introduced (see King 2007; Nölke and Vliegenthart 2009; Myant and Drahokoupil 2011). DMEs are economies which are highly dependent on foreign direct investments (FDIs). Hence, multinational companies and international capital borrowers wield a particularly high influence in setting the formal rules. The institutions are shaped and influenced by external (market) power.

These three main approaches – namely, economic transition, institutional transition and comparative advantages – provide a framework of economic and institutional coherence to evaluate the 30 years of transition, with surprisingly different outcomes. Despite the differences, the new EU Member States will be considered as one group of countries which were exposed to the EU accession process during the transition period. This group (EU-CEE11) will be compared with the two non-EU Member States of Russia and Ukraine, as the economic and institutional achievements in these two groups of countries have been in stark contrast to each other.

Table 8.2   *Years of important steps towards EU accession in the CEE countries*

	EU membership application	Association agreement	Opening of accession negotiations	Accession
Bulgaria	1995	1995	2000	2007
Czech Republic	1996	1995	1998	2004
Estonia	1995	1998	1998	2004
Hungary	1994	1994	1998	2004
Lithuania	1995	1998	1999	2004
Latvia	1995	1998	2000	2004
Poland	1994	1994	1998	2004
Romania	1995	1995	2000	2007
Slovenia	1996	1999	1998	2004
Slovakia	1995	1995	2000	2004
Croatia	2003	2004	2005	2013

Source: Gruševaja and Pusch (2015).

8.2   EU-CEE11: TRANSITION PATTERNS AND APPROACHES

The transition process in EU-CEE11 started after 1989 when the Eastern Bloc of communist countries collapsed politically and economically. The CEE11 countries implemented shock therapy, which was approved by leading economists and the IMF. The primary effects of rapid privatization, liberalization and deregulation were very similar across the EU-CEE11 countries, as evidenced by the strong output decline (approximately 10 per cent annually in CEE in 1989–1991), inflation (up to 249 per cent in Poland in 1990) and high unemployment. To enhance economic growth and avoid the further political influence of former bloc partners, particularly Russia, the CEE countries signed association agreements with the EU and applied for full membership only a few years after the beginning of the transition process (see Table 8.2).

The accession strategy for the enlargement of the EU has been based on the formal *ex ante* harmonization of institutions. The institutional underpinning of market economies is 'a clearly delineated system of property rights, a regulatory apparatus curbing the worst forms of fraud, anti-competitive behaviour, and moral hazard, a moderately cohesive society exhibiting trust and social cooperation, social and political institutions that mitigate risk and manage

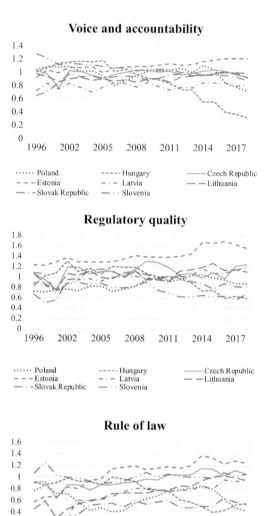

Voice and accountability

.... Poland   ----- Hungary   ——— Czech Republic
— — Estonia   — · — Latvia   — — Lithuania
— · - Slovak Republic   — · · Slovenia

Regulatory quality

.... Poland   ----- Hungary   ——— Czech Republic
— — Estonia   — · — Latvia   — — Lithuania
— · - Slovak Republic   — · · Slovenia

Rule of law

.... Poland   ----- Hungary   ——— Czech Republic
— — Estonia   — · — Latvia   — — Lithuania
— · - Slovak Republic   — · · Slovenia

Source: World Bank Database – Worldwide Governance Indicators.

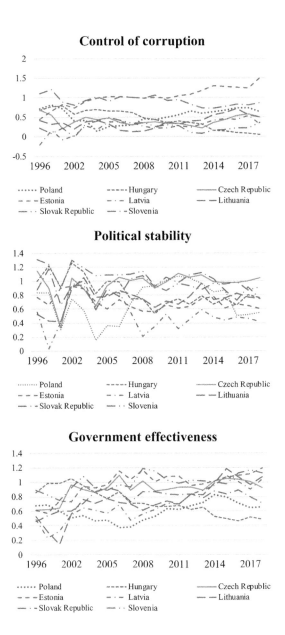

Figure 8.1   *World Bank Governance Indicators in EU-CEE8 (EU Accession 2004)*

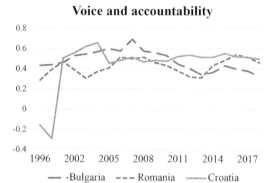

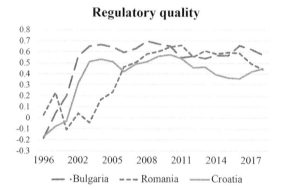

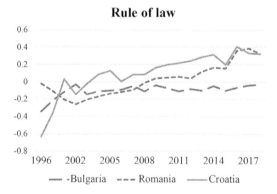

Source: World Bank Database.

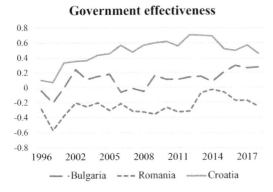

Figure 8.2   *World Bank Governance Indicators in EU-CEE8 (EU Accession 2007 of Bulgaria and Romania; EU Accession 2013 of Croatia)*

social conflicts, the rule of law and clean government' (Rodrik 2000, p. 2). Establishing effective and appropriate market-supporting institutions has been regarded as the necessary condition for an internal common market, and it is reflected in the EU law (*acquis communautaire*). The EU's institutional framework has been assumed to be effective in the first place because it enables an internal common market free of distortion which might help to foster economic growth and integration with the EU. This unified institutional environment, however, has been established in the old EU Member States by interjurisdictional bargaining, informal contracts and cooperation, and mutual learning over a long period of time. The CEE countries also had to converge to this best (praxis proven) coherent combination of effective economic and political institutions (including government profiles) partly before and partly after the EU accession, to ensure macroeconomic stability and enhance economic growth. *Ex post* research showed that this politically enforced institutional convergence had positive and negative dynamics (see Gruševaja and Pusch 2015); however, the positive effects on the transition process outweighed the negative dynamics. Implementation of the EU law and regulations has helped EU-CEE11 to foster economic integration. However, whilst institutional convergence in terms of governance increased before the accession in 2004/2007/2013, since then it has been stagnating or even declining (see Figure 8.1, Figure 8.2).

The persistence on institutional diversity despite institutional *ex ante* harmonization is also visible from the corporate governance (CG) issues of the CEE countries. The varieties of capitalism model suggests that the financial system and CG structure have a highly explanatory power with regard to the differences in market economies, and that the two aspects are tightly interlinked. An assessment of CG in CEE-3 (the Czech Republic, Hungary and Poland) revealed that national peculiarities regarding CG led to differences in outcomes (see Ozsvald 2014) despite the fact that the countries duly followed the EU's initiatives. First, the equity markets of the EU-CEE11 countries (except Poland) were and remain underdeveloped, leading to undercapitalization and hence a strong dependency on domestic and foreign-owned financial institutions. Second, a high inward FDI flow in the CEE countries led to foreign ownership of firms and influenced internal CG in these countries. Foreign ownership also affected the financial restraints of firms in EU-CEE11 and made economies highly dependent on foreign capital. This outcome of the transition period might cause problems in terms of further economic and institutional integration within the EU.

8.3   RUSSIA AND UKRAINE: TRANSITION PATTERNS AND APPROACHES

The transition period in Russia and Ukraine started after the dissolution of the Soviet Union in 1991. Both countries experienced economic collapse upon independence. Gross domestic product (GDP) dropped by approximately 15–20 per cent. Since a centrally planned economy had existed in both countries for more than 70 years, the transition to a market economy proved to be difficult. Taking into account the large sizes of both countries, the sudden breakdown of the collaborations, connections and networks established by central planning among suppliers resulted in remarkable hardships with regard to managing the situation and initiating the transition process. No specific plan existed, and there was no time to adapt any other reform agenda to the situation; initiating the transition had a disruptive influence on the economy on the one hand, and information asymmetry allowed vested interests to pursue their own goals on the other hand. In the initial stage of the transition, both countries followed the same provisions as EU-CEE11 (those of the Washington Consensus). They experienced the same economic outcomes in terms of output decline, high inflation and increasing unemployment (see Figure 8.3).

After a very painful initial period of transition, while implementing the same liberal reform agenda as EU-CEE11, Russia and Ukraine switched from shock therapy to gradualism in the mid-1990s. This change had a negative impact on both countries. The increasing influence of vested interests, weak political leadership and lack of commitment to supranational entities (for example, the EU) created favourable conditions for the evolvement of inefficient economic

Source: World Bank Database – World Development Indicators.

Figure 8.3   GDP per capita in Russia and Ukraine, 1990–2000

Voice and accountability

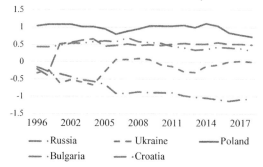

Regulatory quality

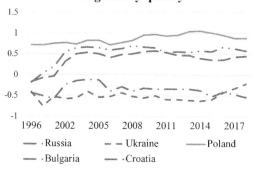

Rule of law

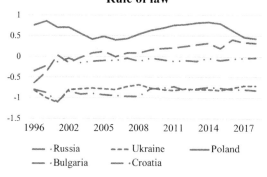

Source: World Bank Database – Worldwide Governance Indicators.

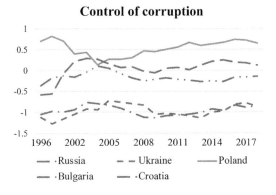

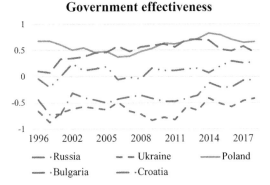

Figure 8.4   *World Bank Governance Indicators in Russia, Ukraine,*
                    Poland (EU accession 2004), Bulgaria (EU accession 2007)
                    and Croatia (EU accession 2013)

structures and interest group-oriented (instead of public interest-oriented) institutional frameworks. The slow and poorly managed privatization of state-owned enterprises favoured the emergence of oligarch ownership. The hasty liberalization of the banking sector, which was non-existent in a unified Soviet Union, led to the establishment of an inefficient banking system with numerous banks (as well as many 'pocket banks'[2]). This system was eventually exposed during the Russian financial crisis in 1998 which had a strong impact on the neighbouring countries. Simultaneously, Ukraine, one of the main trading partners of Russia, experienced a currency crisis which was domestically caused and accelerated by the Russian crisis. The shortcomings of the privatization process as well as the inefficient financial system caused increasing disparities in income distribution. Additionally, both countries were defined by their strong reliance on raw material and natural resources, which increased their vulnerability and exposure to external and internal shocks. All these factors delayed the beginning of economic recovery in terms of GDP only after 2000. In effect, in Russia and Ukraine, the economic recovery during the transition process took significantly longer than in the case of EU-CEE11. Both economies still have not reached their full potential and are very vulnerable with regard to international economic integration.

Likewise, in terms of institutional transition, Russia and Ukraine began with the same transition approach as the other former socialist CEE countries. Later, however, unlike the case of EU-CEE11, they experienced more difficulties in identifying an appropriate institutional transition strategy without the commitment to or pressure of the EU accession. Further, the inconsistency between the rapidly introduced new formal and existing informal institutions was essentially manifested to a stronger extent for these two countries than for the other countries of the Eastern Bloc. More than 70 years of a socialist regime had a very strong influence on the countries' economic, social and political actors. The absence of a legal culture (rule of law), and therefore the lack of familiarity with the new rules recommended by the IMF, immensely increased individual uncertainty and intensified the inconsistency of institutional development, since the old 'shared mental maps' were incompatible with the new formal institutions. Therefore, the adaptation process was impeded considerably. The political actors acted under conditions of radical uncertainty, bounded rationality and immense pressure from inside and outside the country to bring rapid changes under way (see Gruševaja 2010). Instead, asymmetric information, lack of transparency and overwhelming complexity essentially complicated the process. In the initial period of the transition, the political actors were not able – cognitively and organizationally – to establish and effectively enforce the institutions required as part of the framework for a well-functioning market economy. Instead, the strategy of gradualism (as mentioned above) favoured the emergence of strong vested interest groups which were enabled to significantly influence the process of economic and institutional transition for their own benefit. The gradual institutional transition led Russia to a strong institutional and political path dependence, while in Ukraine it caused persistent institutional and political instability. In that context, compared with the three biggest countries of EU-CEE11, the development of market economy-supporting institutions has been lagging in Russia and Ukraine (see Figure 8.4).

With regard to the varieties of capitalism, the findings are quite similar to those for EU-CEE11. Russia and Ukraine experienced the same dependency on FDI during the transition period, with the influence of foreign banks and multinational enterprises dominating CG rule setting (as in the case of DMEs). Although both countries augmented the existing laws with basic provisions for economic companies and created the fundamentals for corporate legislation in the early 1990s, the level of corporate relationship regulation was low and inefficient. Thus, its regulatory functions were not fulfilled. Hence, the coordination of economic activities of companies was disordered and inefficient. Finally, in 2000 and 2002, respectively, the institutional framework of CG in Russia and Ukraine underwent extensive reforms. New corporate legislations were implemented in compliance with the country's own national and international standards and principles of CG. Moreover, after the financial crisis in 1998 and 2007–2008 in Russia and Ukraine, respectively, both countries slowly consolidated and improved their financial systems. However, CG continues to suffer from many weaknesses; *inter alia,* the equity markets remain insufficiently developed. This outcome is expected to impede – at least to some extent – further economic development in Russia and Ukraine.[3]

8.4   CONCLUDING REMARKS

Looking back at the 30-year-long transition in CEE, the overall picture of economic development in the transition countries is a positive one. The transition from planned to market economies was successful: all countries have become wealthier and the living standards of their citizens have improved. All the CEE countries have established market economies and related institutions. All the countries started with the same reform agenda, and the initial effects were quite similar. Later, the two groups of countries analysed in this chapter changed their respective transition strategies. While the EU-CEE11 countries followed the same path by accelerating their commitment to reform through the EU accession process, Russia and Ukraine modified the transition pace by switching to the gradual strategy. In hindsight, the EU accession process in the early transition stage proved to be an important 'reform anchor' for EU-CEE11. Thus, it was expected to have a similar positive impact on Ukraine, which signed the accession agreement with the EU in 2014. Russia and Ukraine had to struggle with economic decline and/or stagnation for a longer period and at a higher cost to their respective populations (as evidenced by the social and economic privation, instability, unpredictability and vulnerability to external shocks).

In regard to institutional changes, all the transition countries struggled to establish and enforce market-related economic and democratic institutions. Here again, the EU accession played an important role in increasing their commitment and ensuring that continuous efforts were undertaken to incorporate the EU law and regulations into the national legislations of the EU-CEE11 countries before accession in 2004, 2007 and 2013. Lack of 'outside pressure' in Russia and Ukraine explains why institutional change, like economic recovery, took much longer than that for EU-CEE11. It is, however, important to mention that the institutional convergence of EU-CEE11 has been stagnating or even declining since the accession to the EU. Although the quality of institutions in EU-CEE11 is higher compared to those in Russia and Ukraine, the overall institutional quality is low and has recently been showing signs of decline in transition countries. This observation also applies to the CG legislation. This aspect is correlated with political development. Some of the transition countries are looking to China's economic development experience and questioning the importance of democratic or liberal market institutions for economic growth. However, economic development without democracy creates its own limits in the long run (see Fukuyama 2012, 2018). Overall, economic transition and institutional transition are intertwined, as together they create a general framework for economic activities. Complementarities within the economic and institutional frameworks enhance economic development, whilst discrepancies exert a negative influence on the social, political and economic development process. Moreover, they make international economic integration more difficult.

The overall economic outlook for EU-CEE11, Russia and Ukraine is positive. All these countries have huge economic potential. They have shown significant growth in recent periods, and the growth forecast predicts additional growth of approximately 2 to 3 per cent for 2020–2021 (with the exception of Russia, whose expected growth is below 2 per cent) (see wiiw 2019). The decrease in FDI inflow poses one of the most important challenges, as FDI translates into improved investment capacity. FDI inflows are expected to be moderate or low, despite their urgent need for further economic development. Additionally, rampant corruption is still an issue in some EU-CEE11 countries and Ukraine, and the geopolitical tensions with Russia will influence overall economic development in the region.[4] Finally, all the countries must improve their institutional settings to create favourable conditions for sustainable economic development.

NOTES

1. For Poland, the Washington Consensus was modified and approved by the IMF as the Balcerowicz Plan. Leszek Balcerowicz was a Polish minister and economist. He adopted the plan for Poland in 1989. The plan was aligned with the liberal economic paradigm (the Washington Consensus) of the IMF and was implemented in different post-communist countries.
2. 'Pocket banks' are known as a post-Soviet phenomenon. These banks were the financial institutions created by privatized companies and industrial groups to finance their own businesses.
3. Despite its very favourable geographical and economic conditions (for example size, population and climate), Ukraine continues to be one of the poorest countries in CEE.
4. There has been an obvious decline in FDI inflow since the Russia–Ukraine conflict in 2014.

REFERENCES

Acemoglu, D. and S. Johnson (2005), 'Unbundling Institutions', *Journal of Political Economy* 115, 949–995.

Aoki, M. (2001), *Toward a Comparative Institutional Analysis*, Cambridge: MIT Press.

Fukuyama, F. (2012), *The Origins of Political Order: From Prehuman Times to the French Revolution*, London: Farrar, Straus and Giroux.

Fukuyama, F. (2018), *Identity: The Demand for Dignity and the Politics of Resentment*, London: Farrar, Straus & Giroux.

Gruševaja, M. (2005), 'Formelle und informelle Institutionen im Transformationsprozess', *Volkswirtschaftliche Diskussionsbeiträge* No. 76, Universität Potsdam.

Gruševaja, M. (2010), 'Governmental Learning as a Determinant of Economic Growth', IWH Discussion Paper 23/2010, Halle Institute for Economic Research.

Gruševaja, M. and T. Pusch (2015), 'The Patterns of European Institutional Convergence in Central and Eastern European Countries and its Relation to Growth', Paper No 7.01, GRINCOH-Project 'Growth-Innovation-Competitiveness: Fostering Cohesion in Central and Eastern Europe', 2012–2015, http://www.grincoh.eu/ (accessed on 27 January 2020).

Hall, P.A. and D. Soskice (2001), *Varieties of Capitalism: The Institutional Foundations of Comparative Advantage*, Oxford: Oxford University Press.

King, L.P. (2007), 'Central European Capitalism in Comparative Perspective', in B. Hancke, M. Rhodes and M. Thatcher (eds), *Beyond Varieties of Capitalism: Conflict, Contradiction and Complementarities in the European Economy*, Oxford: Oxford University Press, 307–327.

Myant, M. and J. Drahokoupil (2011), *Transition Economies: Political Economy in Russia, Eastern Europe, and Central Asia*, Hoboken, NJ: John Wiley & Sons.

Nölke, A. and A. Vliegenthart (2009), 'Enlarging the Variety of Capitalism: The Emergence of Dependant Market Economies in East Central Europe', *World Politics* 61 (4), 670–702.

North, D.C. (1990), *Institutions, Institutional Change and Economic Performance*, New York: Cambridge University Press.

Ozsvald, E. (2014), 'Corporate Governance in Central Eastern Europe – A Comparative Political Economy Approach', Paper No 7.03, GRINCOH-Project 'Growth-

Innovation-Competitiveness: Fostering Cohesion in Central and Eastern Europe',
2012–2015, http://www.grincoh.eu/ (accessed on 28 January 2020).

Rodrik, D. (2000), 'Institutions for High-Quality Growth: What They are and How to
Acquire Them', NBER Working Papers No. 7540, February.

Rodrik, D. (2002), 'After Neoliberalism, What? Remarks at the BNDES Seminar on
"New Paths of Development"', Rio de Janeiro, 12–13 September.

wiiw (2019), 'Braced for Fallout from Global Slowdown', wiiw Forecast Report No.
Autumn 2019, November.

Williamson, J. (1994), 'The Political Economy of Policy Reforms', Institute for
International Economics, Washington, DC.

Williamson, J. (2004), 'The Washington Consensus as Policy Prescription for
Development', Institute for International Economics, Washington, DC.

9. Central, Eastern and Southeastern Europe's reunion with Europe

Andrzej Sławiński

The economic reunion of the Central, Eastern and Southeastern European (CESEE) countries with Europe proved to be a spectacular success (see Grela et al. 2017). The liberalization of their economies in the early 1990s, and joining the European global value chains (GVCs) in the mid-1990s, turned the region into a manufacturing backbone of the European Union (EU) (see Landesmann and Stöllinger 2018).

I was lucky enough to work at the National Bank of Poland (NBP) when our economy was being stabilized and then put on an equilibrium growth path which was significantly facilitated by the country's accession to the EU. For me, it is a pleasure to briefly recount our Polish experiences, which are in many respects typical of all the CESEE countries.

9.1 THE CHOICE OF EXCHANGE RATE REGIME

Leszek Balcerowicz's plan for the liberalization and stabilization of the Polish economy was ready in 1980, but it took a decade until political change permitted it to be launched. In the early stages of its implementation, an unexpected challenge was the inflation rate of 600 per cent. Hence, the initial disinflation measures had to be much tougher than originally planned.

One of the main stabilization tools was the fixed exchange rate introduced in 1990 and intended to dampen inflationary expectations. The message from the monetary authorities was that their determination to fight inflation would suffice to uphold the fixed exchange rate at least for several successive months. The outcome was surprisingly successful. Despite the initial hyperinflation, it was possible to keep the fixed exchange rate unchanged until mid-1991, while inflation was reduced to 40 per cent.

The cost of keeping the fixed exchange rate of the zloty amidst high inflation was its substantial appreciation in real terms. For this reason, in 1991, the NBP implemented the crawling peg regime to slow down the real appreciation of the domestic currency and preserve the economy's international price competitiveness. In 1994, the crawling band was introduced as the first step toward floating the zloty. Subsequently, its trading band was gradually widened to 15 per cent. Meanwhile, the NBP steadily tapered off its interventions on the foreign exchange market to ultimately float the zloty in 2000.

This was in line with the predominant view at the time that, due to the sharply increased scale of short-term capital flows, the choice of exchange rate regimes was between corner solutions: adopting a common currency, as was the case after the exchange rate mechanism (ERM) crisis of 1992–1993, which prompted the creation of the euro area; or choosing a floating exchange rate, which became so common among the emerging economies after the Asian crisis of 1997–1998. In CESEE, some countries chose currency boards (substituting a common currency), while others preferred managed or free floats.

The experiences of the CESEE countries demonstrated, however, that markets were not as invincible as was assumed in the wake of the ERM and the Asian crises. While the Hungarian experiences of 2003 illustrated that markets could attack even a 15 per cent band when they perceived (rightly or wrongly) the macroeconomic policy of a given country as inconsistent (see Barabás 2003), the attack ultimately failed and Hungary floated the forint only in 2008. Likewise, the Czech experiences with containing the appreciation of the koruna in the early 2000s (see Holub 2004) showed that under the floating exchange rate regime, a central bank may choose the right timing for intervention: that is, enter the market when the speculative momentum is fading (see Franta et al. 2014).

The experiences of the CESEE countries revealed that markets are actually disruptive only on rare occasions, and that central banks can 'come to terms' with them by means of properly structured interventions. For example, in 1996, market speculation stabilized the zloty around the level which was assumed to be preferred by the NBP. One of the reasons was that foreign exchange dealers remembered the effectiveness of our interventions in the previous year. A similar situation occurred with the floor for the Czech koruna in 2013–2017, when occasional interventions were sufficient to persuade markets not to break the level set by the Czech National Bank (CNB) (see Baxa and Šestořád 2019).

The floating exchange rate of the zloty served us well. As was the case with the British pound, the Swedish krona and the Czech koruna, the zloty remained fairly stable and floated with the euro against the other main currencies. During the last several years, the zloty has been as stable against the euro, as if Poland had introduced a fixed exchange rate with a narrow band. This resulted from our growing integration with the euro area, and the absence of large macroeconomic imbalances in the Polish economy. Another equally important factor which contributed to reducing the volatility of the zloty was the compression of the interest rate differential between Poland and the developed economies. It substantially narrowed down the opportunities for arbitrage trading (for example, carry trades), which the markets love so much. The stability of the zloty also illustrates the diminishing scale of the Balassa–Samuelson effect.

9.2 STABILIZING INFLATION

In the 1990s, Poland's stabilization policy was pragmatic and eclectic. The NBP controlled both the exchange rate and the money supply, which might not have been elegant, but it was effective. Inflation was being systematically pushed down, while the economy continued to grow at a fairly high rate.

The effectiveness of this policy won the NBP credibility on international financial markets. In the late 1990s, Poland was spared a currency crisis, which was so endemic at that time in emerging economies, including CESEE.

An important change in the monetary policy framework took place in 1998 with the establishment of the Monetary Policy Council (MPC) and the decision to adopt an inflation target regime. Unexpectedly, from the very beginning, the MPC faced a serious challenge. The sharp rise in food prices and a deep depreciation of the zloty during the Russian crisis pushed inflation outside the original target band. The MPC decided to invest in its credibility by hitting the inflationary target despite the changed circumstances. The price paid for the substantial tightening of the monetary policy and the appreciation of the zloty was the significant economic slowdown of 2001–2002. Nonetheless, the slowdown, as was the case in the early 1980s in the developed economies, was the price paid for achieving a decisive change in the long-term inflationary expectations. Since then, the task of the NBP has only been to stabilize inflation around the target level.

The additional factor that pushed the MPC toward a significant tightening of the monetary policy was a substantial deterioration in the current account, with the deficit totalling 8 per cent of GDP in 1999. While the substantial rise in interest rates brought a sharp appreciation of the zloty, the MPC assumed that the increased inflow of foreign direct investments (FDIs) would boost Polish exports anyway. This expectation did materialize. For the first time, Poland's participation in GVCs became more important for our exports than the exchange rate policy (see Ambroziak and Marczewski 2014).

Three important factors contributed to stabilizing inflation in the CESEE region after the disinflation of the 1990s. One of them was the rapidly increasing openness of the CESEE economies when the global inflation rate was fading due to accelerating globalization in the wake of China and India joining the world economy. The second factor was the improved credibility of central banks in the CESEE region due to successful disinflations in the 1990s. Under these circumstances, the NBP was able to effectively stabilize inflation through stabilizing the output gap (see Mackiewicz-Łyziak 2016).

But the crucial factor which helped the CESEE countries to put their economies on an equilibrium growth path was their increasing integration with the European GVCs. This process brought similar positive outcomes to the CESEE region, as did the inflow of United States direct investment to Western Europe after World War II (see Bergeaud et al. 2014). FDIs contributed to the narrowing of the technological and managerial gap between the CESEE and other EU economies. The inflow of new technologies boosted productivity growth rates, which in turn made stabilizing inflation easier. Due to the sharp increase in the CESEE countries' export potential, they were steadily reducing their trade deficits and becoming surplus economies, which facilitated stabilizing their exchange rates.

The integration with GVCs also enabled the CESEE countries to enter the path of export-led growth. For example, in Poland, about half of GDP growth can be attributed to the growth in exports (see Hagemejer and Mućk 2019). The participation in the European GVCs helped the CESEE countries to improve their technological competitive edge and achieve the high rate of growth in exports despite the appreciation of their real exchange rates (see Bierut and Kuziemska-Pawlak 2016). The zloty was appreciating along its equilibrium exchange rate, which gave us the luxury of not engaging in unnecessary interventions on the forex market.

In general, thanks to the economic reforms of the 1990s and the integration with the EU, CESEE became one of the most economically successful regions in the global economy. Among the signs of international markets' trust in the Polish economy's long-term prospects was that a large proportion of foreign-owned Polish T-bonds were in the portfolios of real money (long-term) investors (see Jabłecki et al. 2016).

A telling illustration was also the behaviour of T-bond yields after the European Central Bank (ECB) launched its quantitative easing (QE) policy. In Poland, the outcome was the negative risk premium on the T-bond market. The reason is that our T-bonds are in international bond indices. Hence, when the ECB's QE pushed up the prices of T-bonds in the euro area, the managers in international investment funds were rebalancing their portfolios by buying T-bonds in other countries, including Poland. This gradually pushed down the yields of our T-bonds below the expected level of future short-term interest rates, which made the risk premium negative.

9.3   THE EMERGENCE OF MACROPRUDENTIAL POLICY

A challenging period for monetary policy in CESEE was the global banking crisis caused by the collapse of the unsustainable lending booms in many economies (see Eller et al. 2016). In the CESEE region, the main cause for these booms was foreign exchange lending. It was popular in those countries where the domestic interest rates were comparatively high, for example in Hungary and Poland. The mortgage booms in CESEE were financed largely with wholesale short-term funding which often took the form of credit lines obtained from parent banks.

In Poland, banks offered foreign exchange loans indexed mainly to the Swiss franc. An important reason for the increasing popularity of foreign exchange-denominated loans was the prevailing belief that the zloty will continue to appreciate after Poland's accession to the EU. Unfortunately, it became a self-fulfilling prophecy.

Since Polish banks extended loans indexed to the Swiss franc, they had to hedge their exchange rate risk by selling Swiss francs in forward transactions. As the market for outright forwards is usually illiquid, Polish banks had to engineer synthetic outright forwards through entering foreign exchange swaps and simultaneously selling francs on the spot market.[1] This gradually pushed up the zloty and reinforced the belief that there was indeed an inherent strong trend toward its long-term appreciation.

These foreign exchange lending practices began to tie the NBP's hands. We could not significantly raise the interest rates as this might further encourage the zloty to appreciate, and fuel the credit boom instead of cooling it down. This is why in 2006 the Polish banking supervision initiated its *de facto* macroprudential policy. It introduced Regulation S, which tightened loan-to-value (LtV) and debt service-to-income (DSTI) ratios, especially in the case of foreign exchange-denominated mortgage lending. The regulation did not curb the lending boom, but it directed the majority of foreign exchange loans toward those households that could afford to sustain a sizeable depreciation of the zloty. As a result, Polish banks did not suffer large losses during the global banking crisis. Taxpayers' money did not have to be pledged. The NBP did not resort to any form of unconventional monetary policy. Our assistance provided to commercial banks was limited to a fistful of foreign exchange swaps extended to a couple of smaller institutions which were irresponsible enough to fund a large part of their mortgage loans on the global short-term foreign exchange swap market.

Undoubtedly, there is a future for macroprudential policy in the CESEE countries. Sooner or later, they may enter a period of slower growth and lower interest rates. Hence, during mortgage booms it might be more rational to employ macroprudential measures than to increase interest rates. However, the recent experiences of some countries suggest that a preferred solution should be to empower an independent central bank to decide when to use macroprudential tools (see Borio 2015). A proper solution would be also to leave microprudential policy in banking supervision located outside the central bank. This would protect the central bank's credibility should individual banks encounter problems. Moreover, it would give the central banks leeway in requesting outside impartial opinions on how to structure the most effective set of individual tools (LtV, DSTI, risk weights, and so on) to achieve the best possible results.

Initial experiences with macroprudential policy suggest that it is not a simple substitute for monetary policy, as there are usually long delays between the decision to employ a given tool and the moment it is actually put into action. Hence, macroprudential policy should be treated as an instrument intended to prevent excessive risks from accumulating within the banking system rather than as a handy countercyclical tool.

Polish experiences show that even relatively modest macroprudential measures can be effective in dampening the costs of financial turmoil. In 2007–2009, Poland did not experience a banking crisis but only a periodic asset freeze ordered by foreign parent banks which incurred large losses. Moreover, during the crisis, domestic banks fully complied with the supervisory authority's guidelines not to transfer out liquidity and not to pay out dividends in order to increase their capital.

The fact that other CESEE countries also employed certain macroprudential policy elements before the crisis (see Geršl and Jašová 2014) begs the question why our regulators and supervisors were effective. One of the reasons was that from the very beginning of the economic transformation, Polish authorities were responding promptly to banks' irresponsible lending policies using also unconventional tools.

For example, in the early 1990s, when the rapid growth in corporate debt brought a sharp rise in banks' bad debt portfolios, the government did not cover banks' losses and did not put them in a 'bad bank'. Instead, it gave banks portfolios of treasury bonds to keep them solvent. This forced the banks to live for a long time with the losses on their balance sheets, which effectively worked like a reminder of the risks associated with irresponsible lending.

The other lesson from our experiences, confirmed by academic research, was that while a common European supervision is a necessity in highly integrated banking systems, operational decisions on when and how to apply specific macroprudential tools should be taken at the local level to make such decisions fully informed and effective (see Brzoza-Brzezina et al. 2013).

9.4   THE ADOPTION OF THE EURO

Initially, the accession of the CESEE countries to the euro area was perceived as a challenging task. However, over time, the globally falling inflation and the increasing participation in European GVCs helped the CESEE countries to stabilize their economies, which changed their attitude to the adoption of the common currency. Indeed, the governments in the region were contemplating such a move fairly early.

What made them cautious again as regards the timing of joining the euro area were the lending booms in their economies and the magnitude of the euro area debt crisis. A prompt adoption of the euro was the obvious choice for the Baltic States – having currency boards. In their case, it could be done without substantially modifying their policies, as the unsustainable lending booms of the mid-2000s were not their fault but the outcome of irresponsible lending policies pursued by foreign parent banks whose credit lines overly inflated the balance sheets of banks in the region.

For the other CESEE countries, the timing of the adoption of the euro was not so obvious. In Poland, the floating exchange rate brought certain positive outcomes, such as the stabilization of the trade balance and the real effective exchange rate. Thus, Poland and other CESEE floaters were not losing their cost-competitiveness against the euro area's core countries, unlike the euro area debtor countries.

While, due to the increasing role of the GVCs, the pass-through of the exchange rate has recently declined substantially, the real effective exchange rate (REER) still matters for exports (see Ahmed et al. 2015). Furthermore, in 2008–2009, the floating exchange rate helped our economy to adjust to the global banking crisis and the recession it caused.

Slovakia's experience sheds valuable new light on the problem of CESEE countries joining the euro area. Slovakia fared successfully in the euro area despite the sizeable appreciation of the koruna in the mid-2000s and its large revaluation before the adoption of the euro. There were two reasons behind Slovakia's success. The first was the high productivity growth rate, which enabled the country to stabilize its REER despite the initially demanding accession rate. The other was its participation in the European GVCs. After the outbreak of the global financial crisis, Slovakia experienced a short-lived recession but recovered swiftly with the sharp upturn of the global trade.

The Slovak experience highlights the fact that as the importance of GVCs increases, the role of exchange rate policy declines due to the decreasing pass-through effect on gross domestic product (GDP) and inflation (see Kelm 2016). Keeping the economy on an equilibrium growth path will increasingly depend not on exchange rate adjustments but on undertaking structural reforms which will enable the CESEE countries to increase their supply-side growth resources, such as human capital and innovation potential. In a GVC-dominated global economy, the main goal of economic policy should be to improve an economy's non-price (structural) competitiveness, since it offers the most effective hedge against macroeconomic imbalances (see Kosior and Rubaszek 2014; Benkovskis and Wörz 2012).

9.5   CONCLUDING REMARKS

In the early 1990s, being involved in re-establishing a market economy in Poland was a challenging yet rewarding experience. It was a pleasure to see how in the early 1990s our economy was growing despite the very tight monetary and fiscal policies. This proved that a critical mass of reforms was sufficient to unleash the forces of a market economy.

One may ask about the reasons behind the success of the CESEE region's transformation in comparison with, for example, Latin America's track record in the 1970s. An important factor was that economic reforms in CESEE were introduced simultaneously with the restoration of democracy, which won them social consent. Moreover, shortly after liberalizing and stabilizing their economies, the CESEE countries joined the European supply chains, which enabled them to enter the path of high export-led growth (see Hagemejer and Mućk 2019). Both factors unlocked the potential of fairly well-educated societies with long traditions in manufacturing, of which the Czech Republic is a prominent example.

As far as Poland is concerned, there were several specific factors that helped to put our economy onto a dynamic growth path. The crucial one, which made our transformation more effective, was the method of privatization which ring-fenced the economy from politics and prevented the emergence of oligarchs. The other characteristic of the Polish reforms was the depth of economic liberalization. People from all social backgrounds became entrepreneurs, which imbued our small and medium-sized enterprises sector with an amazing dynamism (see Gardawski 2013). Another important factor was the introduction of the provision into our Constitution that public debt cannot exceed 60 per cent of GDP. Adherence to this rule undoubtedly enhanced Poland's credibility on financial markets (see Belka 2013).

Now, the CESEE countries are confronted with a choice which is discussed by Michael Spence in his book *The Next Convergence* (Spence 2011): they may continue to support the sectors which brought them initial economic success, or embark on a new wave of supply-side reforms aimed at building high-tech industries to improve their position in international GVCs. While the first option is politically tempting, it would definitely mark the beginning of a journey toward the middle-income trap. Hence, choosing the latter option is necessary if we are to avoid the path of slowing and increasingly unbalanced growth.

The present-day challenges faced by CESEE countries are different from those of the 1990s. During the first wave of economic reforms, one of the major challenges was the unprecedented scale of privatization (see Balcerowicz 2014). This time, the governments in the region should strive to build knowledge-based economies in a context in which there are no universal recipes, due to the differences between individual countries rooted in their traditions and cultures (see Gradzewicz et al. 2016).

Nonetheless, a variety of paths may lead to improving the innovation capacity of individual economies; Israel, Taiwan and Ireland being prime cases in point (see Breznitz 2007; Avnimelech et al. 2004). A well-known example of a successful transformation toward knowledge-intensive economies are the Nordic countries (see Ornston 2013). Their success was due to their uniquely high capacity for institutionalized cooperation among authorities, trade unions and the business sector,[2] which enabled them to accumulate supply-side resources (skill formations, basic research and risk capital) necessary to build high-tech industries.

All this begs the question: what are some of the universal conditions conducive to the development of high-tech industries? One factor that must be taken into consideration is that these industries are constantly evolving. For this reason, the state is responsible for supporting enterprises in their unrelenting quest to reinvent themselves. This requires not only a competent but also an adequately independent public service, ready to take the risks associated with promoting innovation, even though the outcomes of such decisions are invariably uncertain. The scope for such independence should be especially ample in the case of public agencies entrusted with nurturing innovation, since political interference is more likely than not to reduce their effectiveness (see Breznitz and Ornston 2013; Breznitz et al. 2018).

We all know the list of the reforms that are necessary to enhance an economy's potential to innovate. Among the critical but difficult issues is, for example, the creation of an incentives system which would match the interest of business and academia in facilitating commercialization of academic research. Other issues, such as a proper system of research and development, and venture capital taxation, do not seem to be complicated but can be difficult to implement in practice.

Hence, the factor which is indispensable to breathe life into reforms promoting innovations is having competent and sufficiently independent public servants who are capable and ready to make the necessary decisions without yielding to the temptation of seeking safety in inaction. Central banks provide a good example of independent public agencies that may serve the economy and society well. One of the reasons is that when you are independent, taking responsibility becomes a challenging pleasure.

NOTES

1. Rolling over short-term foreign exchange swaps is neutral for the exchange rate. Thus, banks selling Swiss francs on the spot market kept pushing up the zloty's value.
2. This factor enabled, for example, the Baltic States to cope amazingly quickly with the dire consequences of the global financial crisis.

REFERENCES

Ahmed, S., M. Appendino and M. Ruta (2015), 'Global Value Chains and the Exchange Rate Elasticity of Exports', IMF Working Paper No. WP/15/252, November.

Ambroziak, Ł. and K. Marczewski (2014), 'Changes in the Polish Foreign Trade in Terms of Value Added' (available in Polish only), *Unia Europejska.pl* 6, 6–17.

Avnimelech, G., M. Kenney and M. Teubal (2004), 'Building Venture Capital Industries: Understanding the US and Israeli Experiences', BRIE Working Paper No. 160, March.

Balcerowicz, L. (2014), 'Poland: Stabilization and Reforms under Extraordinary and Normal Politics', in A. Åslund and S. Djankov (eds), *The Great Rebirth: Lessons from the Victory of Capitalism over Communism*, Washington, DC: Peterson Institute for International Economics, 17–38.

Barabás, G. (2003), 'Coping with the Speculative Attack against the Forint's Band', MNB Background Studies No. 3, May.

Baxa, J. and T. Šestořád (2019), 'The Czech Exchange Rate Floor: Depreciation without Inflation?', CNB Working Paper Series No. 1, February.

Belka, M. (2013), 'How Poland's EU Membership Helped Transform its Economy', Group of Thirty Occasional Papers No. 30, October.

Benkovskis, K. and J. Wörz (2012), 'Non-Price Competitiveness Gains of Central, Eastern and Southeastern European Countries in the EU Market', *Focus on European Economic Integration* Q3/12, 27–47.

Bergeaud, A., G. Cette and R. Lecat (2014), 'Productivity Trends from 1890 to 2012 in Advanced Countries', Banque de France Working Paper Series No. 475, February.

Bierut, B. and K. Kuziemska-Pawlak (2016), 'Competitiveness and Export Performance of CEE Countries', NBP Working Paper No. 248.

Borio, C. (2015), 'Macroprudential Frameworks: (Too) Great Expectations?', in D. Schoenmaker (ed.), *Macroprudentialism*, London: CEPR Press, 29–45.

Breznitz, D. (2007), *Innovation and the State: Political Choice and Strategies for Growth in Israel, Taiwan, and Ireland*, New Haven, CT, USA and London, UK: Yale University Press.

Breznitz, D. and D. Ornston (2013), 'The Revolutionary Power of Peripheral Agencies: Explaining Radical Policy Innovation in Finland and Israel', *Comparative Political Studies* 46 (10), 1219–1245.

Breznitz, D., D. Ornston and S. Samford (2018), 'Mission Critical: The Ends, Means, and Design of Innovation Agencies', *Industrial and Corporate Change* 27, 883–896.

Brzoza-Brzezina, M., M. Kolasa and K. Makarski (2013), 'Macroprudential Policy Instruments and Economic Imbalances in the Euro Area', ECB Working Paper Series No. 1589, September.

Eller, M., F. Huber and H. Schuberth (2016), 'Understanding the Drivers of Capital Flows into the CESEE Countries', *Focus on European Economic Integration* Q2/16, 79–104.

Franta, M., T. Holub, P. Král, I. Kubicová, K. Šmídková and B. Vašíček (2014), 'The Exchange Rate as an Instrument at Zero Interest Rates: The Case of the Czech Republic', Research and Policy Notes No. 3, September.

Gardawski, J. (2013), *Craftsmen and Businessmen: Owners of Small and Medium-Sized Private Firms* (available in Polish only), Warsaw: Wydawnictwo Naukowe SCHOLAR.

Geršl, A. and N. Jašová (2014), 'Measures to Tame Credit Growth: Are They Effective?', *Economic Systems* 38 (1), 7–25.

Gradzewicz, M., A. Stążka-Gawrysiak, M. Rubaszek and J. Growiec (2016), *Innovative Potential of the Polish Economy: The Current State, Determinants, and Prospects* (available in Polish only), Warsaw: Narodowy Bank Polski.

Grela, M., A. Majchrowska, T. Michałek, J. Mućk, A. Stążka-Gawrysiak, G. Tchorek and M. Wagner (2017), 'Is Central and Eastern Europe Converging Towards EU-15?', NBP Working Paper No. 264.

Hagemejer, J. and J. Mućk (2019), 'Export-Led Growth and its Determinants: Evidence from Central and Eastern European Countries', *World Economy* 42 (7), 1994–2025.

Holub, T. (2004), 'Foreign Exchange Interventions Under Inflation Targeting: The Czech Experience', CNB Internal Research and Policy Note No. 1, January.

Jabłecki, J., A. Raczko and G. Wesołowski (2016), 'Negative Bond Term Premia – a New Challenge for Polish Conventional Monetary Policy', *Inflation Mechanisms, Expectations and Monetary Policy* 89, 303–316.

Kelm, R. (2016), 'Exports, Imports and the Zloty Exchange Rate: 2000–2014' (available in Polish only), *Bank i Kredyt* 47 (6), 585–620.

Kosior, A. and M. Rubaszek (2014), *The Economic Challenges of Poland's Integration with the Euro Area*, Warsaw: Narodowy Bank Polski.

Landesmann, M. and R. Stöllinger (2018), 'Structural Change, Trade and Global Production Networks', wiiw Policy Note/Policy Report No. 21, May.

Mackiewicz-Łyziak, J. (2016), 'Active and Passive Monetary Policy in CEE Countries with Inflation Targeting: The Case of the Czech Republic, Hungary, and Poland', *Eastern European Economics* 54 (2), 133–152.

Ornston, D. (2013), 'How the Nordic Nations Stay Rich: Governing Sectoral Shifts in Denmark, Finland, and Sweden', in D. Breznitz and J. Zysman (eds), *The Third Globalization: Can Wealthy Nations Stay Rich in the Twenty-First Century?*, New York: Oxford University Press, 300–322.

Spence, M. (2011), *The Next Convergence: The Future of Economic Growth in a Multispeed World*, New York: Farrar, Straus & Giroux.

PART IV

Lessons from three decades of catching-up in Asia

10. Catching-up in Central and Eastern Europe and East Asia: commonalities and differences

Michael A. Landesmann

This chapter will paint a stylized picture of catching-up processes in East Asia (EA) and in Central and Eastern Europe (CEE). I should start with some words of caution: in a short chapter such as this one, I will not be able to do justice to the highly differentiated historical contexts which the two regions found themselves in, nor will I be able to explore the full range of differentiated experiences across countries within each region.

With regard to the historical contexts in which catching-up took place in these two regions, I will have to refer to rather different phases in post-World War II (WWII) history: for EA economies (that is, Japan, South Korea, Taiwan, Singapore, Hong Kong and Mainland China), the period that I shall consider relevant for this comparative analysis stretches back to the immediate post-war period including the Cold War, while for the Central and Eastern European countries (CEECs), I shall refer to the post-1989 period; that is, the period after the fall of the Iron Curtain.

In the following, I will first look at the role that international economic integration played in catching-up processes in the two regions, covering trade and foreign direct investment (FDI) on the one hand and financial market integration on the other hand. I will then cover macroeconomic issues, particularly external imbalances, which are often an important characteristic of catching-up processes and which act as an important constraint that can lead to severe interruptions of growth and catching-up trajectories. In this context, I will also refer to the choices countries made with regard to exchange rate regimes and monetary policies, and how these affect macroeconomic imbalances. Finally, I will address the issue of institutional developments, particularly the role of the state in economic development processes. In this context, I will return to the very different geopolitical contexts that shaped institutional and political developments in the two regions and that accompanied their exposure to and integration into international economic relations.

10.1   INTERNATIONAL ECONOMIC INTEGRATION AND CATCHING-UP EXPERIENCES IN EAST ASIA AND IN CENTRAL AND EASTERN EUROPE

It is well known that upgrading technological capabilities are a major motor of growth. Technological capabilities should here be interpreted in a rather wide sense: they include not only technologies embodied in production processes, but also know-how in product design, organizational capabilities that affect the efficiency of company performance, and expediency in a variety of inter-actions with markets (such as customer services or marketing).

There are various ways of acquiring such technological capabilities. For countries and companies that are already at the technological frontier in these areas, it means innovating and developing capabilities in the design of new processes, new products and more efficient organizational structures in a competitive environment with other countries and companies at the frontier of global practices.

The situation is different for catching-up economies, as they can utilize the 'advantage of backwardness' (see Gerschenkron 1962), meaning that they do not have to 'reinvent the wheel'. Rather, they can find ways to get access to the know-how that exists in the most or more advanced economies and adapt this know-how to the requirements of their respective economies, taking account of their structural requirements and stage of development. There are a variety of ways of doing this, and they have all been pursued by catching-up economies to differing extents.

In this respect, it is worthwhile to point to the differences in how different catching-up economies in Asia and Central and Eastern Europe (CEE) have obtained access to foreign technology. These differences stem from a number of factors: (1) the international context in which catching-up took place; (2) the level of economic development (in terms of domestic know-how and skills available or acquired); and (3) strategic choices made by governments (local and national).

The first Asian country to embark on catching-up, in the second half of the nineteenth century, was Japan, and its success had a deep impact on the policies adopted by countries that followed in its wake after WWII. Japan pursued a policy that was quite guarded with respect to allowing foreign companies direct access to the domestic economy. Instead, it adopted a policy of copying advanced technologies through imitation, reverse engineering and a particular form of industrial policy (see Johnson 1982). Industrial policy supported the build-up of a few major companies in a succession of industries (see also the recognition of this strategy in an influential study, World Bank

1993). The aim was to succeed in difficult advanced export markets where the mass of global purchasing power was after WWII, and this required not only cost-competitiveness but also strenuous efforts to achieve a quick upgrading of product quality and design. The entry into such markets as well as quality upgrading meant that considerable entry barriers had to be overcome and up-front investment costs covered. The logical strategy therefore was to favour a highly oligopolistic structure of major exporting companies that had strong market power over their many small and medium-scale domestic supplying firms. An important feature of the industrial policy strategy was to allow competition among these highly oligopolistic companies in particular sectors, but also to organize coordinated efforts in domestic research and development (R&D) activities, logistics and strategies to penetrate Western markets. The powerful Ministry of International Trade and Development (MITI) efficiently managed the industrial strategy at this stage of Japan's economic development.

The Japanese industrial policy model was followed by Korea, which equally focused on supporting large companies in a succession of industries (that is steel, shipbuilding, cars, electrical equipment and, more recently, electronics) to become global players. The country also concentrated on building its national 'innovation system' with a strong emphasis on the quality of, *inter alia*, broad-based education and patenting activity.[1] The vast in-house R&D activities of the large industrial companies were complemented by infrastructural and educational support offered by the government. As in the case of Japan, the attitude with respect to FDI was a rather cautious one; for a long time, there was a strict cap on foreign ownership participation in Korean companies. Also, as in Japan, finance for investment was supplied by high domestic savings channelled through a domestic banking system that was strongly aligned with the large domestic industrial companies (often in the form of conglomerates).

The Japanese and Korean models characterized East Asian catching-up strategies until the early 1980s, when the international environment shifted toward trade and financial market liberalization (the so-called 'Washington Consensus'), and the scope for a strongly outward-oriented industrial policy, but that protected domestic markets and adopted a defensive attitude toward FDI, was gradually reduced. By then, of course, Japanese and Korean companies had already achieved a level of technological expertise at par with (if not superior in certain areas to) some of the most successful companies in the West (particularly in the car, electrical equipment and electronics industries).

The other EA economy that I want to cover is China. The country had moved toward a strategy of gradual liberalization and opening-up starting with Deng Hsiao Ping's shift of policies in the early 1980s. China chose a different catching-up model from that of Japan and Korea, thereby following another path of Gerschenkron's 'advantage of backwardness'. After decades of having been shielded from foreign influence, its technological capabilities were much below those of Japan and Korea, which had developed their catching-up strategies after WWII. On the one hand, China placed the same emphasis as Japan and Korea did on developing a successful export strategy in advanced high-income Western markets, which was considered a crucial factor in catching-up. On the other hand, however, in contrast to its two Asian forerunners, China took advantage of the superior know-how of Western companies and developed export-processing industrial zones (EPZs) that provided good logistics, infrastructure and liberalized trade linkages to attract Western companies. The willingness to open up production possibilities for foreign investors, combined with the availability of a huge and cheap labour force willing to migrate to fast-growing urban agglomerations, was a major driver behind the phenomenal growth in China's export capacities. This development turned the country into the 'factory of the world' over a span of only two to three decades, strongly affecting global trading relations.

In China, the ambition to build an improved national innovation system came only at a later stage; that is, after having had to deal with concerns regarding state-owned enterprises (SOEs). Constituting a drag on the domestic economy, SOEs had to be restructured, and thus shrank in their overall importance for the economy. On the other hand, there was a gradual emergence of domestic companies that also had the capabilities to start rivalling advanced foreign companies. This was when China embarked on a strong drive toward improving its national innovation system and setting ambitious targets for it (China's 2025 strategy).

Summing up, depending on a number of factors (such as stages of economic development and international environment), Asian countries pursued different industrial policy strategies. I have described the most prominent of these: the Japanese and Korean strategy, and the Chinese post-Deng strategy.

Let us now come to the CEECs after 1989: 'industrial policy' was – at the start of the transition to become a market economy – associated with the defunct planning system of the Communist era and hence had lost any legitimacy after the start of the transition in 1989. The big driver of 'modernization' became international integration; mostly with the rest of the European economy. The condition for fast integration was the adoption of measures to almost immediately and radically liberalize trade and financial markets. Any type of 'infant industry', 'protectionist' or 'grooming' strategy of domestic companies to become major exporters – as in the Japanese and Korean case – was not on the agenda.

Rather, the CEECs embarked on a strategy of quickly opening up and inviting Western European companies to operate freely in their economies. No explicit differentiated strategy was pursued as to the sectors in which such companies would develop their activities, be they in finance, real estate, wholesale and retail trade, or manufacturing. The fact that the countries in CEE ended up with rather different sectoral distributions of FDI was therefore due to the choices of foreign investors and not due to strategies adopted by the national governments. Thus, foreign investors, particularly German companies, found it very attractive to utilize the opportunity to build up cross-border production chains (particularly in the car industry) in some countries. CEECs could provide, in this early phase of the transition which had started with a big slump in industrial production, a cheap and rather well-trained labour force with a legacy of industrial expertise, as industrial development was highly favoured during the Communist period. The countries and regions in CEE favoured in this respect were those that were geographically close (or adjacent) to the Western European border, so as to keep transport and logistics costs down. Hence, after the massive initial slump in industrial production, some of the Central European economies (particularly the Czech Republic, Hungary and Slovakia) embarked on a rather rapid process of 're-industrialization', almost entirely driven by the incentives of Western manufacturing companies setting up plants integrated into cross-border production chains.

There were attempts in some CEECs to support 'industrial zones' in which foreign companies could benefit from cheap land, better infrastructure and reduced red tape. However, any privileges in such zones that favoured foreign companies had to be gradually reduced or abandoned as the countries moved closer to European Union (EU) integration and thus had to accept the rules of the *acquis* and comply – after accession – with the EU's competition policy.

Summing up, CEE was not guided by an industrial policy of its own, but, in parts, by the rather radical shift toward immediate liberalization and the overriding incentive to integrate with the Western European economy (and the prospects of EU accession). Moreover, the technology transfer necessary for catching-up was due to the operation of foreign (mostly Western European) companies which could offer the advantage of access to high-income markets, had appropriate quality standards and could embed CEE production sites in cross-border production networks.

I should, however, also mention that the CEE countries that benefited particularly from this pattern of catching-up were those that bordered on Western Europe. They formed part of what became known as the 'Central European manufacturing core' (see Stehrer and Stoellinger 2015). Other economies also attracted foreign investment, but much less in manufacturing and more in non-tradables (that is, retail and wholesale trade, domestic banking as well as real estate). This pattern of foreign capital investment led to some of the macroeconomic imbalances that I shall discuss in the next section.

10.2   MACROECONOMIC FEATURES OF CATCHING-UP PROCESSES IN ASIA AND CENTRAL AND EASTERN EUROPE

There is a particular feature that characterizes almost all countries that are on a path of catching-up: they are vulnerable in terms of the external accounts. Although economies benefit from the advantages of interacting with the international environment in terms of both access to technology and access to markets with high levels of purchasing power, this leads – especially in the early stages of such catching-up processes – to imbalances in the external accounts. In the first instance, trade balances are bound to be negative in these early stages, and there are a number of reasons for that: there is a high demand for imported, higher-quality capital goods and in many cases also for consumption goods due to growing incomes (and in some instances, growing income inequality). Export capacities catering to the demand of high-income Western markets, on the other hand, can be built up only gradually. This phase of catching-up is almost bound to be characterized by sustained deficits in the trade accounts, which are the most important component of the current accounts.[2]

The capital accounts, in turn, reveal how any deficits in the current accounts are being financed: through FDI, portfolio investment and credit flows. The capital accounts are a mirror image of the current accounts: if there is a deficit in the current accounts, then there would be a corresponding surplus in the capital accounts, and vice versa.

The major question that arises with external accounts in the context of catching-up processes refers to sustainability. In many instances, the deficits in the current accounts that were building up over a number of years in catching-up economies have turned out to be non-sustainable. This was the case during the Asian crisis in the late 1990s and during various stages of the transition experiences of most of the CEECs (for a detailed discussion of external imbalances in the European context, see Landesmann 2019). Non-sustainability means that, at some point, international capital flows are no longer forthcoming to finance current account deficits. This results in a sudden stop or even a reversal of capital flows (no further lending or rolling over of debts, combined with enforcing debt repayments and repatriating parts of the capital base to the foreign banks' home base).

When a sudden stop happens, the deficit in the current accounts (mostly in the trade balance) cannot easily be remedied through a sudden increase in exports (a sharp devaluation might help; and, in this context, it makes a difference whether a country has adopted a fixed or a flexible exchange rate regime). Hence, the main adjustments initially have to be made through a sharp reduction in imports. This happens through austerity; that is, a fall in domestic disposable income that makes imports no longer affordable and/or a sharp devaluation that makes them too expensive for the domestic population. As the government finds it difficult to borrow in such circumstances (international financial markets will ask for high interest rates), public investment also falls in this situation.

So how did these considerations regarding external imbalances work out in the case of EA and CEE economies during their respective catching-up phases? On the one hand, there are similarities in the trajectories of the CEE economies that form part of the above-mentioned Central European manufacturing core, and in the experiences of the EA economies. These two groups of economies went through phases of significant current account deficits (and thus built up foreign debt), while developing, at the same time, significant export capacities (through domestic companies in Japan and Korea, and through the operation of foreign companies in post-Deng China and in the select group of CEECs). This allowed them to close the gaps in the current accounts over time, reducing the danger of a sudden stop, as net inward capital flows were no longer needed to finance the deficits in the current accounts.

On the other hand, there were also significant differences between the CEECs and the EA economies, as discussed in the previous section. EA economies still operated in a different international economic environment which allowed them to use protectionist trade instruments and regulate international financial flows (into and out of the country). In the case of the CEECs, the instruments required for containing current account deficits were no longer available, as they had opted for full trade and capital markets liberalization.

In the same vein, the EA economies from the 1980s onwards, following the Washington Consensus, gradually abandoned the use of protectionist trade policy instruments (although support for an export-oriented strategy continued in different ways) and opted for capital markets liberalization. One can safely say that the Asian crisis which hit also countries that had built up a sizeable export sector was the result of these policy shifts. They led to a sharp increase in private sector borrowing, and ensuing problems for the domestic banking system when a turn of events led to capital outflows, sharp devaluations and bankruptcies in both the real economy and the domestic banking system (not unlike the case of Ireland, which had similarly built up a strong export base, but experienced a major banking crisis during the 2008–2009 financial crisis).

The CEECs, on the contrary, were exposed to the external imbalances problem in a different way: they had opted for full trade liberalization and very little control over international capital flows. Hence, current account developments were a function of the liberalized choices by investors of which sectors (tradables or non-tradables) they wished to allocate their capital to. Furthermore, as the banking system became mostly foreign-owned in most

CEECs (with the exception of Slovenia), and domestic financial market regulation in a highly integrated European market was not very effective, CEECs – in cases when current accounts were seen as non-sustainable by international financial markets – became the victims of sudden stops, capital flow reversals and (when currencies were flexible) sharp exchange rate depreciations.

Given this overall scenario, we should distinguish between two different groups of CEECs: those that managed to build up sizeable export capacities mostly due to them becoming integrated into cross-border production networks (largely dominated by German companies); and those that, partly due to their geographic location, institutional deficiencies or more protracted policies towards transition, did not attract foreign investment in manufacturing (the main tradable sector, especially for catching-up economies). In the second group of CEECs (countries particularly in Southeast Europe, that is, the Balkans), capital inflows predominantly went into non-tradable sectors. Apart from lacking the support for exporting activities, this had the additional disadvantage of putting an upward pressure on the real exchange rate, the principal measure of price competitiveness of an economy. The capital inflows predominantly into non-tradables thus had the additional impact of making the existing capacities of the tradable sector (both in domestic markets and with respect to exports) less competitive.

Hence, the CEE region was – especially in the pre-2008–2009 financial crisis period – characterized by a division into two groups of economies, with one group being highly vulnerable to changing sentiments of financial markets, and the other group being less vulnerable as it had already built up – like the EA economies – a strong export base.

10.3 THE IMPORTANCE OF INSTITUTIONS IN EAST ASIA VERSUS CENTRAL AND EASTERN EUROPE

The role of institutions as facilitators or inhibitors of economic growth and development has gained high prominence in the development literature (see Acemoglu and Robinson 2012). In fact, many economists now attribute to institutional developments a decisive role in determining whether countries embark on a successful catching-up process and whether, once they have done so, they might or might not get stuck in a middle-income trap.

Taking into account institutional developments, we encounter very different trajectories in EAs (post-WWII) and CEE (post-1989). As already discussed in the cases of Japan and Korea, EA economies built an institutional and governance framework based on technology transfer through reverse engineering and imitation (an important factor was also the American occupation after WWII in Japan, and the presence of American troops following the Korean War).

However, in addition, the two countries developed very specific institutional features of their own, based on a strong commitment to develop their national development strategies.

Thus, Japan's and Korea's industrial policy strategy – discussed above – shaped institutional developments as these were important for economic development. The state, as discussed earlier, took on a very important role as a coordinating agent guiding, in a forward-looking manner, the steps that needed to be taken to succeed in a global economy in which other countries were much more advanced in terms of their technological standards and market power.

Also in China, the role of the state remained very strong, even after the Deng liberalization drive: the development of special industrial zones was an explicit policy pursued by the government, the control over SOEs and the banking system remained very tight, and not only central but also regional and local governments were very actively involved in infrastructure and other location policy decisions. Hence, although foreign companies played a very important role for the impressive catching-up process (through technology transfer and facilitated access to high-income international markets), their position in the Chinese economy was conditioned by the Chinese government taking a strong bargaining stance regarding domestic input content, technology sharing and enforced cooperation with domestic companies. Another important factor was the impact that strict capital markets control exerted on the exchange rate of the Chinese currency, which allowed the Chinese economy to benefit, for a considerable period of time, from an undervalued exchange rate; an important element in successful catching-up, according to development economists (see Rodrik 2008).

The Asian experience during the catching-up phase can thus be seen as characterized by a strong role of nation states in designing and executing development strategies. For a significant part of the catching-up process, the global international environment provided EA economies with certain degrees of freedom as regards the use of trade and industrial policy instruments, and allowed some control over international financial flows and capital markets; something the CEECs did not have in the post-1989 period. So far, however, EA economies have only developed very rudimentary governance structures that would further regional integration processes. The ones that exist, such as the Association of Southeast Asian Nations (ASEAN), often reflect geopolitical interests that do not necessarily support pan-Asian integration (for example, by excluding China from participating in some of these organizations).

The environment that shaped institutional developments in the CEECs in the post-1989 period was a very different one. As a consequence of the disintegration of the Soviet bloc, CEECs had two driving motivations: (1) to establish their national sovereignty after having been controlled by the Soviet Union;

and (2) to attempt as quickly as possible to benefit from a close relationship with and, in due course, from membership in the European Union.

Given the speed of transition, this implied that, after having established national sovereignty fairly quickly, national state apparatuses still carried legacies of the past, and were not well equipped to effectively implement a reformed policy agenda in many areas (such as macroeconomic policy, industrial policy or social policy). The decision towards rapid integration with the West meant that CEECs had the possibility (and at the same time the restriction) to align themselves with an existing institutional and legal set-up that had developed in Western Europe, and in the European Union specifically, over decades. This became very clear when CEECs entered into negotiations to join the EU: the wholesale takeover – although with some transitory arrangements – of the *acquis communautaire* was an absolute condition that had to be met. Since the *acquis* is an extensive collection of legislative and regulatory arrangements, it imposes a very high degree of legal and in many ways also institutional and governance convergence on the Member States.

It is true that the European Union is characterized by political and economic heterogeneity and that there is by no means full convergence among institutional structures and social behavioural patterns (think of Sweden and Germany on the one hand, and Greece and Italy on the other hand). Furthermore, even if similar legal and regulatory frameworks are introduced in different countries, there might still be substantial differences in how these frameworks are implemented. Thus, even with respect to the *acquis*, there might be a big difference between adopting it in legal terms and enforcing it in practical terms.

As regards the CEECs' pattern of integration into the EU, I should also mention that the EU provides scope for differentiated paths of integration into the full policy framework of the EU. In a number of important arrangements, such as membership of the Schengen area and the Economic and Monetary Union (EMU), integration takes place gradually or might even stall. Thus, although in principle all the new Member States are committed to becoming members in both of these arrangements and thus do not have an opt-out clause (as, for example, the United Kingdom had when it was still a member), in practice, membership in these domains is a function of fulfilling certain conditions (such as those on border management in the case of Schengen). Furthermore, it is also a question of policy choice (such as when a country seriously attempts to fulfil the necessary conditions and applies for EMU membership).

Nonetheless, despite the scope for differentiation within the European Union, there is no question that the degree of institutionalized regulatory and legal alignment within the EU is of a far higher degree than that within the Asian context. Thus, when the CEECs embarked on their path toward EU membership, they not only opted for a very high degree of economic integration (in trade, financial markets and labour markets) but also accepted a rather fast takeover of legal and institutional arrangements that had been evolving in Western Europe over a long period. These were and are rather unique as regards the depth and scope of regional integration in today's world. Policymaking in each individual member country is deeply affected by it.

10.4 CENTRAL AND EASTERN EUROPE: FUTURE PROSPECTS AND TRAJECTORIES

In thinking about future trajectories that might impact on the development processes in CEE and in Asia, three issues come to mind that could strongly impact upon these trajectories: (1) demographic challenges; (2) the evolution of the international environment (in the case of CEE, in particular the prospects of future EU integration or disintegration); and (3) the extent to which the 'rise of emerging Asia' will itself significantly shape global international relations which, of course, will not be the case for CEE economies. Let me briefly cover these three points.

Demographic Challenges

The demographic challenges are very severe indeed in the CEE region and one can safely say that it is one of the most important factors affecting long-run economic developments in the region. Many of the CEE countries have lost a significant share of their population through emigration over the past decades, and in quite a few countries these trends are continuing (see, for example, Leitner and Stehrer 2019). On top of that, the initial phase of the transition in the early 1990s has led to a drop in the birth rate, and this in turn has affected the development of the age pyramid thereafter. The outcome of these two factors is a very fast ageing process of the population as a whole, which has consequences for the available labour force (more people over 65), productivity growth (as a young labour force is more open to innovations and organizational change), the sustainability of the social security system (fewer people in the active labour force supporting those outside of it) and the skewness of policymaking to satisfy the interests of the older age cohorts compared to the younger ones.

In this respect, the situation in quite a few of the Asian countries is rather similar to that in the CEECs; not because of outward migration, but because of the fact that several countries (Japan, Korea and China) have experienced a dramatic drop in the birth rate. Hence, similar challenges (named above) are also faced in these Asian countries. One difference between the CEE region and Japan and Korea that one might mention is the high technological level in the latter countries (in particular in relation to the advanced stage of using robots in production, but also increasingly in other areas such as old-age care).

This might allow Japan and Korea to adjust more quickly to the ensuing shortage of an active (human) labour force.

Another factor which the two regions have in common is the rather defensive attitude toward inward migration that could alleviate shortages of the labour force. It will be interesting to see whether a shift in policies will take place in this regard in Asian countries as well as in CEE.

EU Integration or Disintegration

The fate of the European integration process over the coming decades will be crucial for the trajectories of CEE economic development and, of course, for Europe's position in the global economy. The period since the outbreak of the global financial crisis in 2008–2009 has revealed severe fractures in the institutional and policymaking set-up of the EU, and has also resulted in conflictual stances of different countries and country groups vis-à-vis the future of the European integration process. Brexit has been a particularly stark expression of where such tensions could lead, but there are many other instances, such as the lack of further steps toward a banking union, the stalling of the reform of the fiscal policy framework in the EU, and the evolving tensions over the next EU budget.

Thus, political and economic commentators are not even sure whether the current level of EU integration is sustainable, not to mention a significant jump in the degree of EU integration. The impact of a gradual unwinding of the European integration process could have severe repercussions on any further catching-up processes in Europe. In the first instance, any current and future candidates for EU membership (particularly those in the Western Balkans and, in the more distant future, Ukraine and countries in the Caucasus) will no longer be able to take up the advantages of EU membership which the current CEE EU members received in the form of a relatively fast closure of the income gap, the benefits of deepening trade relationships combined with integration into cross-border production chains, substantial transfers, and the significant impact of convergence on institutional and legal structures. All of these will not be completely absent but will proceed at a much slower speed and will not gain the same degree of intensity compared to being a member of the Single Market.

An unscrambling or even further stalling of EU reforms will also have significant impacts on current EU Member States. It will continue to reveal significant shortcomings in the EU's policymaking frameworks and show their dysfunctionality in the case of renewed shocks (as was apparent during the recent financial and economic crisis). As a result, parts of the population in EU countries will no longer have a positive view of the benefits of EU membership, which will be exploited by populist parties (as has already happened over the past decade). This, in turn, would strengthen the nationalist stance that countries might take in intra-EU negotiations, thus making reforms even more difficult and setting into motion a self-enforcing spiral of disintegration (see Szekely and Ward-Warmedinger 2018). This might still not be the most likely outcome; yet, it is a non-negligible possibility.

From a regionalist international relations point of view, this will weaken the soft power position of EU institutions and the political weight of the EU, thus exposing European Member States, current candidate countries and regions in the EU's immediate neighbourhood to an increased influence of other geopolitical powers, such as Russia, China and Turkey.

The Rise of Asia and Global International Relations

Finally, we come to the possible scenarios that the rather dramatic trends as regards Asia's (and particularly EA's) weight in the global economy might entail for the future of international (economic and political) relations. Most analysts expect the trends observed over the past decades to continue, albeit at a somewhat reduced pace. However, while past shifts in global gross domestic product (GDP) have been, above all, driven by EA economies (China in particular), it is likely that populous Southern Asian economies (India in particular) will leave their mark on the world stage to a greater extent (see Table 10.1).

This has already had, and will continue to have, important repercussions for both political international relations as well as global and regional economic relations. Various scenarios are possible: a likely one would lead to a more entrenched emergence of regional blocs in the global economy, which could in turn lead to two subscenarios: one in which relationships between the regional blocs would move toward relatively stable and peaceful relationships; and one in which there would be increased frictions between the regional blocs (dominated by the two countries leading two of the blocs, that is, China and the United States). This would also lead to a scrambling regarding the influence on regions that are not part of any of the blocs (such as countries in the Middle East, Africa and Central Asia). Europe, lacking a true hegemon, will have to find its place in such a scenario by using its still considerable economic weight and other forms of 'soft power', albeit having little in terms of political clout. Europe's foreign and security policy will remain difficult to coordinate, given the lack of a strong commitment to concentrate resources in this field. Most analysts believe that this will remain to be the case (see, for example, Tocci 2017).

Thus, while in principle Europe has the economic potential to act as a significant agent to support development processes in its neighbourhood, such as in Northern and sub-Saharan Africa, as well as in the Middle East, the lack

Table 10.1   Asia, East Asia and South Asia in the global economy (global shares in %)

	1970	1980	1990	2000	2010	2016
Population						
East Asia	24.1	24.1	23.7	22.5	21.1	20.3
South Asia	19.3	20.2	21.3	22.6	23.1	23.7
Asia	53.7	55.4	56.8	58.6	58.4	58.0
GDP						
East Asia	3.3	3.7	4.1	6.8	11.9	17.9
South Asia	2.5	1.9	1.8	1.8	3.1	3.8
Asia	8.7	11.4	10.2	13.5	22.9	29.9
GDP per capita (in % to industrialized world)						
East Asia	4.3	4.2	3.7	6.2	13.1	21.1
South Asia	4.0	2.7	1.8	1.6	3.1	3.9
Asia	5.0	5.7	3.9	4.7	9.1	12.3
Manufacturing value added						
East Asia	0.6	1.4	3.0	4.4	22.5	29.9
South Asia	1.4	1.4	1.5	1.7	3.1	3.5
Asia	3.6	5.8	8.3	10.9	32.8	40.8
Merchandise exports						
East Asia	2.2	3.8	8.0	12.1	17.8	21.3
South Asia	1.1	0.7	0.8	1.0	1.8	2.1
Asia	8.4	18.0	17.0	24.0	33.0	36.0
Foreign direct investment flows (annual averages)			1981–1990	1991–2000	2001–2010	2011–2015
Inward flows: East Asia			5.2	10.3	11.9	16.1
South Asia			0.3	0.5	2.0	2.4
Asia			13.0	16.0	22.9	28.9
Outward flows: East Asia			3.8	6.1	8.7	17.9
South Asia			0.0	0.1	0.9	0.5
Asia			4.8	8.2	14.0	25.1

Notes: Country groups: East Asia – China, Hong Kong, Macao, Mongolia, Republic of Korea and Taiwan; South Asia – Afghanistan, Bangladesh, Bhutan, India, Nepal, Pakistan and Sri Lanka; Asia – includes all countries in Asia with the exception of the ex-Soviet Union, Israel and Japan. Calculations are all based on current price data at market exchange rates (to the USD); definition of country groupings as in Nayyar (2019).
Sources: United Nations, National Accounts, Population Statistics, UNCTAD International Trade and Foreign Direct Investment Statistics.

of political clout might prevent it from doing so. It is thus likely that political and security instability will continue to characterize Europe's neighbourhood.

The situation in Asia will not be easy, either, as China will wield significant clout over the coming decades; yet, China will not be unchallenged: the United States will continue to try to form alliances in the Pacific and in Asia to act as a counterweight to China; and another, even more populous country – that is, India – will also increase its economic and political weight in the Asian arena.

All in all, the dynamics of international economic and political relations are anything but easy to predict.

NOTES

1. The classic text on the Korean experience is Amsden (1989).
2. The current accounts – in the income accounts – also show additional flows, such as the repatriation of profits by international companies, and remittances of nationals living and working abroad.

REFERENCES

Acemoglu, D. and J.A. Robinson (2012), *Why Nations Fail: The Origins of Power, Prosperity and Poverty*, London: Crown Publishers.

Amsden, A. (1989), *Asia's Next Giant: South Korea and Late Industrialization*, Oxford: Oxford University Press.

Gerschenkron, A. (1962), *Economic Backwardness in Historical Perspective*, Cambridge, MA: Harvard University Press.

Johnson, C. (1982), *MITI and the Japanese Miracle, the Growth of Industrial Policy 1925–1975*, Stanford, CA: Stanford University Press.

Landesmann, M. (2019), 'External Imbalances and European Integration', in C. Marcuzzo, A. Palumbo and P. Villa (eds), *Economic Policy, Crisis and Innovation: Beyond Austerity in Europe*, New York: Routledge, Taylor & Francis, 84–112.

Leitner, S. and R. Stehrer (2019), 'Demographic Challenges for Labour Supply and Growth', wiiw Research Report No. 439, Vienna Institute for International Economic Studies (wiiw), Vienna.

Nayyar, D. (2019), *Resurgent Asia, Diversity in Development*, New York: Oxford University Press.

Rodrik, D. (2008), 'The Real Exchange Rate and Economic Growth', Brookings Papers on Economic Activity, Fall, 365–412.

Stehrer, R. and R. Stoellinger (2015), 'The Central European Manufacturing Core: What is Driving Regional Production Sharing?', FIW Studien No. 2, Forschungsplattform Internationale Wirtschaft (FIW), Vienna.

Szekely, I.P. and M.E. Ward-Warmedinger (2018), 'Reform Reversal in Former Transition Economies of the European Union: Areas, Circumstances and Motivations', IZA Policy Paper No. 142, Institute of Labor Economics (IZA), Bonn.

Tocci, N. (2017), *Framing the EU Global Strategy, A Stronger Europe in a Fragile World*, London: Palgrave Macmillan.

World Bank (1993), *The East Asian Miracle*, New York: Oxford University Press.

11. Chinese multinationals in East Central Europe: structural, institutional or political considerations?[1]

Ágnes Szunomár

Europe has emerged as one of the top destinations for Chinese investments. According to Rhodium Group's statistics, annual foreign direct investment (FDI) flows in the 28 European Union (EU) economies have grown from €700 million in 2008 to €30 billion in 2017, representing one-quarter of total Chinese FDI outflows in 2017. In 2018, partly as a result of capital controls in China, FDI outflows to the EU fell to €17.3 billion. However, China's approach toward Europe is far from being unified since China pursues different motives and uses different approaches when dealing with different countries or regions in Europe (see Szunomár 2017): having access to successful brands, high technology and know-how motivates China when entering Western European markets; investments in the green energy industry and sustainability bring Chinese companies to Nordic countries; while greenfield investments (manufacturing), acquisitions and recently also infrastructural projects attract them to Central and Eastern Europe (CEE), including the non-EU member Western Balkan countries.

In recent years, Chinese multinational enterprises (MNEs) have increasingly targeted CEE countries, with East Central Europe[2] (ECE) – that is, Czechia, Hungary, Poland, the Slovak Republic and Slovenia – being among the most popular destinations. Although compared with the Chinese economic presence in the developed world, or even in Europe, China's economic impact on ECE countries is still small, it has accelerated significantly in the past decade. This development is quite a new phenomenon but not an unexpected one. On the one hand, the transformation of the global economy and the restructuring of China's economy are responsible for growing Chinese interest in the developed world, including Europe. On the other hand, ECE countries have become more open to Chinese business opportunities, especially after the global economic and financial crisis of 2008, with the intention of decreasing their economic dependency on Western (European) markets.

In line with the above, this chapter aims to map out the main characteristics of Chinese investment flows and types of involvement, and to identify the host-country determinants of Chinese FDI in the ECE region, with a focus on structural, institutional and political pull factors. According to this chapter's hypothesis, pull determinants of Chinese investments in the ECE region differ from that of Western companies in terms of specific institutional and political factors that seem to be important for Chinese companies. This hypothesis echoes calls to combine macroeconomic and institutional factors to gain a better understanding of the internationalization of companies (see Dunning and Lundan 2008). The novelty of this research is that besides macroeconomic and institutional factors it also incorporates political factors into the analysis, which may also have an important role to play in attracting emerging, especially Chinese, companies to a certain region.

To gather the corresponding data, face-to-face as well as online interviews were conducted with representatives of various Chinese companies in the ECE region.[3] This approach was chosen as the topic of Chinese FDI in European peripheries is new and has sparked academic interest only recently. Moreover, the available literature is rather limited and mostly based on secondary sources.

After the introductory section, the existing theories and literature on the topic are briefly summarized. The next section describes the changing patterns of Chinese outward FDI in the ECE region, while the following section contains the author's findings on the characteristics and motivations behind Chinese FDI in the ECE countries. The final section presents the author's conclusions.

11.1 THEORY AND LITERATURE REVIEW

The majority of research papers and journal articles on motivations behind FDI apply the eclectic paradigm, also known as the OLI model ('OLI' stands for ownership, location and internalization) by Dunning (1992, 1998). This paradigm states that firms will venture abroad when they possess firm-specific advantages – namely, ownership and internalization advantages – and when they can benefit from the advantages particular locations provide. Different types of investment incentives attract different types of FDI, which Dunning (1992) divided into four categories: (1) market-seeking (tariff-jumping or export-substituting FDI is a variant of market-seeking FDI; see Campos and Kinoshita 2008); (2) resource-seeking; (3) efficiency-seeking; and (4) asset-seeking. The factors attracting market-seeking MNEs usually include market size, as reflected in gross domestic product (GDP) per capita and market growth (GDP growth). MNEs often acquire particular types of resources – for example, natural resources or raw materials – that are not available in their home country or that are offered at a lower cost, such as unskilled labour. Investments aimed at seeking improved efficiency are, for example, determined by tax incentives (see Resmini 2005, p. 3). Finally, the companies interested in acquiring foreign assets might be motivated by a common culture and language as well as trade costs (see Blonigen and Piger 2014; Hijzen et al. 2008).

It should be emphasized that some FDI decisions may be based on a complex mix of factors (see Resmini 2005, p. 3; Blonigen and Piger 2014). Much of the existing research and theoretical discussion is based on FDI outflows from developed countries, for which market-seeking and efficiency-seeking FDI are most prominent (see Buckley et al. 2007; Leitão and Faustino 2010). Chinese outward FDI is characterized by natural resource-seeking, market-seeking (see Buckley et al. 2007) and recently also by strategic asset-seeking motives (see Di Minin et al. 2012; Zhang et al. 2012). The rapid growth of outward FDI from emerging and developing countries has been subject to numerous studies trying to account for special features of emerging-country MNEs' behaviour which is not captured by mainstream theories. For example, Mathews (2006) extended the OLI paradigm with the 'linking, leverage, learning framework' (LLL) that explains the rapid international expansion of companies from the Asia-Pacific region.

Nevertheless, traditional economic factors seem to be insufficient in explaining MNEs' FDI decisions, especially when it comes to emerging MNEs. In the past decade, international economics and business research has acknowledged the importance of institutional factors in influencing the behaviour of MNEs (see, for example, Tihanyi et al. 2012). According to North (1990, p. 3), institutions are the 'rules of the game', 'the humanly devised constraints that shape human interactions', as they serve to reduce uncertainties related to transactions and minimize transaction costs. As a result, Dunning and Lundan (2008) extended the OLI model with institution-based location advantages, explaining that institutions developed in home countries, and that host economies shaped the MNEs' geographical scope and organizational effectiveness.

When analysing the impact of institutional characteristics – such as forms of privatization, capital market development, state of laws and country risk – on CEE (including ECE) countries, the studies show varying results. According to Bevan and Estrin (2004, p. 777), institutional aspects were not a significant factor in investment decisions of foreign firms. Carstensen and Toubal (2004) argue that these aspects could explain the uneven distribution of FDI across CEE countries. Fabry and Zeghni (2010) point out that in transition countries, FDI agglomeration may be explained by institutional weaknesses – such as poor infrastructure, the lack of developed subcontractor networks and an unfavourable business environment – rather than by positive externalities resulting from linkages, such as spillovers, clusters and networks. Based on a study of 19 Latin American and 25 Eastern European countries in the period

1989–2004, Campos and Kinoshita (2008) found that structural reforms, especially financial reforms and privatization, had a strong impact on FDI inflows.

11.2   CHANGING PATTERNS OF CHINESE OUTWARD FDI IN THE ECE REGION

The transition of CEE – including ECE – countries from centrally planned to market economies resulted in increasing inflows of FDI to these countries. During the transition, the region went through radical economic changes which had been largely induced by foreign capital. Foreign MNEs realized significant investment projects in this region and established their own production networks. Although the majority of investors arrived from Western Europe, the first phase of inward Asian FDI also occurred right after the transition: Japanese and Korean companies indicated their willingness to invest in the ECE region before the fall of the Iron Curtain. Their investments took place during the first years of the democratic transition. The second phase came after the New Millennium, when the Chinese government initiated the 'Go Global' policy, which was aimed at encouraging domestic companies to become globally competitive. Therefore Europe – including European peripheries – also became a target region for Chinese FDI (see Szunomár 2017).

As Figure 11.1 shows, Chinese outward investment stock in the five ECE countries has steadily increased in the last one-and-a-half decades, particularly after 2004 and 2008, as well as after the countries' accession to the EU and the economic and financial crisis, respectively. According to Chinese statistics, there was a real rapid increase from US$9.6 million in 2004 to US$673 million in 2010. By 2017, the amount of Chinese investments had further increased and reached US$1009 million according to data published by the Ministry of Commerce of the People's Republic of China (MOFCOM). It is, however, also true that FDI flows are rather hectic (see Figure 11.2) and are connected to one or two big business deals per year.

Although China considers the CEE region as a bloc (this is one of the reasons for creating the 16+1 initiative, which is a joint platform for the 16 CEE countries and China), some countries seem to be more popular investment destinations than others: the selected five ECE countries, for example, host almost 55 per cent of total Chinese FDI stock in the 16 CEE countries (see Figure 11.3). Among them, Czechia, Hungary and Poland have received the bulk of Chinese investment in recent years. In contrast, there are countries, such as Albania, the Baltic states and Macedonia, where the stock of Chinese FDI is still negligible.

At this point, it is important to note that Chinese MOFCOM statistics are adequate to show the main trends of Chinese outward FDI stocks and flows; however, apart from this, they proved to be a less reliable data source, as they

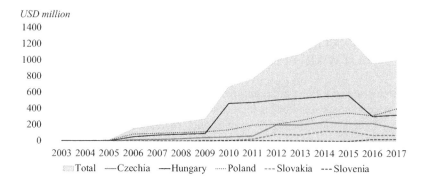

Sources: MOFCOM / NBS, PRC.

Figure 11.1   Chinese FDI stock in ECE countries, 2003–2017

do not show the Chinese investments that have flowed to a country through a foreign country, company or subsidiary. To identify the home country of the foreign investor who ultimately controls the investments in the host country, the new International Monetary Fund (IMF) guidelines recommend compiling inward investment positions according to the ultimate investing country (UIC) principle. For example, if we compare the Chinese MOFCOM database with two other databases – in our case, the China Global Investment Tracker (CGIT) and the Organisation for Economic Co-operation and Development

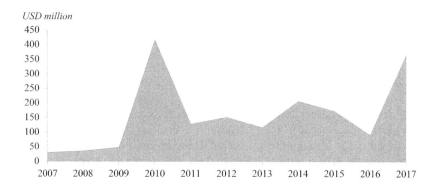

Sources: MOFCOM / NBS, PRC.

Figure 11.2   Chinese FDI flow to ECE countries, 2007–2017

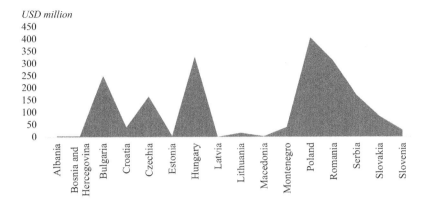

Sources: MOFCOM / NBS, PRC.

Figure 11.3   Chinese FDI stock in CEE countries, 2017

(OECD) databases – that track back data to the ultimate parent companies (see Figure 11.4), we find major differences regarding the main recipients of Chinese outward FDI in ECE (Czechia, Hungary and Poland). In most cases, the difference between the lowest (MOFCOM) and the highest (CGIT) dataset is more than tenfold. On the one hand, this discrepancy justifies the assumption that Chinese companies are indeed using intermediary companies when investing in Europe, including in ECE countries. On the other hand, it also confirms that Chinese FDI is much more significant in the ECE region – especially in Czechia, Hungary and Poland – than previously thought.

Based on the UIC principle, we can also calculate the percentage share of Chinese FDI stocks of total inward FDI stocks in ECE countries. It was decided to use OECD data for these calculations as CGIT statistics often contain various infrastructure projects, such as the planned costs for the Budapest–Belgrade railway, which should be considered separately as these projects are credit agreements. As expected, the percentage shares were definitely higher when calculated using ultimate data (OECD) instead of direct investment amounts (MOFCOM). However, China's share of total FDI in ECE is still far from being decisive: it is below 1 per cent for Czechia and Poland (0.7 and 0.3, respectively) and below 3 per cent (2.4) for Hungary. It is even less (below 0.3 per cent) in the case of Slovakia and Slovenia. In these countries, (Western) European investors are still responsible for more than 70 per cent of total FDI stocks, while among non-European investors, companies

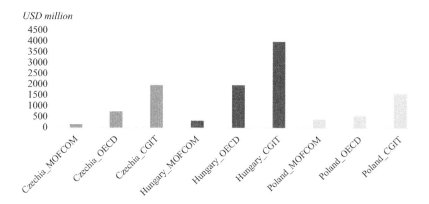

USD million

Note: MOFCOM and CGIT data are from 2017, while OECD data show the 2016 stock of
Chinese FDI.
Sources: MOFCOM / NBS, PRC, CGIT, OECD.

*Figure 11.4   Comparing MOFCOM, CGIT and OECD data on China's
                  outward FDI stock in Czechia, Hungary and Poland,
                  2016/2017*

from the United States, Japan and South Korea are more important players than
those from China.

As presented in Table 11.1, Chinese investors typically target secondary
and tertiary sectors of the selected five ECE countries. Initially, Chinese
investment flowed mostly into manufacturing (assembly), but over time,
services have attracted more and more investment as well. For example, in
Hungary and Poland there are branches of the Bank of China and the Industrial
and Commercial Bank of China, as well as offices of some of the largest law
firms in China, such as Yingke Law Firm (established in Hungary in 2010
and in Poland in 2012) and Dacheng Law Offices (established in Poland in
2011 and in Hungary in 2012). The main Chinese investors targeting these
five countries are primarily interested in telecommunication, electronics, the
chemical industry and transportation. Although the main form of investment
used to be greenfield in the first years after Chinese companies had discovered
the ECE region, mergers and acquisitions (M&A) became more frequent later
on, especially after the global financial crisis of 2008. The main reason behind
this shift is that investments by Chinese companies are increasingly motivated
by gaining access to brands and new technologies, and by discovering market
niches that they can fill on European markets.

Table 11.1   Major characteristics of Chinese investment in the ECE region

	Hungary	Poland	Czechia	Slovakia	Slovenia
Main form of investment	Greenfield / brownfield, (M&A), joint ventures	Greenfield and M&A	Greenfield and M&A	Greenfield and M&A	Greenfield and M&A
Main sectors	Chemical, IT/ICT, electronics, wholesale and retail, automotive, banking, hotels and catering, logistics, real estate	IT/ICT, electronics, heavy machinery, publishing and printing, real estate, municipal waste processing	Electronics, IT/ICT, transport equipment, automotive, shipping, engineering, food, media, platemaking	Automotive, IT/ICT	Chemical, automotive, airport construction/ aeroplane production industry, electronics/ high technology, IT/ ICT
Most important Chinese companies	Wanhua, Huawei, ZTE, Lenovo, Sevenstar Electronics, BYD Electronics, ZMJ, Comlink, Yanfeng, China–CEE Fund	Liu Gong Machinery, Huawei, ZTE, Haoneng Packaging, Shanxi Yuncheng Plate-making Group, Sino Frontier Properties Ltd, China Everbright International Ltd	Shanxi Yuncheng, Changhong, SaarGummi, Noark, Huawei, ZTE, Shanghai Maling, COSCO, YAPP, CEFC, Buzuluk Komarov, China CNR	SaarGummi, ZVL Auto, Inalfa Roof Systems, Mesnac, Lenovo, Huawei	Zhejiang Jinke Culture Industry, Elaphe, Sino-Pipistrel Asia Pacific, TAM Durabus, Fotona, Arctur, Acies Bio, Chiho Tiande Group, China– CEE Fund, Huawei

Note: IT/ICT = information technology/information and communication technology.

The selected five ECE countries account for a major share of the population (around 66 million) and economic output (more than US$1000 billion, according to the World Bank) of CEE. Moreover, all of the five countries have strengthened their relations with China in recent years. Hungary still receives the majority of Chinese investment in the region, followed by Poland and Czechia, while Slovakia and Slovenia lag a little behind due to their small size and lack of efficient transport infrastructure. The main forms of and sectors targeted by Chinese investment are similar in all countries, despite being more diverse in the more popular target countries (Hungary and Poland). With regard to certain sectors, such as tourism, Chinese companies have preferred to target Slovenia.

11.3   HOST COUNTRY DETERMINANTS OF CHINESE OUTWARD FDI IN THE ECE REGION

Host country determinants – or pull factors – are those characteristics of the host country markets that attract FDI. Pull factors, just like push factors, can be grouped into institutional and structural factors. 'While international and regional investment and trade agreements, as well as institutions such as banks or IPAs [investment promotion agencies] involved in outward FDI, are counted as institutional pull factors, structural pull factors include low factor costs, markets, and opportunities for asset-seeking companies' (Schüler-Zhou et al. 2012, p. 163).

Based on the literature mentioned in the theory and literature review section as well as on the interviews conducted with company representatives and experts, the main structural and macroeconomic pull factors for Chinese MNEs (that is, host-country determinants that 'pull' them to developed markets) are:

- market access;
- low factor costs (such as the relatively low cost of labour force);
- qualifications of labour force;
- various opportunities for asset-seeking companies (such as access to brands, know-how, networks, distribution channels and global value chains);
- company-level relations; and
- the high level of technology.

The most important institutional pull factors are:

- international and regional investment and trade agreements, free trade agreements of the host country (or that of the EU);
- host government policies (including strategic partnership agreements between the government and certain companies);
- tax incentives;
- special economic zones;
- 'golden visa' programmes: residence visa in exchange for a certain amount of investment;
- institutions: such as banks and government-related IPAs;
- institutional stability: such as intellectual property rights (IPR) protection and product safety standards;
- possibilities for more acquisitions through privatization opportunities;

- opportunities to participate in public procurement processes; and
- home-country diaspora in the host country.

When searching for possible pull factors that could make ECE countries a favourable investment destination for Chinese investors, the labour market is to be considered as one of the most important elements: a skilled labour force is available in sectors for which Chinese interest is growing, with labour costs being lower than the EU average. However, there are differences within the broader CEE region as well: unit labour costs are usually cheaper in Bulgaria and Romania than in the five ECE countries. Corporate taxes can also play a role in the decision of Chinese companies to invest in the region. Nevertheless, the differences in labour costs and corporate taxes within the broader CEE region do not really seem to influence Chinese investors. After all, there is more investment from China in ECE countries (especially in Czechia, Hungary and Poland) than in Romania or Bulgaria where labour costs and taxes are lower. This can be explained by the theory of agglomeration, as outward FDI in ECE countries is the highest in the region (see McCaleb and Szunomár 2017).

Although the above-mentioned efficiency-seeking motives play a role, the main type of Chinese FDI in ECE countries is definitely market-seeking investment: by entering these markets, Chinese companies have access to the whole EU market; moreover, they might also be attracted by free trade agreements between the EU and third countries, such as Canada, and the EU neighbouring country policies as they claim that their ECE subsidiaries are to sell products in the ECE host countries, the EU and North American or even global markets (see Wiśniewski 2012, p. 121). For example, the subsidiary of Nuctech (a security scanning equipment manufacturer) in Poland also sells to Turkey; the subsidiary of Guangxi LiuGong Machinery in Poland targets the EU, North American and Commonwealth of Independent States (CIS) markets; while Huawei's logistics centre in Hungary supplies over 50 countries located in Europe and North Africa.

Based on the interview results (see Table 11.2), Chinese companies wanted to operate in ECE due to their already existing businesses in Western Europe and to strengthen their presence in the wider European market. In addition, there are also cases of Chinese companies following their customers to the ECE region, as in the case of Victory Technology (supplier to Philips, LG and TPV) or Dalian Talent Poland (supplier of candles to IKEA) (see McCaleb and Szunomár 2017, p. 125). Moreover, through their ECE subsidiaries, Chinese firms can participate in public procurements and access EU funds. As a case in point, Nuctech established its subsidiary in Poland in 2004, initially targeting mainly Western European markets, before focusing more on the ECE (CEE) region, which benefits from different EU funds. Recently, Chinese firms have also become interested in investing in the food industry as a result of the growing awareness about food safety standards and certificates. They are interested in exporting agricultural products which meet EU safety certificates to China, where food safety causes problems. These factors lead us to the institutional host-country determinants of the ECE region.

Institutional factors can be further specified by dividing them into two levels: the supranational level and the national level. Both levels are important elements in the location decisions of Chinese companies investing in the five ECE countries (see McCaleb and Szunomár 2017). As for supranational institutional factors, that the change in the ECE countries' institutional setting due to their economic integration into the EU has been the most important driver of Chinese outward FDI in the region, especially in the manufacturing sector. EU membership of ECE countries allowed Chinese investors to avoid trade barriers, and ECE countries could serve as an assembly base for Chinese companies. Moreover, not only actual EU membership but also the prospects of EU membership attracted Chinese investors to the region: thus, some companies made their first investments before 2004; that is, in the early 2000s. New investments arrived in the year of accession too. The second wave of Chinese FDI in CEE dates back to the global economic and financial crisis, when financially distressed companies all over Europe, including ECE, were often acquired by Chinese companies.

Another aspect of EU membership that has induced Chinese investment in the five ECE countries was institutional stability (including, for example, the protection of property rights). This was important for early investors from Japan and Korea, and was one of the drivers of FDI by Chinese firms, given the unstable institutional, economic and political environment in their home country. These findings are in line with those of Clegg and Voss (2012, p. 101), who argue that Chinese outward FDI in the EU shows 'an institutional arbitrage strategy' as 'Chinese firms invest in localities that offer clearer, more transparent and stable institutional environments. Such environments, like the EU, might lack the rapid economic growth recorded in China, but they offer greater planning and property rights security, as well as dedicated professional services that can support business development'.

Institutional factors at the national level include, for example, strategic agreements, tax incentives and privatization opportunities. The significance of such factors has begun to increase only recently as the majority of ECE countries – with the exception of Hungary – neglected relations with China in the early 2000s, starting to focus on the potential of this relationship only since the aftermath of the global financial crisis of 2008. Based on observations as well as responses from interviewees, Chinese companies indeed appreciate business agreements that are supported by the respective host-country government. Thus, the high-level strategic agreements with foreign companies

Table 11.2   Major characteristics of Chinese companies in the ECE region

Location	Year of investment	Company type	Industry	Entry mode	Employees direct (indirect)	Pull factors
Central Hungary	2004/ 2008	private	telecommunications	greenfield	330 (over 2500)	macroeconomic, institutional (supranational, national)
Mazovian (north-eastern) region of Poland	2007	private	telecommunications	greenfield	425	macroeconomic, institutional (supranational, national)
Northern Hungary	2007	state-owned enterprise (SOE)	chemical	M&A	Over 2500	macroeconomic, institutional (supranational)
Central Hungary	2010	private	printer manufacturing, imaging technology	M&A (acquisition of a company that had a Hungarian subsidiary)	372	macroeconomic, institutional (supranational)
Northern Hungary	2017	SOE	automotive	greenfield	n.a.	macroeconomic, institutional (supranational, national)
Mazovian (north-eastern) region of Poland	2010	SOE	industrial machinery	greenfield	77	macroeconomic, institutional (supranational, national)
Maolpolska (southern) region of Poland	2009	private	other miscellaneous manufacturing	greenfield	n.a.	macroeconomic, institutional (supranational, national)

Source: Based on data from the Amadeus Database.

investing in Hungary offered by the Hungarian government could have also spurred Chinese investment in the region. Moreover, personal (political) contacts between representatives of the respective host-country government and Chinese companies also proved to be important when choosing a host country in the ECE region.

It was also found that less quantifiable aspects play a significant role in the decision of Chinese MNEs to invest in the ECE region. These aspects include the size and feedback of Chinese ethnic minorities in the host country, investment incentives and subsidies, possibilities of acquiring visas and permanent residence permits, as well as the quality of political relations and the respective government's willingness to cooperate. These aspects are exemplified by the stock of Chinese investment in Hungary, which is the highest in the ECE region (as well as in the broader CEE region).

Hungary is a country where the combination of traditional economic factors and institutional factors seems to play an important role in attracting Chinese investors. The country has historically had good political relations with China, established earlier than by other ECE countries. From 2003 onward, the Hungarian government has intensified bilateral relations to attract Chinese FDI. Moreover, Hungary is the only country in the region that has introduced special incentives for foreign investors from outside the EU: that is, a 'golden visa' programme which enables investors to acquire a residence visa in exchange for investing a certain amount of money. What is more, Hungary has the largest Chinese diaspora in the region, which is an acknowledged attracting factor for Chinese FDI in the extant literature; in other words, a relational asset that constitutes an ownership advantage for Chinese firms when they invest in countries with a significant Chinese population (see Buckley et al. 2007). An example of this is Hisense's explanation of the decision to invest in Hungary, which besides traditional economic factors was motivated by 'good diplomatic, economic, trade and educational relations with China; big Chinese population; Chinese trade and commercial networks, associations already formed' (CIEGA 2007).

In addition to the above-mentioned pull factors, Hungary also seems to be politically committed to China. In fact, Hungary was among the first countries to establish diplomatic relations with China (3 October 1949); since then, diplomatic gestures have been made and confidence-building measures taken from time to time. For example, Hungary was the first European country to sign a Memorandum of Understanding with China on promoting the Silk Road Economic Belt and the Maritime Silk Road during the visit of China's Foreign Minister Wang Yi to Budapest in June 2015. The Hungarian government was also very keen on promoting the Budapest–Belgrade railway project. When signing the construction agreement in 2014, prime minister Viktor Orbán called it the most important moment for the cooperation between the EU and

China (see Keszthelyi 2014). In 2016, Hungary (and Greece) prevented the EU from backing a court ruling against China's expansive territorial claims in the South China Sea (see *The Economist* 2018); while in 2018, Hungary's ambassador to the EU was alone in not signing a report criticizing this Chinese One Belt, One Road (OBOR) initiative for benefiting Chinese companies and Chinese interests, and for undermining principles of free trade through its lack of transparency in procurement (see Sweet 2018).

Starting from a rather cold and critical stance, Czechia's relationship with China changed a few years ago. Since then, similar political factors – compared to the Hungarian case – have been observed in Czech–Chinese relations: after Czech 'political sympathy' emerged, inflows of Chinese FDI to Czechia started to increase. As a case in point, the Czech president, Milos Zeman – who was the only high-level European politician visiting Chinese celebrations of the end of World War II in 2015 – now wants his country to be China's 'unsinkable aircraft-carrier' in Europe (*The Economist* 2018). Zeman also has a Chinese adviser on China who comes directly from a Chinese company with a controversial background. Moreover, as a potential result of the improving political relations, the Chinese company CEFC recently invested sizeable amounts – €1.5 billion – in Czechia. It has to be added, however, that this company is now under investigation by Chinese authorities for 'suspicion of violation of laws' (Lopatka and Aizhu 2018). Since then, Czech–Chinese relations have been cooling off again.

Contrary to Hungary and Czechia, Poland used to be more enthusiastic about the potential of its economic relationship with China. Recently, however, the country has taken a more critical – or even cautious – stance. For Poland, high trade deficits represent the biggest problem with regard to the country's bilateral ties with China: Poland imports from China goods to a value of some 12 times that of Poland's exports to China, with the deficit reaching €20 billion according to Eurostat. Potential security risks of Chinese investments caused the Polish government to reconsider its rather positive approach toward China and to use firm rhetoric about trade deficits as a serious political problem. This reconsideration was signalled by the cancellation of a tender in February 2018 for land in Łódź where a transhipment hub was to be built and in which a Polish–Chinese company expressed interest. Another example was a government adviser's statement in connection with the Central Communication Port, a current flagship project of the Polish government, saying that Chinese (party) financing in return for control over the investment would be rejected (see Szczudlik 2017).

11.4   CONCLUSIONS

Chinese investment in ECE countries constitutes a relatively small share of China's total FDI stock in Europe and is quite a new phenomenon. Nevertheless, Chinese FDI in the ECE region is on the rise and may increase further due to recent political developments between China and certain countries of the region, especially Hungary, Czechia and – albeit to a lesser extent – Poland. The analysis of the motivations behind Chinese outward FDI in ECE shows that Chinese MNEs mostly search for markets. ECE countries' EU membership allows them to treat the region as a 'back door' to the affluent EU markets; moreover, Chinese investors are attracted by the relatively low labour costs, skilled workforce and market potential. It is characteristic that their investment patterns in terms of country location resemble that of the world's total FDI in the region.

As demonstrated in the analysis above, macroeconomic or structural factors do not fully explain the decisions behind Chinese FDI in the broader CEE region, including ECE countries. For example, Hungary, Czechia and Poland, the three largest recipients of Chinese investment in CEE, are not the most attractive locations in terms of cutting costs nor when searching for potential markets in the broader CEE region. This indicates that institutions may be crucial for Chinese companies when deciding on investment locations.

To map out the real significance of institutional factors, they were divided into two levels: the supranational level and the national level. Supranational institutional factors that attract Chinese companies to the ECE region are linked to the EU membership (economic integration) of ECE countries, especially to the institutional stability provided by the EU. Country- or national-level institutional factors that impact upon location choice within ECE seem to be privatization opportunities; investment incentives such as tax incentives, special economic zones, 'golden visas' or resident permits in exchange for a given amount of investment; as well as the size of the Chinese ethnic population in the host country.

Although clear evidence could not be found for causal links between the level of political relations and the amount of Chinese investment in ECE countries, good political relations between the respective host country and China seem to play an important role in attracting investment from Chinese state-owned as well as private companies. Examples are: (1) Hungary's good political relations with and strong political commitment to China, while hosting the biggest stock of Chinese FDI in the ECE and the broader CEE region; and (2) the positive political shift in Czech–Chinese relations that induced increasing amounts of Chinese FDI in Czechia.

NOTES

1. This research was supported by the research project 'Non-European emerging-market multinational enterprises in East Central Europe' (K-120053) of the National Research, Development and Innovation Office of Hungary, as well as by the Bolyai János Research Fellowship of the Hungarian Academy of Sciences and the ÚNKP-19-4-BCE-12 New National Excellence Program.
2. Throughout the literature, ECE is referred to as a term encompassing the five new EU Member States which are also members of the Organisation for Economic Co-operation and Development (OECD), namely: Czechia (the Czech Republic), Hungary, Poland, the Slovak Republic and Slovenia. The term 'Central and Eastern Europe' (CEE) is broader, comprising Albania, Bulgaria, Croatia, Czechia, Hungary, Poland, Romania, the Slovak Republic, Slovenia and the three Baltic states: Estonia, Latvia and Lithuania. Therefore, the chapter does not focus on the entire CEE region; however, in some cases, examples of the ECE countries will be supplemented with some of the CEE countries.
3. Interviews with major Chinese investors in the region were conducted anonymously. The author conducted semi-structured interviews with four companies, that is, she drew up a questionnaire and structured the interview based on questions concerning the reasons behind investments, motivations prior to investment decisions being made and their significance a few years after the investments had taken place. Several further questions arose based on the original questions and answers, which is why the structure of each interview was unique. In cases where interviews were not applicable (three companies, in addition to the already mentioned four companies), the author relied on other sources, such as business professionals, experts and academics from ECE countries.

REFERENCES

Bevan, A.A. and S. Estrin (2004), 'The Determinants of Foreign Direct Investment into European Transition Economies', *Journal of Comparative Economics* 32 (4), 775–787.

Blonigen, B.A. and J. Piger (2014), 'Determinants of Foreign Direct Investment', *Canadian Journal of Economics* 47 (3), 775–812.

Buckley, P.J., L.J. Clegg, A.R. Cross, X. Liu, H. Voss and P. Zheng (2007), 'The Determinants of Chinese Outward Foreign Direct Investment', *Journal of International Business Studies* 38 (4), 499–518.

Campos, N.F. and Y. Kinoshita (2008), 'Foreign Direct Investment and Structural Reforms: Evidence from Eastern Europe and Latin America', IMF Working Paper No. 08/26, January.

Carstensen, K. and F. Toubal (2004), 'Foreign Direct Investment in Central and Eastern European Countries: A Dynamic Panel Analysis', *Journal of Comparative Economics* 32 (1), 3–22.

CIEGA (2007), 'Investing in Europe: A Hands-On Guide', available at http://www.e-pages.dk/southdenmark/2/72 (accessed on 4 November 2016).

Clegg, J. and H. Voss (2012), 'Chinese Overseas Direct Investment in the European Union', available at http://www.chathamhouse.org/sites/default/files/public/Research/Asia/0912ecran_cleggvoss.pdf (accessed on 17 August 2017).

Di Minin, A., J.Y. Zhang and P. Gammeltoft (2012), 'Chinese Foreign Direct Investment in R&D in Europe: A New Model of R&D Internationalization?', *European Management Journal* 30, 189–203.

Dunning, J. (1992), *Multinational Enterprises and the Global Economy*, Wokingham: Addison-Wesley Publishers.

Dunning, J. (1998), 'Location and the Multinational Enterprise: A Neglected Factor?', *Journal of International Business Studies* 29 (1), 45–66.

Dunning, J. and S.M. Lundan (2008), 'Institutions and the OLI Paradigm of the Multinational Enterprise', *Asia Pacific Journal of Management* 25 (4), 573–593.

The Economist (2018), 'China has Designs on Europe. Here is how Europe should Respond', Print edition of 4 October 2018.

Fabry, N. and S. Zeghni (2010), 'Inward FDI in Seven Transitional Countries of South-Eastern Europe: A Quest of Institution-Based Attractiveness', *Eastern Journal of European Studies* 1 (2), 77–91.

Hijzen, A., H. Görg and M. Manchin (2008), 'Cross-Border Mergers and Acquisitions and the Role of Trade Costs', *European Economic Review* 52 (5), 849–866.

Keszthelyi, C. (2014), 'Belgrade–Budapest Rail Construction Agreement Signed', *Budapest Business Journal*, 17 December.

Leitão, N.C. and H.C. Faustino (2010), 'Portuguese Foreign Direct Investments Inflows: An Empirical Investigation', *International Research Journal of Finance and Economics* 38, 190–197.

Lopatka, J. and C. Aizhu (2018), 'CEFC China's Chairman to Step Down; CITIC in Talks to Buy Stake in Unit', Reuters, 20 March, available at https://www.reuters.com/article/us-china-cefc-czech/cefc-chinas-chairman-to-step-down-citic-in-talks-to-buy-stake-in-unit-idUSKBN1GW0HB (accessed on 28 November 2018).

Mathews, J.A. (2006), 'Dragon Multinationals: New Players in 21st Century Globalization', *Asia Pacific Journal of Management* 23, 5–27.

McCaleb, A. and Á. Szunomár (2017), 'Chinese Foreign Direct Investment in Central and Eastern Europe: An Institutional Perspective', in J. Drahokoupil (ed.), *Chinese Investment in Europe: Corporate Strategies and Labour Relations*, Brussels: ETUI, 121–140.

North, D. (1990), *Institutions, Institutional Change and Economic Performance*, Cambridge: Cambridge University Press.

Resmini, L. (2005), 'FDI, Industry Location and Regional Development in New Member States and Candidate Countries: A Policy Perspective', EURECO final Conference, Brussels, 26 October.

Schüler-Zhou, Y., M. Schüller and M. Brod (2012), 'Push and Pull Factors for Chinese OFDI in Europe', in I. Alon, M. Fetscherin and P. Gugler (eds), *Chinese International Investments*, London: Palgrave Macmillan, 157–174.

Sweet, R. (2018), 'EU Criticises China's "Silk Road", and Proposes its Own Alternative', Global Construction Review, 9 May, available at http://www.globalconstructionreview.com/trends/eu-criticises-chinas-silk-road-and-proposes-its-ow/ (accessed on 28 November 2018).

Szczudlik, J. (2017), 'Poland's Measured Approach to Chinese Investments', in J. Seaman, M. Huotari and M. Otero-Iglesias (eds), *Chinese Investment in Europe – A Country-Level Approach*, ETNC Report, December.

Szunomár, Á. (2017), 'Driving Forces behind the International Expansion Strategies of Chinese MNEs', IWE Working Paper 237.

Tihanyi, L., T.M. Devinney and T. Pedersen (2012), *Institutional Theory in International Business and Management*, Advances in International Management, Vol. 25, Bingley: Emerald Group Publishing.

Wiśniewski, P.A. (2012), 'Aktywność w Polsce przedsiębiorstw pochodzących z Chin' (Activity of Chinese companies in Poland), *Zeszyty Naukowe* 34, Kolegium Gospodarki Światowej, SGH, Warszawa.

Zhang, Y., G. Duysters and S. Filippov (2012), 'Chinese Firms Entering Europe: Internationalization through Acquisitions and Strategic Alliances', *Journal of Science and Technology Policy in China* 3 (2), 102–123.

PART V

Challenges for CESEE's near future: monetary and financial stability

12. Did macroprudential policies play a role in stabilizing the credit and capital flow cycle in CESEE?

Markus Eller, Helene Schuberth and Lukas Vashold[1]

Almost all the empirical analyses on the effectiveness of macroprudential policies (MPPs) investigate the impact on domestic variables, such as credit growth as well as asset and housing prices, and whether MPPs are capable of increasing the resilience of the banking system and financial stability in general. Research on the more global dimension of MPPs, such as international spillovers, leakages and capital flow cycle stabilizing effects, has only recently attracted scientific interest (see Portes et al. 2020). Studying these issues is particularly appealing from a policy perspective. The effectiveness of policies adopted at the domestic level may be weakened when excessive lending moves outside of the regulatory perimeter to non-covered entities (inward spillovers) or if domestic MPPs induce externalities on foreign countries, for example, through adjustments in the lending behaviour of domestic banks toward foreign borrowers (outward spillovers). Cerutti and Zhou (2018) show for a large global panel of countries over the period from 2006 to 2015 that the implementation of macroprudential policies in borrower countries results in stronger direct cross-border inflows linked to circumvention motives. A macroprudential tightening in lender countries would curb this effect; yet, at the same time, lending from foreign-owned local affiliates increases. Ahnert et al. (2018) show for a sample of 48 countries over the period from 1996 to 2014 that macroprudential regulations targeting the foreign currency (FX) exposure of banks are effective in terms of reducing FX borrowing by banks. Simultaneously, however, these regulations also have the unintended consequence of causing firms to increase FX bond issuance, thus shifting FX exposure to other sectors of the economy. If these spillovers have a material knock-on effect, coordination between countries and reciprocity arrangements may be called for (see ECB 2015; Buch and Goldberg 2017).

The main focus of this chapter, however, is on another, and so far less researched, aspect of the global dimension of MPPs: it relates to the question of whether MPPs are indirectly capable of taming a strong capital inflow boom. While MPPs are not directly set to target the financial account, they can nonetheless have an impact on capital flows, especially if they consist to a considerable extent of bank flows (see IMF 2017). Frost et al. (2020), for example, find for a large panel of countries for the period 2000–2017 that capital inflow volumes are lower once FX-based MPPs have been activated.

Countries in Central, Eastern and Southeastern Europe (CESEE) provide excellent case studies for the analysis of both the effectiveness of MPPs and their impact on capital flows. First, most CESEE countries belong to the relatively small group of countries that had used macroprudential policy tools already prior to the global financial crisis (GFC). Hence, we can exploit the rich information provided by a longer time series. Second, the countries are relatively similar in terms of their financial sector structure, notably in terms of the importance of foreign-owned banks as providers of funding. The remarkable catching-up process in many CESEE countries was based, to a substantial degree, on foreign funding, as was similarly observed in earlier boom–bust cycles in other emerging markets. The boom–bust cycle in capital flows and credit that started to affect the whole CESEE region from 2004 onward was particularly significant. In the boom phase, cumulated gross capital inflows into the CESEE European Union (EU) countries were substantial and even higher relative to gross domestic product (GDP) than in Southeast Asia prior to 1997 (see Bakker and Gulde 2010). This was followed by a very pronounced impact of the bust phase: the collapse of foreign demand coupled with a sudden stop of capital inflows led to a sharp economic downturn and a sizeable depreciation of floating currencies, leaving the banking sector with rising non-performing loans, predominantly denominated in foreign currency.

Taking into account the significant boom–bust cycle in capital flows and domestic credit in the CESEE region, this chapter raises the questions of whether MPPs have been effective in containing credit extension to households and firms in CESEE, and whether MPPs have had an impact on gross capital inflows into the region.

The remainder of the chapter is structured as follows. Section 12.1 gives an overview of the MPP measures taken in 11 CESEE countries using an intensity-adjusted macroprudential index for each country. Section 12.2 discusses the transmission channels through which MPPs may affect capital flows, before section 12.3 presents empirical evidence on the effectiveness of MPPs with respect to the domestic credit and capital flow cycle. Section 12.4 concludes.

12.1   CAPTURING THE INTENSITY OF MACRO-PRUDENTIAL POLICY MEASURES IN CESEE

To evaluate the impact of MPPs, it is a necessary condition to come up with a quantification of the macroprudential policy stance. However, in contrast to (conventional) monetary policy, macroprudential policy relies on many different instruments and is subject to numerous policy interactions. Composite indicators can be useful in describing the overall macroprudential policy stance. We contribute to the existing literature by relying on a novel index (see Eller et al. 2020) for measuring not only the occurrence of implemented MPPs – as is done in most of the literature – but also the strength of the implemented measures, following the approach of Vandenbussche et al. (2015) and Dumičić (2018). For instance, it should make a difference if limits on the loan-to-value (LTV) ratio are decreased from 100 per cent to, say, 70 per cent or just to 90 per cent. To come up with an intensity-adjusted index to describe the overall macroprudential stance of the eleven EU member states in the CESEE region,[2] we integrated the information provided by four different databases (see Budnik and Kleibl 2018; Vandenbussche et al. 2015; Alam et al. 2019; Kochanska 2017), applying suitable weighting and aggregation rules. In the following, we describe developments of macroprudential policies in CESEE based on the broadest ('extended') version of the macroprudential policy index (MPPI) provided by Eller et al. (2020). It includes: (1) system-wide (uniform) minimum capital requirements; (2) minimum reserve requirements (as they have often been used for macroprudential purposes); (3) various capital buffer requirements reflecting the incorporation of Basel III regulations; (4) risk weights determining banks' risk-weighted assets; (5) liquidity-based measures (including liquidity requirements and limits on banks' exposure to single clients, specific sector and market segments or FX mismatch); and (6) borrower-based measures (including limits on LTV ratios for collateralized house purchase loans and on debt-service-to-income (DSTI) ratios as well as outright FX loan provisioning bans).

Figure 12.1 displays the MPPI for a CESEE aggregate by simply averaging over all countries. A gradual tightening of the overall macroprudential stance can be observed in the years from the late 1990s up to the GFC. The stance remained unchanged until 2010 but was tightened thereafter, with increased intensity after 2014. The tightening in the late 1990s to levels that have mostly not been reverted later on was mainly due to an increase in minimum capital requirements, and to some extent due to liquidity-based measures. The tightening since 2010 mainly reflects the introduction of borrower-based measures, while the somewhat accelerated tightening since 2014 can be explained by the introduction of various capital buffers. Borrower-based measures gained

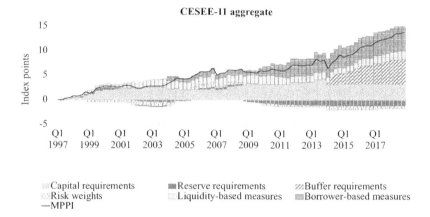

Sources: Calculations by Eller et al. (2020) based on data by Alam et al. (2019), Budnik and Kleibl (2018), Kochanska (2017) and Vandenbussche et al. (2015).

Figure 12.1   CESEE-11 aggregate

importance especially after the crisis, but their use has stagnated in recent years. Finally, minimum reserve requirements were often eased countercyclically in the wake of the crisis and have then largely remained at these levels.

The experiences of countries in the CESEE region as regards MPPs are quite heterogeneous, both with respect to when and which MPPs were implemented. In general, we can roughly distinguish between three country groups. The regional 'frontrunners' – that is, Bulgaria, Croatia and Romania – had already started to implement MPPs in an advanced manner in the late 1990s and/or early 2000s (see Figure 12.2). The early-on increases in their respective indices can be mainly traced back to a substantial tightening in their capital requirements. However, another important MPP category for Bulgaria and Croatia was liquidity-based, most notably including limits on banks' exposure to single clients and specific sector and market segments. Romania also significantly tightened borrower-based measures in the pre-crisis period, such as LTV and DSTI limits, being one of the very few countries to use such instruments in the pre-crisis period. While Bulgaria's stance remained largely unchanged, with only small deviations, in the post-crisis period, Croatia and Romania eased their stance quite substantially after the onset of the GFC. Croatia, in particular, did so by lowering its reserve requirements repeatedly. Hence, Croatia and Bulgaria acted countercyclically, partly to diminish the credit crunch following the GFC. For these countries – as for the rest of the investigated CESEE countries – the introduction of various buffer rates has

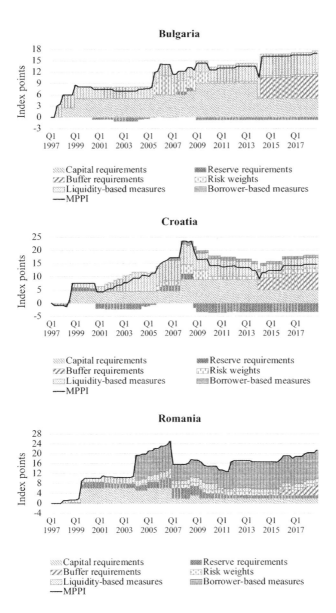

Sources: Calculations by Eller et al. (2020) based on data by Alam et al. (2019), Budnik and Kleibl (2018), Kochanska (2017) and Vandenbussche et al. (2015).

Figure 12.2   Bulgaria, Croatia and Romania

played an important role in the tightening of their macroprudential environment in the recent past.

Estonia, Poland and Slovenia represent another group of countries that
exhibited quite substantial changes in their macroprudential environment,
though not as pronounced as the regional 'frontrunners' mentioned above did.
Moreover, the toolkit that these countries applied was less diverse, as can be
seen in Figure 12.3. While in Estonia and Slovenia pre-crisis tightening can be
attributed mainly to capital and reserve requirements as well as risk weights,
Poland in fact eased its macroprudential policy stance by lowering the applicable risk weights on mortgage and consumer loans compared to the initial
situation in 1997. With the onset of the GFC and thereafter, however, Poland
then proceeded by substantially tightening its macroprudential environment.
A large share of this evolvement can be associated with the introduction of
'Recommendation S' by the Polish authorities that included lower LTV and
DSTI limits as well as higher risk weights on loans denominated in foreign
currency. In the more recent past, the introduction of various buffer rates has
also played a substantial role. This also holds true for Estonia and Slovenia,
which experienced quite diverging patterns after the GFC. While Estonia
eased its risk weights and reserve requirements quite substantially in this
period, it has strongly tightened borrower-based measures in the recent past by
introducing lower LTV and DSTI limits. Slovenia was not as active as others,
but has similarly introduced buffer rates and some stricter requirements for
borrower-based measures in the recent past.

The third group of countries (shown in Figure 12.4) is characterized by
much less pronounced activity or tightening in the early pre-crisis period,
which is partly followed by a stronger usage of MPPs thereafter. The Czech
Republic, Hungary and Slovakia experienced a pronounced tightening in the
macroprudential environment after the GFC. However, the main drivers of
the tightening differed across the countries. While Hungary introduced an
interim outright ban of FX lending in 2010, which was deactivated in 2015,
the increased tightening in the other two countries took place in a more gradual
manner and was mainly driven by the introduction of buffer rates and stricter
requirements for bank lending in the form of lower LTV and DSTI limits or
by at least issuing recommendations regarding these borrower-based measures. Additionally, the Czech Republic also ramped up liquidity requirements
for banks and raised general capital requirements. After having deactivated
the aforementioned ban, Hungary also tightened liquidity requirements and
introduced various buffers, yet in a slightly less pronounced way by slowly
phasing in, for example, the capital conservation buffer. The two Baltic States,
on the contrary, had already been quite active in the pre-crisis period, when
they implemented a broad set of MPPs. While Lithuania experienced some net
easing due to loosened risk weights and reserve requirements, Latvia recorded

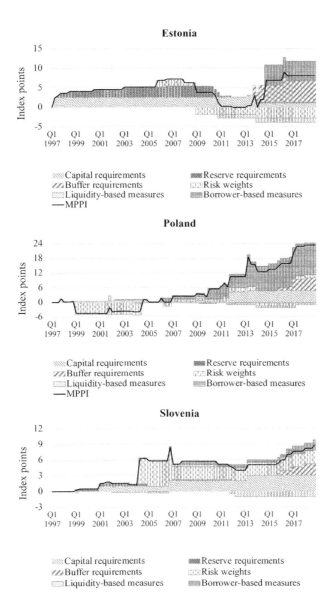

Sources: Calculations by Eller et al. (2020) based on data by Alam et al. (2019), Budnik and Kleibl (2018), Kochanska (2017) and Vandenbussche et al. (2015).

Figure 12.3 Estonia, Poland and Slovenia

Czech Republic

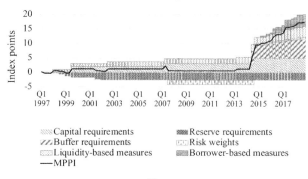

Capital requirements   Reserve requirements
Buffer requirements   Risk weights
Liquidity-based measures   Borrower-based measures
—MPPI

Hungary

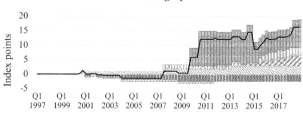

Capital requirements   Reserve requirements
Buffer requirements   Risk weights
Liquidity-based measures   Borrower-based measures
—MPPI

Lithuania

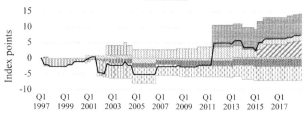

Capital requirements   Reserve requirements
Buffer requirements   Risk weights
Liquidity-based measures   Borrower-based measures
—MPPI

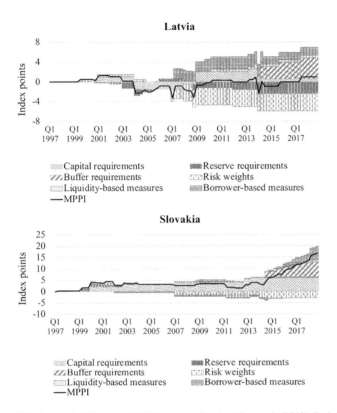

Sources: Calculations by Eller et al. (2020) based on data by Alam et al. (2019), Budnik and Kleibl (2018), Kochanska (2017) and Vandenbussche et al. (2015).

Figure 12.4   Czech Republic, Hungary, Lithuania, Latvia and Slovakia

no clear trend toward a considerable tightening or loosening of the situation in the period before the crisis. Lithuania introduced stringent lending restrictions in the form of LTV and DSTI limits in 2011, which largely explains its tighter macroprudential stance thereafter. At the same time, however, Lithuania removed its limits on open FX positions due to the harmonization of national legislation with the EU's Capital Requirements Directive (CRD) IV package prior to the country's accession to the euro area in 2015. In our sample, Latvia has exhibited the least pronounced tightening in the overall macroprudential environment in the more recent past, as gradual increases in buffer rates have just substituted eased minimum capital requirements.

12.2   HOW DO MACROPRUDENTIAL POLICY MEASURES IMPACT UPON THE FINANCIAL ACCOUNT?

In this section, we review the transmission channels of MPP measures to capital flows, as discussed in the literature (see Eller et al. forthcoming). In principle, macroprudential tools, which do not target the financial account per se, can nevertheless have an impact on capital flows (see IMF 2017). Disregarding for a moment the potential circumvention of and leakages from macroprudential measures, the more general channels that link MPP tools to the financial account can be described as follows.

First, MPP tools can more generally increase resilience and help contain the build-up of systemic financial risks during capital inflow surges and reversals of flows. Excessive capital inflow episodes may be limited by containing the procyclical interplay between asset prices, private credit and non-core bank funding. By restricting increases in leverage and volatile funding, the resilience against the global financial cycle may be enhanced. Cesa-Bianchi et al. (2018), for instance, found that countries featuring lower limits on LTV ratios and limits on FX borrowing are less vulnerable to global credit supply shocks. During financial stress, the incidence of disruptive capital outflows may be reduced.

Second, MPPs can help dampen procyclical dynamics triggered by capital inflows. The latter may result in unsustainable increases in credit, asset prices, unhedged FX exposures, a further increase in cross-border non-core funding of the banking system and interconnectedness. The likelihood of strong gross capital inflows leading to a systemic crisis is higher if funded by other investments (OIs) which mostly reflect direct foreign lending to resident banks and include more volatile funding sources, such as short-term funding sourced on wholesale markets (see Hahm et al. 2013). In almost all the considered CESEE countries, there is a strong correlation between capital flows and the share of FX lending by households, non-financial corporations and banks.

It follows that tighter MPPs may not only negatively affect credit extension to households and non-financial corporations, but may also have an effect on capital flows, while impacting upon different flow categories in different ways. OI inflows are expected to decline, insofar as MPP measures restrict bank lending in local and/or foreign currency. As a consequence, cross-border funding from parent banks or, in general, from financial institutions and financial investors abroad, is less needed for domestic credit extension. Nevertheless, the case that OI inflows do not react negatively to tighter MPPs could be interpreted in such a way that the measures were not effective in reining in an overly excessive inflow of OI. But even if the impact of MPPs on bank inflows is negative, the effectiveness of the macroprudential tools can be limited by direct cross-border borrowing, as shown by Cerutti and Zhou (2018). This was, in particular, the case prior to the GFC when large foreign banks extended direct cross-border credit to non-financial corporates in some of the CESEE countries. In general, to the extent that capital flows are not intermediated by banks, lender-based MPPs would not be effective to rein in excessive leverage in the economy. Borrower-based measures, on the contrary, are likely to be more appropriate. Concerning the impact of MPP measures on credit extension to households and non-financial corporations, it might also be the case that the effects are limited; in particular, during periods of excessive capital inflows that allow banks to generate capital through retained earnings or issuing own capital (see Basten and Koch 2015).

In this chapter, we put a focus on OI inflows next to gross total capital inflows, as they typically have the most robust relationship with credit growth (see Blanchard et al. 2016). Restraining credit growth should affect bank inflows negatively, as argued above. The impact of an MPP tightening on foreign direct investment (FDI), on the other hand, is a priori ambiguous. FDIs related to the financial sector may decline as a consequence of stronger regulation. Conversely, the need for capitalizing the local subsidiaries of foreign banks may have a positive impact on FDI inflows. An ambiguous effect may also be expected with regard to portfolio inflows. As regards corporate bonds, firms may, as a consequence of MPP measures, substitute borrowing from banks for issuing corporate bonds that are sold abroad (see Ahnert et al. 2018). To the extent that wholesale funding of banks is contained by MPP measures, the issuance of bank bonds (that are probably sold to foreign investors) may decline, yielding a negative impact on portfolio inflows.

12.3 EMPIRICAL EVALUATION OF MACRO-PRUDENTIAL TIGHTENING AND ITS IMPACT ON CREDIT GROWTH AND CAPITAL FLOWS

In this section, we evaluate the effectiveness of MPPs in reining in excessive credit growth and capital inflows. While there are several papers that investigate the effect of MPPs on macrofinancial quantities, such as credit growth or housing prices (see, for example, Cerutti et al. 2017; Akinci and Olmstead-Rumsey 2018), or on other macroeconomic quantities (see, for example, Richter et al. 2019), the literature on the impact of MPPs on capital flows is rather sparse. Aysan et al. (2015) conclude that MPPs helped to dampen the sensitivity of capital inflows into Turkey with respect to global factors. Analysing the joint impact of macroprudential policies and capital flow management tools for a large panel of countries, Cerutti and Zhou (2018) find that MPPs reduce direct cross-border bank flows. Ahnert et al. (2018) and

Frost et al. (2020) provide evidence that MPPs targeting the FX exposure of banks are effective with respect to stabilizing the volumes of capital inflows. Ahnert et al. (2018) also find that asset-side MPPs (such as LTV and DSTI limits and risk weights) have a stronger dampening effect on capital inflows than liability-side measures (such as liquidity and reserve requirements). On the other hand, Avdjiev et al. (2017) find that a tightening of LTV limits in a destination country is associated with an increase in international bank lending to the residents of that country. Eller et al. (forthcoming) apply a non-linear factor-augmented VAR model and find that a tightening MPP shock results in lower credit growth and reduced capital inflow levels in most of the investigated CESEE countries, while the volatilities of capital inflows show a rather mixed response. We contribute to the existing literature by evaluating the consequences of a tightening in the macroprudential environment – which is reflected by an increase in the intensity-adjusted MPPI – on private sector credit growth and capital inflows by conducting a simple empirical exercise.

As is common in the literature on the effects of macroprudential policies on macroeconomic quantities (for a recent survey see Galati and Moessner 2018, and for a similar application see Eller et al. 2020), we employ panel regressions augmented by country-fixed effects. Specifically, the model takes the following form:

$$y_{i,t} = \beta MPPI_{i,t-1} + \boldsymbol{X}_{i,t}\boldsymbol{\gamma} + \tau_i + \varepsilon_{i,t} \quad (12.1)$$

where $y_{i,t}$ denotes as dependent variable either total private sector credit growth, gross total capital inflows or gross other investment inflows of country i ($i=1,...,N$ for N countries) in quarter t ($t=1,...,T$ for T observation periods) and $MPPI_{i,t-1}$ denotes the lag of the included measure of macroprudential policy. Besides the extended version of the MPPI, introduced in section 12.2, we also investigate whether narrower MPP instruments have a different impact. We thus also use a narrow version of the index (N-MPPI) that, compared to the overall index, does not cover minimum capital requirements and minimum reserve requirements. Moreover, as the narrowest category, we also focus on borrower-based measures (BB-MPPI) only. τ_i captures unobserved, country-fixed effects and $\varepsilon_{i,t}$ denotes a normally distributed error term with potentially varying variance. The matrix of control variables, $\boldsymbol{X}_{i,t}$, contains country-specific information about GDP growth and short-term interest rates (lagged by one quarter) as well as a dummy for the GFC to control for possible crisis-driven variation (not lagged). A detailed description of the included variables can be found in Table 12A.1 in the Appendix. For analysing the short-term effects of macroprudential policies, we include the respective index lagged by one quarter in our model. For medium-term effects of MPPs, we include a simple moving average over the previous four quarters, similarly to Alam et al. (2019). The analysed period covers Q1 1998 to Q4 2018 in all specifications. Ordinary least squares with heteroscedasticity-robust standard errors and country-fixed effects (OLS-FE) is used as a baseline estimator.

The inclusion of lags of the policy measures and other covariates addresses the problem of endogeneity (see, for example, Galati and Moessner 2013), at least to a certain degree. Furthermore, as already pointed out in section 12.2, there is quite some heterogeneity with respect to the development of MPPs across countries. Supported by several pre-estimation diagnostic tests (available from the authors upon request), we also estimated two other models that allow for heterogeneous slope parameters across countries. These are labelled as the dynamic-fixed effects (DFE) and the mean group (MG) estimation models. However, a caveat in applying these estimators is the fact that they are mostly designed for datasets with large N and T dimensions. As our dataset comprises only 11 countries, this may lead to outlier-driven results and should thus be interpreted with caution.

Table 12.1 summarizes our estimation results based on the combination of different dependent variables, different definitions of the MPPI and different estimation techniques. First, as already shown in Eller et al. (2020), tighter macroprudential policies – no matter which of the three indices is considered – are indeed associated with lower credit growth (first panel). Strikingly, the magnitude of the negative effects widens the narrower the investigated policy instrument. Statistical significance of these results across all three indices can be found in the baseline OLS-FE specification. The DFE and MG specifications, instead, while confirming a negative sign across all indices, indicate statistical significance only in the case of the borrower-based index.

Second, looking at the impact of macroprudential measures on gross capital inflows, we can again identify negative signs, and the coefficients become larger with narrower instruments across all specifications; however, statistical significance is given only in the case of borrower-based MPPs. Interestingly, the effects on other investment inflows (third panel) are smaller than those for total capital inflows (second panel). The lack of statistical significance in the case of the wider MPPIs may reflect the fact that refinancing needs of banks (stemming from borrowing from abroad) are more strongly reduced when borrower-based measures are tightened than when a broader set of instruments, including also capital-based measures, are tightened. This again may be related to the somewhat higher effectiveness of borrower-based measures in containing credit growth compared to capital-based measures which, *ceteris paribus*, implies less need for banks to borrow from abroad.

Table 12.1   Macroprudential policy, credit growth and capital flows: panel regression results

Dependent variable   Private sector credit (year-on-year change)

Included policy index	MPPI			N-MPPI			BB-MPPI		
	(1)	(2)	(3)	(4)	(5)	(6)	(7)	(8)	(9)
Estimation method	OLS-FE	DFE	MG	OLS-FE	DFE	MG	OLS-FE	DFE	MG
First lag of respective policy index	-0.580*	-0.297	-0.797	-0.850**	-0.590	-0.331	-1.695***	-1.530***	-4.776**
Standard error	[0.283]	[0.406]	[0.768]	[0.303]	[0.469]	[0.624]	[0.405]	[0.458]	[2.052]
Moving avg of previous four quarters	-0.569*	-0.261	-0.701	-0.884**	-0.607	-0.169	-1.780***	-1.611***	-5.276**
Standard error	[0.292]	[0.443]	[0.953]	[0.317]	[0.501]	[0.766]	[0.424]	[0.461]	[2.273]
No. of observations	913	913	913	913	913	913	830	830	830

Dependent variable   Gross total capital inflows (in % of GDP)

	(1)	(2)	(3)	(4)	(5)	(6)	(7)	(8)	(9)
First lag of respective policy index	-0.242	-0.300	-0.399	-0.443	-0.586	-0.500	-1.161**	-1.407**	-2.942*
Standard error	[0.290]	[0.401]	[0.517]	[0.305]	[0.419]	[0.382]	[0.511]	[0.579]	[1.537]
Moving avg of previous four quarters	-0.240	-0.295	-0.315	-0.453	-0.594	-0.418	-1.185**	-1.428***	-3.247*
Standard error	[0.301]	[0.417]	[0.595]	[0.309]	[0.424]	[0.448]	[0.485]	[0.539]	[1.760]
No. of observations	913	913	913	913	913	913	830	830	830

Dependent variable	Gross other investment inflows (in % of GDP)								
First lag of respective policy index	-0.020	-0.061	-0.201	-0.111	-0.195	-0.135	-0.468**	-0.644***	-2.121*
Standard Error	[0.144]	[0.184]	[0.414]	[0.151]	[0.183]	[0.267]	[0.197]	[0.189]	[1.233]
Moving avg of previous four quarters	-0.033	-0.078	-0.208	-0.129	-0.220	-0.091	-0.523**	-0.709***	-2.392*
Standard error	[0.152]	[0.196]	[0.496]	[0.161]	[0.196]	[0.315]	[0.212]	[0.200]	[1.407]
No. of observations	913	913	913	913	913	913	830	830	830

Notes: All models include lags of GDP growth and the short-term interest rate as additional covariates as well as an unlagged crisis dummy, all at quarterly frequency. Robust standard errors are in brackets below the coefficients. Models (1), (4) and (7) were estimated using OLS with heteroscedasticity-robust standard errors and include country-fixed effects (OLS-FE); models (2), (5) and (8) with dynamic-fixed effects (DFE); and models (3), (6) and (9) with the mean group estimator (MG). For models (7)–(9) BG was excluded due to its lack of variation in the BB-MPPI. F-tests for joint significance are all highly significant.
Significance level: *** - 1%, ** - 5%, * - 10%.

12.4   CONCLUSIONS

Countries in the CESEE region are a particularly interesting sample for studying the impact of MPPs on capital flows, given: (1) pronounced boom–bust cycles in capital flows and credit over time; (2) the important role of bank flows for total capital flow dynamics; and (3) the fact that several CESEE countries have been active in implementing MPPs over a considerably longer time compared to countries in Western Europe. This chapter, alongside ongoing research efforts (see Eller et al. 2020, forthcoming), tries to provide value added to the existing literature by introducing a novel index for measuring the strength of MPPs and by empirically evaluating the impact of macroprudential intensity on credit and capital flow dynamics.

The descriptive analysis reveals a gradual increase in the intensity of macroprudential policy use with considerable shifts in the role of different instruments across all of the 11 CESEE EU Member States on average. The macroprudential tightening in the years after the GFC can be mainly traced back to tighter borrower-based measures and a stronger role of capital-based measures that have been implemented since 2014 to cope with Basel III regulations and the respective EU directives. The aggregate picture conceals pronounced heterogeneity across countries, though. Three groups of countries can be identified. First, Bulgaria, Croatia and Romania experienced a comparatively strong macroprudential policy tightening in the late 1990s or early 2000s that was reinforced in the years before the GFC, mostly motivated by extraordinarily strong credit growth at that time. Second, Estonia, Poland and Slovenia also experienced considerable MPP activity before the crisis, yet a less pronounced tightening compared to the first group of countries, and partly applied a less differentiated instrument toolkit. Third, the remaining countries – the Czech Republic, Hungary, Lithuania, Slovakia and, partly, Latvia – experienced a largely unchanged overall macroprudential policy stance for a long period, before considerably tightening their MPPs just after the crisis and especially in the past few years.

Using the intensity-adjusted MPPI (and some of its components) in a panel regression framework allows us to reach some conclusions on the effectiveness of MPPs in stabilizing the credit and capital flow cycles across the investigated CESEE region. In line with already existing empirical evidence, we find that MPPs could be effective in containing private sector credit growth and gross capital inflows into CESEE. Strikingly, this evidence is stronger for borrower-based measures than for broader sets of measures which also include lender-based instruments. Further research is needed to study more closely the role of different transmission channels, to better understand the reasons for cross-country heterogeneity, and to explore the effectiveness of different sets of macroprudential instruments and their possible interactions with other policy instruments (especially those of monetary policy). The index and its components presented here could serve as an important contribution to the quickly evolving literature in this field of research.

NOTES

1. Opinions expressed by the authors of studies do not necessarily reflect the official viewpoint of the Oesterreichische Nationalbank (OeNB) or of the Eurosystem. This chapter largely builds on ongoing research efforts documented in Eller et al. (2020, forthcoming).
2. The CESEE-11 aggregate comprises the following countries: Bulgaria, Croatia, the Czech Republic, Estonia, Hungary, Latvia, Lithuania, Poland, Romania, Slovakia and Slovenia.

REFERENCES

Ahnert, T., K. Forbes, C. Friedrich and D. Reinhardt (2018), 'Macroprudential FX Regulations: Shifting the Snowbanks of FX Vulnerability?', NBER Working Paper No. w25083.

Akinci, O. and J. Olmstead-Rumsey (2018), 'How Effective are Macroprudential Policies? An Empirical Investigation', *Journal of Financial Intermediation* 33 (C), 33–57.

Alam, Z., A. Alter, J. Eiseman, R. Gelos, H. Kang, M. Narita, E. Nier and N. Wang (2019), 'Digging Deeper – Evidence on the Effects of Macroprudential Policies from a New Database', IMF Working Paper No. 19/66.

Avdjiev, S., C. Koch, P. McGuire and P. von Goetz (2017), 'International Prudential Policy Spillovers: A Global Perspective', *International Journal of Central Banking* 13 (S1), 5–33.

Aysan, A.F., S. Fendoğlu and M. Kilinc (2015), 'Macroprudential Policies as Buffer against Volatile Cross-Border Capital Flows', *Singapore Economic Review* 60 (1), 1–26.

Bakker, B.B. and A.M. Gulde (2010), 'The Credit Boom in the EU New Member States: Bad Luck or Bad Policies?', IMF Working Paper No. 10/130.

Basten, C.C. and C. Koch (2015), 'Higher Bank Capital Requirements and Mortgage Pricing: Evidence from the Countercyclical Capital Buffer (CCB)', BIS Working Paper No. 511.

Blanchard, O., J.D. Ostry, A.R. Ghosh and M. Chamon (2016), 'Capital Flows: Expansionary or Contractionary?', *American Economic Review* 106 (5), 565–569.

Buch, C.M. and L.S. Goldberg (2017), 'Cross-Border Prudential Policy Spillovers: How Much? How Important? Evidence from the International Banking Research Network', *International Journal of Central Banking* 13 (S1), 505–558.

Budnik, K.B. and J. Kleibl (2018), 'Macroprudential Regulation in the European Union in 1995–2014: Introducing a New Data Set on Policy Actions of a Macroprudential Nature', ECB Working Paper No. 2123.

Cerutti, E., S. Claessens and L. Laeven (2017), 'The Use and Effectiveness of Macroprudential Policies: New Evidence', *Journal of Financial Stability* 28, 203–224.

Cerutti, E. and H. Zhou (2018), 'Cross-Border Banking and the Circumvention of Macroprudential and Capital Control Measures', IMF Working Paper No. 18/217.

Cesa-Bianchi, A., A. Ferrero and A. Rebucci (2018), 'International Credit Supply Shocks', *Journal of International Economics* 112, 219–237.

Dumičić, M. (2018), 'Effectiveness of Macroprudential Policies in Central and Eastern European Countries', *Public Sector Economics* 42 (1), 1–19.

ECB (2015), 'A Framework for Analyzing and Assessing Cross-Border Spillovers from Macroprudential Policies', Financial Stability Review, May.

Eller, M., N. Hauzenberger, F. Huber, H. Schuberth and L. Vashold (forthcoming), 'Capital Flows and the Stabilizing Role of Macroprudential Policies in CESEE', ESRB Working Paper.

Eller, M., R. Martin, H. Schuberth and L. Vashold (2020), 'Macroprudential policies in CESEE – an intensity-adjusted approach', Focus on European Economic Integration, Q2/20, 65–81.

Frost, J., H. Ito and R. van Stralen (2020), 'The Effectiveness of Macroprudential Policies and Capital Controls against Volatile Capital Inflows', BIS Working Paper No. 867.

Galati, G. and R. Moessner (2013), 'Macroprudential Policy – a Literature Review', *Journal of Economic Surveys* 27 (5), 846–878.

Galati, G. and R. Moessner (2018), 'What Do We Know about the Effects of Macroprudential Policy?', *Economica* 85 (340), 735–770.

Hahm, J., H.S. Shin and K. Shin (2013), 'Noncore Bank Liabilities and Financial Vulnerability', *Journal of Money, Credit and Banking* 45 (S1), 3–36.

IMF (2017), 'Increasing Resilience to Large and Volatile Capital Flows: The Role of Macroprudential Policies', IMF Policy Paper, September.

Kochanska, U. (2017), 'The ESRB Macroprudential Measures Database', IFC Bulletins, Chapter 46.

Portes, R., T. Beck, W. Buiter, K. Dominguez, D. Gros, C. Gross, S. Kalemli-Ozcan, T. Peltonen and A. Sánchez Serrano (2020), 'The Global Dimensions of Macroprudential Policy', European Systemic Risk Board, Reports of the Advisory Scientific Committee No. 10, February.

Richter, B., M. Schularick and I. Shim (2019), 'The Costs of Macroprudential Policy', *Journal of International Economics* 118, 263–282.

Vandenbussche, J., U. Vogel and E. Detragiache (2015), 'Macroprudential Policies and Housing Prices: A New Database and Empirical Evidence for Central, Eastern, and Southeastern Europe', *Journal of Money, Credit and Banking* 47 (S1), 343–377.

Table 12A.1 *Appendix: Description and availability of variables used in the panel regressions*

Variable	Description	Main sources	Data availability
Credit growth	Claims on domestic private sector, CPI-deflated, seasonally adjusted, in logarithms, year-on-year change	IMF-IFS, BIS	Q1 1998–Q4 2018
Capital flow levels	Cumulative four-quarter sums of gross total capital or gross other investment inflows (BPM6 definition) as percentage of GDP	IMF-IFS	Q1 1998–Q4 2018
MPPI	Extended intensity-adjusted macroprudential policy indicator, no further transformations	own calculations	Q1 1997–Q4 2018
N-MPPI	Narrow intensity-adjusted macroprudential policy indicator, no further transformations	own calculations	Q1 1997–Q4 2018
BB-MPPI	Borrower-based intensity-adjusted macroprudential policy indicator, no further transformations	own calculations	Q1 1997–Q4 2018
GDP growth	GDP volume, 2005=100, seasonally adjusted, in logarithms, quarter-on-quarter change	IMF-IFS	Q2 1997–Q4 2018
Short-term interest rate	Typically, three-month money market rate (per annum), no further transformations	IMF-IFS, ECB, Eurostat	Q1 1997–Q4 2018

Notes: The table shows the variables included in the various panel regressions, together with a short description of their transformations, the sources used to obtain them as well as the respective period for which they are available. Seasonal adjustment was conducted using the Census X12 method. A few capital flow series were not satisfactorily available at quarterly frequency at the beginning of the sample; we used the corresponding annual figures and the quarterly dynamics of the rest of the sample for data interpolation. Moreover, in cases where the short-term interest rate was not available, we used the dynamics of the deposit rate for data interpolation. In cases where few observations were missing at the beginning or the end of the sample, we used the average of the subsequent or previous four quarters to fill these gaps.

13. 30 years of monetary and exchange rate regimes in Central and Eastern Europe: what has changed, and what is next?

Johannes Wiegand[1]

Let us start out with a thought experiment. Suppose a person not familiar with Central and Eastern Europe (CEE) was asked what monetary and exchange rate regimes (MERRs) they expected countries in the region to have. A sensible response would be, 'the regimes are probably rather similar'. After all, countries in the region are on broadly the same monetary journey: a journey that began in the late 1980s and early 1990s with the transition from centrally controlled to market-based economies. And a journey that has a common endpoint, at least in principle: euro adoption. Some CEE countries are already members of the euro area, others have signed accession agreements that oblige them to eventually adopt the euro, and yet others are negotiating or getting ready to negotiate agreements that will likely contain a similar commitment.[2]

However, MERRs in the region are, in fact, vastly different from one another. Take any MERR that one can think of, and the chances are that one will find it in CEE. Some CEE countries are part of a currency union: the euro area. Others have floating exchange rates and conduct monetary policy via inflation targeting. Yet others manage the exchange rate of their currency against the euro. A couple of countries – Kosovo and Montenegro – have even adopted the euro unilaterally, using it as legal tender without being members of the euro area, and hence without having access to the liquidity facilities of the European Central Bank (ECB).

The MERRs' diversity raises a number of questions:

1. Why are MERRs so different from one another?
2. Is the diversity of MERRs a good outcome?
3. How are MERRs likely to evolve going forward, especially as regards the prospects for euro adoption?

13.1   WHY ARE MONETARY AND EXCHANGE RATE REGIMES SO DIFFERENT FROM ONE ANOTHER?

To understand the CEE's MERRs as they are today, it is key to understand the region's monetary history, especially in the 1990s, the early phase of transition. In this period, CEE countries struggled with enormous monetary challenges, such as the freeing-up of prices and wages and the release of pent-up inflationary pressures that had built up under socialism over decades. They had to address the challenges with young, untested institutions, such as treasuries and central banks that lacked a track record in managing decentralized economies.

Monetary transition did not advance in the same manner everywhere. In one group of countries, it went relatively smoothly (not shaded in Figure 13.1). While these economies also experienced sizeable price pressures during transition, inflation never spiralled out of control. In response, these countries typically engaged in 'exchange rate-based stabilization': they tied their currency to an established currency – often the Deutsche mark – and built their institutions in the meantime. Once inflation had been brought under control, they moved on to flexible exchange rates with inflation targeting. The first CEE country to do so was the Czech Republic in 1997, followed by Poland, Hungary, and so on.[3]

In a second group of countries, monetary transition was not smooth, however. These countries suffered hyperinflation during transition. There are three subgroups: (1) the Baltics, which experienced hyperinflation in 1992/1993, right at the onset of transition;[4] (2) most countries of the former Yugoslavia in 1992–1994, in the context of civil war and the eventual break-up of the country;[5] and (3) Bulgaria, which suffered an intense hyperinflationary period in 1997.

Also, in hyperinflation countries, inflation came down eventually, also by means of exchange rate-based stabilization. But there are two important differences. First, most – though not all – countries used very rigid exchange rate pegs to defeat inflation: currency boards (in Bosnia and Herzegovina, Bulgaria, Estonia and Lithuania), or unilateral adoption of the euro. Second, once inflation had been defeated, these economies did not move on to floating but stayed with their fixed exchange rate regimes.

Figure 13.2 illustrates the evolution of MERRs over time, according to the International Monetary Fund's (IMF) Annual Reports on Exchange Arrangements and Exchange Restrictions (AREAER). In the 1990s, most countries in the region used some type of managed exchange rate to combat inflation. In the late 1990s and early 2000s, the first economies switched to floating and inflation targeting. By the 2010s, more countries had adopted

162 *30 years of transition in Europe*

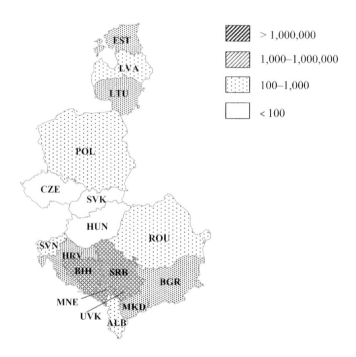

Note: Country codes: ALB = Albania, BGR = Bulgaria, BIH = Bosnia and Herzegovina, CZE = Czech Republic, EST = Estonia, HRV = Croatia, HUN = Hungary, LTU = Lithuania, LVA = Latvia, MKD = Republic of North Macedonia, MNE = Montenegro, POL = Poland, ROU = Romania, SVK = Slovak Republic, SVN = Slovenia, SRB = Serbia, UVK = Kosovo.
Source: Belhocine et al. (2016).

Figure 13.1   Maximum annual inflation during transition (%)

flexible exchange rates, and another group of countries – Slovenia, the Slovak Republic and the Baltics – had joined the euro area.

A number of countries in Southeastern Europe stayed with their fixed exchange rate regimes, however, either *de jure* or *de facto*. *De facto* refers, for example, to Serbia, whose currency officially floats, but whose central bank continues in practice to stabilize the exchange rate to the euro – at least to a larger degree than central banks in other countries with floating currencies do (Figure 13.3).

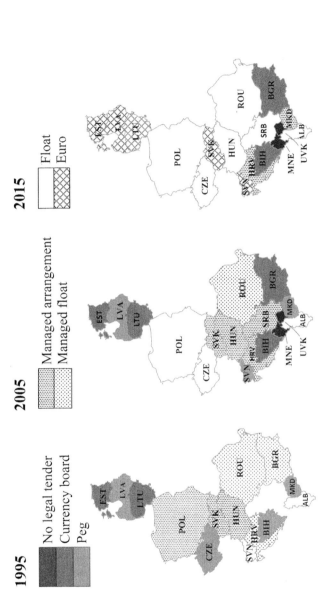

Note: Country codes: ALB = Albania, BGR = Bulgaria, BIH = Bosnia and Herzegovina, CZE = Czech Republic, EST = Estonia, HRV = Croatia, HUN = Hungary, LTU = Lithuania, LVA = Latvia, MKD = Republic of North Macedonia, MNE = Montenegro, POL = Poland, ROU = Romania, SVK = Slovak Republic, SVN = Slovenia, SRB = Serbia, UVK = Kosovo.
Source: Belhocine et al. (2016).

Figure 13.2   Evolution of exchange rate regimes (IMF AREAER classification)

Why did countries with a hyperinflationary past stick to fixed and quasi-fixed exchange rates? Hyperinflation has an unfortunate long-term consequence: it destroys trust in the domestic currency (see Reinhart and Savastano 2003). In CEE, this is visible along several dimensions. For example, deposit euroization tends to be very high in former hyperinflation countries: the population is prepared to save only in euros, even though returns on euro deposits are (typically) lower than those on local currency deposits (see Geng et al. 2018). Moreover, survey-based results show that in former hyperinflation countries, a large part of the population still expects the currency to depreciate in the next 12 months and inflation to surge (see Brown and Stix 2015); even in countries that maintain currency boards, that is, countries that have adopted an institutional setting which gives the fixed exchange rate priority over all other macroeconomic policy objectives.

In such circumstances, a central bank has little choice but to stabilize the exchange rate. Otherwise, it risks that savers would take their money out of the country as soon as the currency comes under depreciation pressure, thus triggering capital flight and monetary instability.

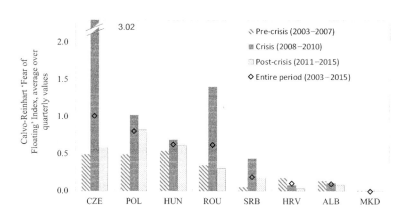

Note: Country codes: ALB = Albania, CZE = Czech Republic, HRV = Croatia, HUN = Hungary, MKD = Republic of North Macedonia, POL = Poland, ROU = Romania, SRB = Serbia.
Source: Belhocine et al. (2016).

Figure 13.3   Effective exchange rate flexibility in 2007–2015

13.2 IS THE DIVERSITY OF MONETARY AND EXCHANGE RATE REGIMES A GOOD OUTCOME?

To answer this question, one first needs to define 'good for what?'. What is the key monetary challenge that economies in the region have been facing ever since transition inflation was defeated? This chapter argues that the challenge is managing convergence, that is, managing the process of CEE economies closing the income gap vis-à-vis Western Europe, specifically the euro area.

There are solid theoretical arguments that for convergence, a flexible exchange rate regime has advantages (see Lipschitz et al. 2002; Backé and Wójcik 2008; Magud et al. 2014). The reasoning is as follows:

- A converging economy grows faster than the economy it is converging to. This implies that its natural rate of interest is higher, meaning the interest rate at which the economy grows free of inflation.
- A flexible exchange rate grants the central bank monetary autonomy, and therefore the ability to align its monetary stance with the natural rate of interest. Thus, if monetary policy is conducted well during convergence, inflation will be low, and convergence will happen mostly through appreciation of the nominal exchange rate.
- By contrast, a country with a fixed exchange rate imports the monetary stance of the economy it is pegged to; in this case, the ECB's stance. The latter will be misaligned by design, and it will typically be too loose as the respective CEE economy is growing structurally faster than the euro area. This, in turn, means that convergence will happen through inflation differentials.
- Elevated inflation generates low real interest rates, however. This can provoke excessive demand, overly fast credit growth and debt accumulation. Overall, convergence with a fixed exchange rate is more likely to give rise to boom–bust growth cycles.

A recent IMF paper (see Belhocine et al. 2016) analysed whether the region's experiences match these theoretical predictions. The answer is clearly 'yes'. While all CEE countries went through a boom–bust cycle between 2003–2015 – reflecting to a large part shifts in global financial conditions – the pattern was significantly more pronounced in countries with fixed or quasi-fixed exchange rates. Their boom experienced prior to the global financial crisis (GFC) was larger, their post-GFC recession was deeper and longer. For example, while it took countries with flexible exchange rates one year, on average, to come out of recession after the GFC, countries with fixed exchange rates were in recession for almost three years, on average (see Figure 13.4).

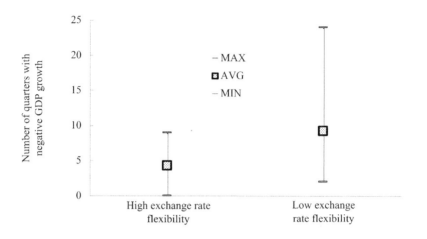

Note: Countries with 'high exchange rate flexibility' include the Czech Republic, Hungary, Poland and Romania.
Source: Belhocine et al. (2016).

Figure 13.4   Length of recession in 2008–2014

To summarize the main results:

•   Broadly speaking, CEE countries fall into two groups with respect to their 1990s transition experience: those that experienced hyperinflation, and those that did not.
•   Countries that did not suffer from hyperinflation are largely unconstrained in their choice of the MERR. Most chose flexible exchange rates and inflation targeting, which helps to manage the convergence process.
•   Countries that suffered hyperinflation were – and still are – constrained by the hyperinflation trauma. Given that constraint, adopting a fixed rate regime has been a rational choice, prioritizing monetary stability over fine-tuning monetary conditions. There is a cost, though, in the form of a bumpier convergence process that is more prone to dislocations.

13.3   LOOKING AHEAD: WHAT ABOUT EURO ADOPTION?

The question of whether and when euro adoption is advisable presents itself differently for countries with different MERRs. For countries with flexible exchange rates, the key issue is whether convergence is still ongoing, as monetary autonomy helps during the convergence process (see above). And it clearly is ongoing: the most recent IMF forecasts from October 2019 indicated that flexible exchange rate CEE countries would grow significantly faster than the euro area in the period ahead.[6] Such a growth differential provides a solid economic rationale for staying outside the euro area – for now. Once growth rates have become more aligned, the question will present itself in a new light (see Figure 13.5).

For countries with fixed and quasi-fixed exchange rates, convergence is also expected to continue, possibly at an even faster pace.[7] Yet, there is more interest among these countries in adopting the euro, with Bulgaria and Croatia having applied for Exchange Rate Mechanism (ERM) II membership recently. What explains this apparent paradox?

Fixed rate economies have – in contrast to their flexible rate peers – no monetary policy autonomy to give up or preserve. Both inside and outside the euro area, they import the ECB's monetary stance, and therefore monetary conditions that are (most of the time) misaligned. At the same time, euro adoption removes a critical part of the hyperinflation legacy: the lack of a trusted currency. This eliminates foreign currency deposits and the need to hold and manage foreign currency reserves; instead, banks have institutionalized access to ECB liquidity – changes that make for a more robust macroeconomic and financial framework.

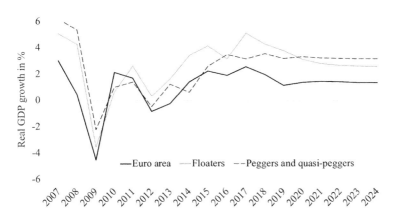

Source: IMF, World Economic Outlook and author's calculations.

Figure 13.5   Convergence

The argument for caution, however, is that euro adoption is irreversible. Once inside the euro area, countries forego the possibility of regaining monetary autonomy for good.[8]

Is there a possibility? The previous sections argued that in the past 20 years, countries with a hyperinflation legacy had little choice but to stabilize their exchange rates. But this does not necessarily mean that they will not have a choice in the next 20 years. There are two arguments supporting this assertion.

First, by now, the CEE's monetary transition dates back more than 20 years. The (limited) evidence from Latin America and other regions suggests that the grip of past hyperinflation lasts about one generation; that is, 20–30 years. Thereafter, prospects improve for the grip of hyperinflation to gradually loosen, provided that the economy has enjoyed monetary stability since, as all CEE economies have. As the memory of hyperinflation fades, monetary authorities regain degrees of freedom.

Second, for former hyperinflation countries, experimenting with the monetary anchor is especially risky during periods of depreciation pressures as depreciation can bring back memories of hyperinflation and trigger destabilizing behaviour of savers (see above). In the 8–9 years after the GFC, currencies in the region were indeed under depreciation pressures. Since 2016 or so, however – that is, with the resumption of convergence – currencies in the region have again been appreciating, providing a more conducive environment for more exchange rate flexibility (see Figure 13.6).

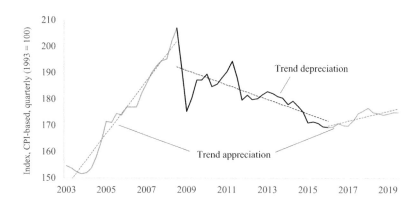

Source: ECB and author's calculations.

Figure 13.6   Real effective exchange rate of CEE floaters

This is not to argue that potential euro adoptees should necessarily forego the option of membership and instead seek to regain monetary autonomy. Compared with the tangible short-term benefits of euro area membership, such a strategy is complex and its prospects for success are uncertain.[9] Moreover, choosing one or the other includes aspects that go beyond basic monetary reasoning (including, for example, geopolitical considerations).

However, where euro adoption is no near-term option, countries need a long-term monetary strategy. And as a longer-term strategy, de-euroization, seeking to increase exchange rate flexibility where possible and improving monetary management of the convergence process are conceptually appealing. Among the countries pursuing a similar strategy is Serbia, which will be an important case to watch in the period ahead.

Another important case are the Baltics. As other former hyperinflation countries, the Baltics defeated inflation with hard pegs/currency boards, sticking to them thereafter. They converged at the fastest pace in CEE prior to the GFC, and suffered the largest boom–bust cycles. The Baltics joined the euro area in the first half of the 2010s, even though convergence is clearly incomplete also in this region.

It is too early to assess whether the Baltic approach has been a success. To do so, one would need to observe these economies for at least one or two business cycles. Yet, available indicators suggest that 'so far, so good'. Price and wage inflation pressures have returned to the Baltics, but this by itself is not a problem; rather, it is implied by converging with a fixed exchange rate (see above). What would be a problem – and has not (yet) returned – are financial imbalances: excess credit growth, debt accumulation and current account deficits.

This may reflect an important lesson that the Baltics have drawn from the GFC: the adoption of strong macroprudential policy frameworks and their proactive use, supported by adequate fiscal and structural policies. When a country imports a monetary stance not aligned with its needs, it requires something else to manage financial conditions.

NOTES

1. This chapter summarizes the results of work conducted over many years with colleagues both inside and outside the International Monetary Fund (IMF). I would like to mention especially my co-authors Nan Geng and Tiberiu Scutaru; Philip Gerson who oversaw the work on the 2016 paper (see Belhocine et al. 2016) and co-authored a blog (see Gerson and Wiegand 2016); Poul Thomsen who steered me toward working on exchange rate regimes; more recently, my colleagues in the Development Strategy Unit in the IMF's Strategy, Policy and Review Department; colleagues in the IMF's European Department who provided helpful comments on an earlier draft; and Helene Schuberth from the Oesterreichische Nationalbank.

This said, the views expressed in this chapter are mine and should not be attributed to the IMF.
2. The term 'CEE' is limited to countries that are, in a broad sense, part of the European integration process. The chapter does not cover countries from the Commonwealth of Independent States (CIS). Nor does it cover Turkey, whose historical path is fairly different from that of the countries discussed in this chapter.
3. The pace and circumstances of these shifts differed from country to country. For a more detailed narrative see, for example, Khachatryan (2014).
4. In Latvia, inflation peaked at 970 per cent. Thus, while dotted in Figure 13.1, for practical purposes, it is also a former hyperinflation country.
5. The exception is Slovenia, which broke away early.
6. In the period between when this chapter was first written and publication, these growth forecasts have been overtaken by events, notably the Covid-19 crisis. Note that growth rates are simple averages for the Czech Republic, Hungary, Poland and Romania.
7. Simple averages for Albania, Bulgaria, Croatia and Serbia. Figure 13.6 does not include smaller countries where floating may not be a realistic option, given size and (therefore) capacity constraints.
8. One lesson to take from the euro area crisis is that adopting the euro without sufficient economic convergence and compatibility with economic policies carries risks.
9. It requires, *inter alia*, a de-euroization strategy; see Belhocine et al. (2016).

REFERENCES

Backé, P. and C. Wójcik (2008), 'Credit Booms, Monetary Integration and the New Neoclassical Synthesis', *Journal of Banking and Finance* 32 (3), 458–470.
Belhocine, N., E. Crivelli, N. Geng, T. Scutaru, J. Wiegand and Z. Zhan (2016), 'Taking Stock of Monetary and Exchange Rate Regimes in Emerging Europe', IMF Departmental Paper Series No. 16/12, November.
Brown, M. and H. Stix (2015), 'The Euroization of Bank Deposits in Eastern Europe', *Economic Policy* 30 (81), 95–139.
Geng, N., T. Scutaru and J. Wiegand (2018), 'Carry Trade vs. Deposit-Driven Euroization', IMF Working Paper No. 18/58, March.
Gerson, P. and J. Wiegand (2016), 'A Field Guide to Exchange Rate Regimes in Central, Eastern and Southeastern Europe', IMFBlog – Insights & Analysis on Economics & Finance, available at https://blogs.imf.org/2016/11/29/a-field-guide-to-exchange-rate-regimes-in-central-eastern-and-southeastern-europe/ (accessed on 18 January 2010).
Khachatryan, A. (2014), 'Monetary and Exchange Rate Policy', in J. Roaf, R. Atoyan, B. Joshi, K. Krogulski and an IMF Staff Team (eds), *25 Years of Transition – Post-Communist Europe and the IMF*, Washington, DC: International Monetary Fund, 15–19.
Lipschitz, L., T. Lane and A. Mourmouras (2002), 'Capital Flows to Transition Economies: Master or Servant?', IMF Working Paper No. 02/11, January.
Magud, N.E., C.M. Reinhart and E.R. Vesperoni (2014), 'Capital Inflows, Exchange Rate Flexibility and Credit Booms', *Review of Development Economics* 18 (3), 415–430.

Reinhart, C. and M. Savastano (2003), 'The Realities of Modern Hyperinflation', *Finance and Development* 40, 20–23.

PART VI

The future of CESEE: the impact of megatrends

14. At the start of a new leadership of the European Commission and the European Central Bank: where is the place of Central and Eastern Europe?

Martin Selmayr

In November 2019, we celebrate the 30 years anniversary of the fall of the Berlin Wall and the end of the Iron Curtain. It is certainly highly symbolic that at the very moment of this important anniversary, a new leadership is taking office in the European Union: in Frankfurt with Christine Lagarde at the helm of the European Central Bank (ECB), and in Brussels with Ursula von der Leyen as the new President of the European Commission. This is therefore a very good moment for a broader reflection: where do we stand 30 years after the end of the Cold War? What is the position of Europe now, after our continent was lucky to become reunited? And where is the place of Central and Eastern Europe in this new constellation, and in the new mandate of the European Union (EU) institutions?

At first glance, the situation appears to be rather disappointing for Central and Eastern Europe. The region appears to be absent in the new constellation of power that is meant to govern Europe for the next five years from 2019 onward. Today, the EU institutions seem to be led by French, German, Belgian, Spanish and Italian nationals; this means, in essence, by a Western European leadership. The new leadership of our Union thus appears to look more like the Carolingian Empire than like the united Europe that we should have had since 1989. This holds in particular true for the ECB, where a representative from Central and Eastern Europe or from a newer Member State has yet to become a member of the Executive Board.

14.1 CENTRAL AND EASTERN EUROPE: STRONGLY REPRESENTED IN THE NEW COMMISSION

On second glance, however, we can observe that Central and Eastern Europe is nevertheless strongly represented. From a Central and Eastern European perspective, the fact that we have, with Ursula von der Leyen, a German as

President of the European Commission could be a first advantage. After all, Germany has a particular affinity for Central and Eastern Europe, historically and economically, since it is a country that was itself divided and thus looks to the East much differently and probably with more sympathy and understanding than many other European countries do. We can thus expect from the Commission a strong sensitivity to the concerns and challenges of Central and Eastern Europe in the 2019–2024 period.

Secondly, let us take a look at the key positions of the new European Commission: one of the three Executive Vice-Presidents of the new Commission (the 'triumvirat' that is supporting President von der Leyen in the management of the Commission) is the former Latvian Prime Minister Valdis Dombrovskis, who successfully steered his country through the financial crisis and who is now – just as he was in the Commission presided by Jean-Claude Juncker from 2014 to 2019 – in charge of the Economic and Monetary Union and of the Capital Markets Union. His experience was extremely valuable already during the 2014–2019 period when the European Commission had to deal with preventing 'Grexit' by means of a third stability support programme for Greece and by adding a necessary social dimension to the development of the Economic and Monetary Union. Valdis Dombrovskis can thus be expected to play a key role in the von der Leyen Commission, notably in defining its economic policy strategy. He also continues to represent the European Commission in the meetings of the Governing Council of the ECB.

If we continue to analyse the leadership of the new European Commission, we find that three of the remaining four ordinary Vice-Presidents are from Central and Eastern Europe.

Maroš Šefčovič from Slovakia is in charge of interinstitutional relations and strategic foresight. He has a key position in conducting relations with the European legislators (the European Parliament and the Council of Ministers) and in defining the work programme and the strategic orientation of the Commission in the 2019–2024 period. As a third-time Commissioner, he is also (next to Budget Commissioner Johannes Hahn from Austria) the most senior member of the College of Commissioners, which gives him a lot of influence due to his vast experience within the institution.

Then, there is Dubravka Šuica, Vice-President for Democracy and Demography, who is from Croatia. Her mandate can be explained by the strong interest Central and Eastern European countries have shown in bringing the subject of demographic change to the strategic forefront of the Commission. This issue is not only about the ageing populations in Western European societies, but notably about the over 5 million Poles and the 4 million Romanians that today live and work outside their country. In the mission letter to her Croatian Vice-President, President von der Leyen explicitly says that Ms Šuica should address the brain drain from East to West to bring back balance in the single market. Dubravka Šuica is also in charge of the new push for democracy, which is a very important project in the programme of the new Commission President. From 2020 to 2022, in view of the many changes we are facing as a European Union, a conference on the future of Europe will take place to define how the European Union could become more democratic, more efficient and a stronger actor in the world. The Croatian Vice-President will organize this conference in close cooperation with Member States, stakeholders, the European Parliament and national parliaments, and in this task she will certainly be able to draw on her experience as Mayor of Dubrovnik.

Last but not least, the Czech Vice-President Věra Jourová is in charge of Values and the Rule of Law, which are both subjects at the very heart of the current discussions – and sometimes controversies – in the European Union. It can certainly be understood as a symbol that Jourová, a second-time Commissioner, is in charge of this thematic priority, on which she will be closely cooperating with Didier Reynders, the new Justice Commissioner, a very experienced politician from Belgium.

14.2 A VISIBLE FOCUS ON THE CHALLENGES FOR CENTRAL AND EASTERN EUROPE

If we go beyond the people and look at the subjects and what the big priorities for the new Commission are – they were outlined in the Political Guidelines issued by Ursula von der Leyen in July 2019 – we see that the Central and Eastern European dimension is extremely present, as is illustrated by five examples.

First, there is the European Green Deal, a key priority of the Commission and of all EU institutions in the 2019–2024 period. It poses a particular challenge in Central and Eastern Europe, as the pollution caused by the companies operating in this region is more than 25 per cent higher than the Organisation for Economic Co-operation and Development (OECD) average. This is why in the Political Guidelines of the von der Leyen Commission we find not only the objective of making Europe carbon-neutral by 2050, but also the establishment of a Just Transition Fund, which is a concrete offer of solidarity meant to help Central and Eastern Europe, both financially and operationally, move faster from coal to carbon-neutrality without negative social consequences. The central banking community will have to watch the development of the European Green Deal closely, as legislative decisions regarding the taxonomy of green investments may, over time, also have an impact on the composition of central bank investments and of the assets purchased under the ECB's asset purchase programme.

A second priority for the von der Leyen Commission is the digital agenda: once the digital single market in the European Union is finally completed, it will add an annual benefit of €170 billion or more to the European economy. The Central and Eastern European countries are frontrunners in this field, and we can learn a lot from what they have done so far, starting with the experiences in Estonia.

A third and very sensitive subject is migration, which the von der Leyen Commission wants to tackle by means of a new approach. At the moment, after years of controversy, this subject appears to stand in the way between East and West without an easy solution on the horizon. To a certain extent, the controversy about migration is a false debate. It is simply not true that Europe was flooded with migrants in the last few years. We had a migration situation in 2015, but at the end of the day it was still a relatively small percentage of the world's population that came to Europe – the richest continent in the world – from war-torn Syria and other countries, and the situation was blown out of proportion in the media and by populist forces. The challenge is now to overcome the ideological divide and make a fresh start. In doing this, we need to find a sound combination of solidarity and responsibility in every country. Those in the front line have a responsibility to make sure their borders are protected; at the same time, they also need support in organizing humane and orderly procedures for asylum seekers that have a right to seek asylum in Europe; a fact we need to recognize as long as the European Union is part of the Geneva Convention, which was, in fact, created for the Europeans during the terrors of World War II. A new approach to migration also means that the Member States of the European Union need to find new forms of burden-sharing between them. In this context, we should recall that the story of some bureaucrats in Brussels wanting to impose an obligation on Central and Eastern European countries to take in hundreds of thousands of migrants is only a myth. In reality, a decision was taken by the majority of Member States in the Council of Ministers to receive and distribute a maximum of 160 000 migrants from Italy and Greece, which were clearly overburdened in 2015. It was for political reasons that one country rejected the offer that the rest of the EU would take in 58 000 asylum seekers that had arrived in this country, while this country was asked to take just 2500 asylum seekers. If we recall these figures, we see that there was no East–West conflict as regards the numbers, but instead an attempt to organize solidarity in a fair manner. We need to remember that solidarity and responsibility must always go hand in hand in the European Union. Solidarity is part of the history, of the DNA, of the European Union. We witnessed it in the financial crisis: one cannot stabilize a monetary union without both solidarity and responsibility; and we see it again with issues such as migration, where every country once in a while can be on the receiving side, only depending on its geographic location.

A fourth important subject in the 2019–2024 period that East and West will have to discuss and agree on will be the rule of law, which is probably the most important foundation of the European Union. In the European Union, common decisions are taken every day, sometimes by unanimity, and most of the time by majority. However, in contrast to a state, the EU does not have any direct execution instrument to enforce the decisions commonly taken vis-à-vis the Member States against their will. It is nothing more and nothing less than the mutual trust in the commonly agreed rules that holds the Union together. None of these rules are 'dictated by Brussels', as populists often claim, but all Member States have, at some point, agreed to them democratically; including to the possibility of being overruled by a majority in certain cases. The respect for these commonly agreed rules is of vast importance, as is the respect for independent courts, which are the institutions mandated to enforce the law at national and European Union level. There is no place in this European Union for illiberal democracy, because the Union itself is based on the rule of law and on democracy. This is why, over the last few years, the Commission has had an important dispute with some Member States on the role of national courts and their independence. This dispute was in many respects similar to the regular challenge of the role and independence of central banks. It is rather normal that central banks are challenged by politicians, as for some, interest rates are too high, for others they are too low, and for some, there is too much monetary easing, and for others, there is too little of it. The existence of such challenges is the very reason for having independent central banks in the first place. Hence, how can we defend monetary institutions and their independence in view of such challenges?

The EU Treaties and the Court of Justice in Luxembourg are the strongest forms of protection central banks have against their national governments. This became evident in the course of 2019 when the Court of Justice upheld the independence of the Governor of the Central Bank of Latvia against a challenge by his own government. The question is whether similarly strong legal protection is available if the independence of national courts is challenged. In all Member States, politicians sometimes criticize court decisions, as they consider them either too harsh or too lenient, either too conservative or too progressive. This is a rather normal situation in all democracies and a necessary part of a pluralistic discussion. However, the borders of democratic discourse are clearly crossed when judges are personally attacked, slammed via the media or even directly prevented from independently exercising their judicial functions. Although, unlike in the case of central banks, there is no explicit legal provision in the EU Treaties, the European Commission believes that the independence of national courts is also protected by means of EU law, as courts are the only institutions that can decide whether commonly agreed European rules are correctly applied at national, regional or local level. Unlike in the United States, which has, within a two-layer system, federal courts with branches in each state entrusted with enforcing federal legislation in addition to state courts entrusted with applying state legislation, the European Union has a one-layer system, which means that EU law is primarily applied and enforced by the national courts of each Member State. Over the past years, the European Commission therefore argued that national courts are 'wearing two hats': they are nationally born courts that exercise, at the same time, a European function. And it is the function of acting independently as 'Union courts' exercised by national courts that needs the protection of EU law. Otherwise, we cannot trust each other within the Union. How could we travel to another country in the European Union as an EU citizen if we were not sure that we are protected there in our rights in the same way as we are at home? How could we invest in another country in the European Union if we were not sure that we are protected there by an independent court in the same way as we are protected at home? How could we accept that a European Arrest Warrant for a fellow national issued in another EU Member State is executed in our home country if we were not sure that it was issued by an independent judicial authority? For some, surprisingly, the Court of Justice of the EU agreed with the European Commission on this important point of principle. It is now settled EU law that national courts must be independent and are protected in their independence by means of EU law. This is a small legal revolution, even though it is a rather logical one if we see the Union as a Community based on the rule of law. This development makes the EU stronger and will hopefully help make this emotionally charged debate more factual in the future.

There is one strongly distinguishing feature of the Union: whatever Member States argue about in Europe, whatever we have argued about in the last 60 years of the European process, all Member States have always respected the judgments of the Court of Justice, in spite of many debates and controversies and even though they may have disliked the final outcome of a legal dispute in Luxembourg. This respect for the 'European Supreme Court' is a sign of the maturity of our continent, and it will hopefully help us to settle the pending rule of law conflicts on the basis of the judgments of the Court of Justice, which will have to be fully implemented.

The fifth issue between East and West that will be on the agenda for at least the next five years from 2019 onward is geopolitics. The new European Commission of Ursula von der Leyen strives to be 'a geopolitical Commission'. That means that after years of crises, be they financial or other, we will now take a broader look at the world. How will Europe position itself in this world which has become much more volatile and uncertain over the past years? There are some disagreements here, for example concerning Russia. In Central and Eastern Europe, we have both the greatest enemies of Vladimir Putin and his greatest fans. This sometimes causes trouble in European decision-making processes. We therefore need to have a very honest debate in the next years about how to deal with Russia, as recently called for by

France's President Emmanuel Macron. The different experiences with Russia in Central and Eastern Europe will hopefully help the Commission to find the right, balanced way forward. The respect for the rule of law internationally and Europe's long-term strategic interests will certainly be an important guiding principle in this respect.

14.3 FIVE RECOMMENDATIONS FOR THE NEXT FIVE YEARS

Let us conclude with five recommendations with regard to the new leadership at the EU level, both in Brussels and in Frankfurt, taking into account the particular situation of Central and Eastern Europe 30 years after the fall of the Berlin Wall.

Number one takes up an important statement that was made by Ursula von der Leyen in a speech in Berlin in 2019. She said that Europe must learn the language of power in order to position itself in the world. This may sound rather dramatic, but it is spot on, since after World War II we Europeans have lived in a comfort zone, relying on the security umbrella of the United States, which will always be our ally, but probably not the ally that we knew – at least for the time being. Therefore, Europe needs to grow up, also in view of increasing power competition from Russia and China. As a precondition, we need to be strong and united as Europeans; otherwise, we are weak. A strong Europe can make balanced trade deals, also with United States President Donald Trump, but only if we are united, if everybody stands behind the EU institutions. Europe can respond to Russia's illegal annexation of Crimea with sanctions, but only if we are united and if we speak with one voice. Therefore, the most important challenge for the next months and years will be to reconcile the pending disputes between East and West, and not to allow third countries to sow the seeds of division among us. Thirty years after the fall of the Iron Curtain, new divisions between Western and Eastern Europeans are not worthy of Europe. We have to sit down together, we have to discuss in all honesty, and we have to overcome our difficulties by looking at the many points we have in common that can make us stronger on the basis of our common values. Europe must breathe from both its lungs, East and West; and this is today, in a more uncertain world, more important than ever before.

Secondly, we must continue something that is probably more cherished in Central and Eastern Europe than in Western Europe: the successful process of enlargement. The further West we go in Western Europe, the more people consider enlargement to be 'a big mistake'. We should strongly disagree with this position. How can we say such a thing 30 years after the Iron Curtain fell? We should remember the fall of the Iron Curtain as one of the greatest moments of freedom and democracy on our continent. Every transition brings, without any doubt, difficulties, both in the West and in the East. But no one can disagree with the fact that the enlargements of 2004, 2007 and 2013 were an unprecedented success. They were certainly not an undivided success, as they increased the heterogeneity of our continent, but they were a historical necessity and brought about the long-awaited reunification of our continent. We have to open our eyes more to the immense benefits that came along with enlargement, in both political and economic terms. This, in consequence, also means that we need to continue working with our neighbourhood. It is a historic mistake not to start accession talks now with North Macedonia and Albania. Of course, starting accession talks does not mean that membership will be granted tomorrow. All of this is about the beginning of a long process, which is, however, key for the reforms in our immediate neighbourhoods, for keeping the positive momentum, and for keeping the European perspective of the Western Balkans. This is why the new European Commission, which has proposed opening accession talks in May 2020, will continue to pay attention to this subject. However, we also need to listen carefully. In view of the resistance in parts of Western Europe regarding some of the fallouts of the enlargement process, we must consider ways of addressing some of these concerns. For example, the European Commission has proposed that in future accession talks, the rule of law must be at the very beginning of every process and throughout the process, alongside the economic chapters. The rule of law cannot be separated from good institutions, and is therefore essential for participation in the single market and the Monetary Union. We should support this proposal. In addition, we should not set artificial deadlines for the enlargement process. We cannot promise today that a certain country will be a member of the Union in 2025. This would create wrong expectations. We can only help to make sure that all conditions necessary for membership are progressively fulfilled, and that they are sustainably and irreversibly fulfilled. Once this has happened, accession should happen as the final step of a merit-based process supported by the EU institutions and all Member States.

Enlargement should also be possible for the euro area. For two countries, it is rather logical to become members of the euro area: for Bulgaria and for Croatia. For Bulgaria, because it has an exchange rate pegged to the euro; and for Croatia, because it is *de facto* 'euroized' in most respects. Therefore, we can be rather optimistic that in the mandate of the next Commission, we can see both countries first join the Exchange Rate Mechanism II and the Banking Union, and in the end introduce the euro. This is rather necessary. Europe must not be artificially divided between those that have the euro and those that do not. The euro is not simply something nice to have, something that one can choose to add to one's integration with the other EU Member States – or not. Instead, the EU Treaties deliberately foresee that one day, every Member State will have the euro. The euro is not a side issue but the heart of the European project and the coronation of the single market. Therefore, we should support our Central and Eastern European colleagues in their efforts to converge with the euro area and to join the euro, including financially.

This brings us to the third recommendation for the 2019–2024 period, which concerns a matter of key importance for the future of our continent: the multiannual framework for the common EU budget. Occasionally, central bankers laugh a little about the EU budget, because it is almost ridiculously small in size. It is too small to really have a visible macroeconomic effect. Yet, that is but a bird's eye perspective. In fact, the EU budget amounts to around €160 billion per year. Not all of it goes into agriculture, as some may think, but only about one-third. The budget is also there for investment programmes, such as the Juncker Plan and investEU, which were very welcome complements to the accommodative monetary policy of the ECB over the last years, and which we want to maintain. The exact numbers of the budget, however, do not really matter that much. What matters is how the EU budget of the future is focused on projects of European added value and how efficient the common management of this money is. The common EU budget could be geared more toward investment as well as growth and jobs in the European Union. Here, again, the Central and Eastern European perspective is extremely valuable. All the Central and Eastern European countries are currently asking for a higher budget, as the EU budget has a positive connotation eastward from Vienna, where the budget negotiations are currently seen from a more frugal perspective. However, in the West and also in Vienna, we have to understand that the investment of Member States in the EU budget is not a financial burden, but that it brings a very good return. In Austria, the fall of the Iron Curtain added around 1 per cent to the country's gross domestic product (GDP) per year, mainly because of the positive effects that this event has had in the East of our continent. One hundred thousand jobs were created in Austria, just because of the new freedom and the transition to market economies in Central and Eastern Europe. As a result, Austria is clearly a strong net beneficiary of enlargement, similar to most Western European countries. Therefore, a couple of cents more invested in the EU budget return a tenfold value. In this respect, it is very good that in the von der Leyen Commission, an independent Commissioner from Austria – Johannes Hahn – is now in charge of the budget negotiations. Notably, after his experience as Regional Policy Commissioner, he understands perfectly well the very beneficial functioning of the EU budget on the ground. To illustrate this, the so-called Visegrad Four countries (Czechia, Hungary, Poland and Slovakia) received, between 2010 and 2016, EU funds amounting net to between 1.5 and 4 per cent of their GDP, while during the same period, the outflow of dividends and income from property for investors based in the 15 countries that were already EU members before 2004 amounted to between 4 and 8 per cent of GDP.

For Central and Eastern Europe, it will be important to underline during the forthcoming budget negotiations that not everything is about numbers. The EU budget is policy in numbers. It is solidarity in numbers. It is solidarity when Austrian taxpayers' money is invested in the EU budget, which is spent eastward. This is a positive investment, which has a strong return on investment for Austria; but this requires also that we all, East and West, never forget why and on what basis we are investing together in our common future. The European Union is certainly not a supermarket where everybody can get some money out of common funds and does not realize that solidarity must apply not only financially, but also in other contexts, whether that might be foreign policy, the development of a common asylum policy or the support of our common values. We need unanimity for the new budget for the years 2021–2027. Unanimity among 27 countries is difficult to achieve, but it is also a very good disciplinary force to arrive at such fundamental decisions, since all sides will have to move a little toward a compromise, while keeping in mind the imperative to secure our common European future. Hopefully, we will soon move toward a good compromise, while keeping in mind that compromises are nothing bad, but rather a necessity in a Europe where 27 democracies are working together to pave the way for a common future based on common values and generating mutual benefits.

The fourth recommendation concerns a theme that should bring East and West closer together during the 2019–2024 period: the definition of a growth-oriented EU economic policy. While everyone is searching for new sources of growth, whether in renewables or in the digital economy, we must not forget that we have a tremendous source of growth on our own continent. Europe can grow on its own, better than it does today, if we invest more in Central and Eastern Europe. This region continues to be our economic locomotive: most of our Central and Eastern European Member States have above-average growth rates, and their labour force is highly skilled and mobile. What is more, we should note with some satisfaction that all these countries are currently characterized by an increase in wages, which should boost domestic consumption and hopefully result in Europe's trade growing more independently. Trade will always remain an important source of growth on our continent. But we cannot rely on it in times of certain threats emanating not only from economic rivals, but also from political and economic allies. Therefore, Europe needs to take its economic destiny more into its own hands, and this is why the sources of growth in Central and Eastern Europe are so important for our common future.

The fifth and last point of importance that should make a difference in the years 2019–2024 – both in the West and in the East of our continent – concerns the ECB; more specifically, the fact that the ECB will, with Christine Lagarde, for the first time have a woman as President. It is remarkable that we still have to underline this. The Commission has been used to this for a while already, since it already has a great number of women in the Commission's leadership, having reached the target of 40 per cent of female managers defined by President Juncker in 2014. Almost half of the new Commissioners that now serve in the von der Leyen Commission are women. And for the first time, the President of the European Commission is a woman. However, when we take a look at the pictures of central bankers' meetings in Europe, we note that this is something central bankers will still have to get used to. Gender equality should not be seen as an ideological topic, but as a necessary sign of modernity of all institutions in our democratic European societies. In Europe, whether in the West or in the East, independent institutions must be representative, or they will lose acceptance and respect among the population. Therefore, central banks will also have to change in this regard, and with Christine Lagarde at its helm the ECB will soon lead the way on this.

These are interesting times. On 27 November 2019, a large majority of the Members of the European Parliament had their say and elected the new European Commission, voting in favour of the von der Leyen Commission after a long democratic process. Some might say that there were many delays, arguments and compromises. However, getting to a new Commission is akin to the formation of a government at the European Union level, and this in a rather challenging multidimensional democratic system. It is remarkable that we Europeans get this done. We Europeans should sometimes be a little prouder of ourselves for getting things done. We are very good in talking ourselves down. But achieving the formation of a new Commission is a very important moment of our European democracy, and shows one thing: that Europe's political leadership does not comprise unelected bureaucrats. Instead, the leadership of the European Commission was elected by our common Parliament that we could all elect in May 2019. Prior to the election of the Commission, every Commissioner had to pass a process of hearings in the competent committees of the European Parliament, lasting between two to three hours; a process that is unknown to national ministers who, most of the time, are simply appointed by their Prime Minister or Chancellor.

Democracy is very much alive at the European Union level, which is why one should give the new Commission some benevolent support during its beginnings. Criticize the Commission when it is not doing the right thing, but also remember the miracle that is behind the fact that we have an elected Commission in place, mandated to steer our continent on the basis of commonly agreed rules. Thirty years after the fall of the Iron Curtain, we have a European Commission, we have a European Central Bank for our whole continent, and all countries that were behind the Iron Curtain three decades ago are in key positions in this new Europe and will shape it over the next five years from 2019 onward. Central and Eastern Europeans are no longer objects in this new Europe, they are actively shaping it. We can all be proud to have come this far over the past 30 years. And we should all remain committed to continuing this successful process with energy and determination, with responsibility and solidarity, creating mutual benefits on the basis of common values. Europe is never easy in its day-to-day operations. But if we did not have it, we would have to invent it.

REFERENCE

von der Leyen, Ursula (2019), 'A Union that Strives for More. My Agenda for Europe. Political Guidelines for the next European Commission 2019–2024', Brussels.

15. Will the EU overcome the East–West divide?

Ada Ámon

The Visegrad Group[1] (V4) started gloriously and served for quite some time as a good platform of political change, contributing to the democratic development of Central Europe. By now, however, this has changed. European Union membership with all its benefits and obligations has had a great impact on the climate policies of the Visegrad countries, which would not have happened outside of the Union. Today's Visegrad cooperation is based on ignoring climate threats, attempting to extend fossil fuel burning, violating air pollution limits and undermining the development of renewable energies. In doing so, these countries not only hurt the interests of the European Union but also hurt the interests and health of their own citizens.

The V4 play a significant role in setting the agenda for the rest of the Central and Eastern European (CEE) Member States. It is therefore interesting to examine the dynamics of this group of countries and the way they are dealing with energy and climate policy. Three countries of this region – the Czech Republic, Hungary and Poland – were responsible. at the European Council in the summer of 2019, for blocking the European Union's (EU) ambition to become climate neutral by 2050, hindering a clear and united voice of the European Union in international climate negotiations. Yet, it is not only the EU's credibility that is at stake. The negotiations are at a critical stage and the momentum should be maintained, ratcheting up the nationally determined contributions to cut greenhouse gas emissions for mitigating the future impact of climate change. The international community is far from fulfilling the Paris promise and the EU would be the only player brokering further deals, but it will not be credible with a disputable ambition. Therefore, getting the support of the V4 and the wider CEE region is essential for a sufficient global deal.

CEE Member States are also important in delivering the European Union promise. These countries (11 countries out of the 27) are responsible for one-fifth of the EU's greenhouse gas emissions. Thus, a significant delay of the green transition in CEE – as it stands at the beginning of 2020 – would slow down the EU's pace and lower the chance of meeting the Paris commitment.

A recent report published by E3G, an independent climate think tank, on 'The Political Economy of Energy in Central Eastern Europe – Supporting the Net Zero Transition' gives a comparative overview based on the findings from in-depth analyses conducted in six countries (Bulgaria, the Czech Republic, Hungary, Poland, Romania and Slovakia) using E3G's Political Economy Mapping Methodology (PEMM) (see Heilmann et al. 2020). The report looks at selected aspects of these assessments and compares and contrasts the dynamics of and similarities between the different policy approaches, while an in-depth analysis can be found in previously published country reports.[2]

Renewable energy policies are the focus of this chapter, as they are often debated and seen as controversial in the CEE region, which demonstrates the attitude of policymakers toward the wider context of climate policy. At the end of the chapter, recommendations are given in priority action areas for targeted political and diplomatic interventions by both European and national policymakers.

15.1   THE LOW-CARBON ECONOMY IS WEAK AND DIVIDED

Some of the main aspects that were assessed in the six countries under review were the tendencies and dynamics of the low-carbon economy, and the development of renewable energy policy. It can be stated that the green and blue sectors of the economy are generally weak and/or very much divided in all of the countries concerned. At the same time, the high interest in carbon is evident, with the incumbent companies in question having good and historic connections to the state, as most of them are still or – surprisingly enough – again owned by the state. They traditionally represent the establishment of the conventional energy industry and, as such, still manage to lay the institutional, economic as well as legislative framework in a 'Soviet' style of policymaking. 'Soviet' style refers to the lack of a culture of evidence-based public policy design and to centralized and supply side-oriented infrastructure planning where conventional technologies and energy sources play the overwhelming role. This style of policymaking exists despite EU values, rules and long-term climate targets as well as corresponding cohesion and structural funds aimed at supporting the transition.

15.2   FINANCING THE LOW-CARBON TRANSITION

European cohesion and structural funding in CEE is important for two main reasons: (1) a major part of the funds are spent in CEE Member States; and (2) these funds provide around half of public investments of these countries (see Table 15.1).

Table 15.1   The importance of EU funding

	Bulgaria	Czech Republic	Hungary	Poland	Romania	Slovakia
Total allocation (2014–2020)	€9.90	€23.80	€25.00	€85.20	€30.60	€15.30
Share of public investment (2015–2017)	48.50%	42.50%	55.50%	61.20%	44.90%	54.60%

Source: European Commission (2020).

The overarching theme here is obviously the suspicion of mismanagement and misuse of EU funds; corruption, state capture and kleptocracy can be mentioned as synonyms. It is a fair expectation of European taxpayers, though, that their money is spent purposefully and according to legal requirements. So far, however, it has been proven that numerous projects that were carried out with the aim of supporting cohesion policy or structural developments in CEE countries rather contributed to the additional wealth of some oligarchs in Eastern Europe (see Emerging Europe 2019). The other main concern is what is referred to as climate mainstreaming. In the current funding period (2014–2020), 20 per cent of EU expenditure was allocated to climate-related spending, which was increased to 25 per cent for the overall Multiannual Financial Framework (MFF) and more for the share of the respective funds flowing into these countries for the following period (2021–2027) according to the recent proposal on the table. Yet, the question remains of whether the CEE Member States intend to spend more than one-third of their budgeted EU funds on real climate measures and programmes. And even if they agree to do so on paper, one may wonder whether they will turn rhetoric into action (see Reitzenstein et al. 2018).

Recent negotiations show that the MFF plays an important role when it comes to agreeing on the common goal of making the European Union climate neutral by 2050, a goal also known as the European Green Deal. The conditions of using the Just Transition Fund, a key financial component of the European Green Deal, as well as the overall size and the particular slice of the cake, are all part of the bargaining process (see Simon 2019). The terms of the Just Transition Fund have been a crucial bargain as some of the most-impacted Member States wanted to use the money for switching from coal to natural gas as a temporary replacement of fuel. At the same time, a real transition needs the commitment of the Member States by declaring a close enough date to phase out coal from their entire energy generation repertoire. As is shown in Table 15.1, EU funding has a high significance in CEE, as a result of which reasonable conditionality, which is high on the political agenda, can be attached to it. The European Green Deal is likely to accelerate the transition to climate neutrality of the entire region in the coming months and years. The deal combines high levels of climate ambition with financial support for the transition through what is referred to as the Just Transition Mechanism. However, it is only a first step, and the mechanism and rules of the new deal are not yet fully known. To achieve a more ambitious EU climate position and to ensure its implementation in all EU Member States, a nuanced understanding of the political dynamics of the transition to climate neutrality in CEE is necessary. This is especially important in light of the upcoming negotiations on an increased climate target for 2030 and on the new EU budget.

15.3   RENEWABLE ENERGY: VAST UNTAPPED POTENTIAL

There is great potential for expanding renewable energy capacities across CEE countries, but it is not yet exploited, as there is no commitment to a systemic renewable energy transition (see IRENA 2017). In its assessment of the draft National Energy and Climate Plans (NECPs), the European Commission has criticized the renewable energy targets for 2030 of all the countries studied as being too low.[3] An accelerated expansion of renewable energy faces serious barriers, as governments are sceptical toward renewable energy and often favour the expansion of centralized power generation, such as nuclear.

A distinction needs to be made between renewable energy used for heating, and renewable energy used for electricity production. Renewable heating is encouraged by governments, and its expansion is often pursued as the main strategy for meeting renewable energy targets. This happens primarily through increased burning of biomass, including firewood, which is unsustainable, as forests are an important carbon sink (see Sandbag 2019).

Electricity generation from renewable energy sources, such as wind and solar photovoltaic (PV), by contrast, is facing significant opposition from governments and incumbent electricity producers who fear the associated changes to the electricity system. The policy framework for renewable electricity generation is subject to frequent changes in all countries. In Bulgaria, the Czech Republic, Romania and Slovakia, initial support frameworks were introduced in the late 2000s and early 2010s but the governments underestimated the pace of capacity additions that these new policies would trigger. They caused increases in energy prices, and governments responded by abolishing the frameworks instead of improving their design. The hike in energy prices led to a negative public perception of renewable energy, and the retroactive abolishment of support schemes significantly undermined investor trust in these countries. The obstructive and unstable policy environment causes insecurity among investors and leads to a lack of investment in renewable energy. The

Table 15.2   Share of renewable electricity generation in total fuel generation, 2017

	Bulgaria (%)	Czech Republic (%)	Hungary (%)	Poland (%)	Romania (%)	Slovakia (%)
Hydro	7.7	3.5	0.7	1.9	23.1	16.7
Solar	3.1	2.5	1.1	0.0	2.9	1.8
Wind	3.3	0.7	2.3	8.7	11.5	0.0
Biomass	0.9	5.6	6.0	3.8	0.8	6.0
Total	15.0	12.3	10.1	14.4	38.3	24.5

Source: International Energy Agency (2019).

VISEGRAD+ for Renewable Energy platform of regional renewable energy associations seeks to overcome these barriers by building regional coalitions for the clean energy transition (see VISEGRAD+ for Renewable Energy 2019).

An additional problem is the large share of hydro power and biomass in the energy mix of CEE countries (see Table 15.2). The prominent role of hydro power in the energy mix in Romania and Slovakia is debated domestically, as planned hydro power projects with potentially large environmental impacts lie within protected Natura 2000 areas. More recently, changes to policy frameworks have been implemented across the region to expand wind and solar capacities: Bulgaria, the Czech Republic, Hungary and Poland have introduced new small-scale support schemes for renewable energy, but only Poland is promoting investment in wind projects (offshore), and has held large auctions for solar and onshore wind.

15.4 'THREATENED BY GREEN ELECTRICITY'

When it comes to the share of renewables in the EU, the Czech Republic, Hungary, Slovakia and Poland are sitting in the last row. Their share is well below 20 per cent. The situation gets even worse if one digs deeper and wants to know the share of renewables in electricity consumption. Hungary is second to last, while Poland and the Czech Republic rank fifth and sixth from the bottom. Slovakia stands out in the region thanks to its extensive use of hydro capacity built back in Communist times.

One could say that the region lags behind because of its geographical location. Yet Austria, which borders three of the four Visegrad countries, plays a leading role in the use of renewables and spearheads developments in renewable electricity generation on the continent. Since wind does not stop at geographical borders, what could be the reason for such tremendous differences between the countries?

The answer is political will. Austria's successful development of renewables is rooted in the political and societal consensus that a clean and sustainable energy policy is beneficial for the country regardless of any current ideological, political direction. It brings prosperity, clean air to all people, and many benefits for the economy. This notion and understanding supports high climate ambitions by providing the needed institutional set-up.

This was not the case 25 years ago; not even in Austria. At the time, the common attitude was the one that is widespread in CEE Member States today: renewables are expensive, unreliable and not able to deliver. Back in the last century when climate change was not widely acknowledged, renewable technologies were much less developed, investment costs were much higher, and project management as well as financing were still in a very early stage. Thanks to the forerunners, such as Austria, Germany and the Scandinavian countries, the opposite now applied. Wind and solar investments are routine projects and integrate well into the grids. The overall costs of these investments have dropped below most of the costs of the conventional power plants.

At the same time, the V4 governments and the political establishment of these countries still believe that only huge and baseload powerplants can reliably supply electricity (see Ámon 2018). The incumbent power sector feels threatened by solar and wind. It is right to feel so, since the costs of coal-based electricity production as well as nuclear investment are increasing, while the overall price of renewable technologies is falling. As a response, these governments use their legislative power and hold back the development of renewables, thus maintaining the hegemony of conventional technologies.

Some of these countries have also introduced extreme regulations unprecedented in the EU. In Hungary, for example, wind parks will not be permitted within 12.5 km of any settlement, which makes the whole country a no-go zone for wind parks. In fact, it is easier to obtain a licence for a 2 GW nuclear power plant than for a 30 MW wind park. Slovakians are allowed install their own household-size renewable power plant (in practical terms, PV on the roof) but need to consume at least 90 per cent of the generated power themselves.

The NECPs submitted to the European Commission at the end of 2019 mirror the insufficient idea of energy policy and very low climate ambitions. The share of renewable energy sources in the final energy consumption for 2030 only ranges from 19 per cent to 21 per cent in these countries, and the supporting documents of the NECPs are generally of very low quality. According to a new study applying the Commission's own methodology based on the revised Renewable Energy Directive, all Member States in question should have come up with a share that is at least four percentage points higher (see CEE Bankwatch Network 2019). In other words, according to the rules, these countries would be required to generate at least one-quarter of their energy needs based on renewable sources by 2030. Moreover, it is certain that the economically viable potential is well above this figure.

15.5 HOW TO DIAL UP AMBITION

All in all, what would be possible drivers of the needed change? When looking at all the actors in this field, one can conclude that the European Union is in practice the only active and forceful agent at the moment that pushes the development of new renewable energy production and green electricity generation systems. The question, however, is what room remains for the EU institutions to insist on and advocate for high climate ambitions. Eastern European Member States like to refer to national sovereignty in terms of deciding on the ideal mix of energy sources. This argument is always there for them to parry and call for protecting their choice of maintaining the status quo and the hegemony of conventional technology at the Member State level. Infringement would be the next logical response, if these Member States do not fulfil the obligations, reach the targets or comply with the rules. But do the sanctions or penalties the countries would need to pay in cases of non-compliance act as a deterrent? It is quite doubtful that the stick would have the desired impact; rather, the carrot might be a better option.

By combining high levels of climate ambition with the offer to financially support the transition, the European Green Deal is likely to accelerate the transition to climate neutrality in CEE countries in the coming years. The following measures will help to speed up the energy transition and set the right conditions in all countries of the region, despite varying levels of support for the implementation of the Green Deal.

The next EU budget (2021–2027) will offer ample opportunity to improve climate action by providing the core of the financial support for the green transition. According to recent plans, at least 25 per cent of the budget needs to be spent on climate-related projects and investment. Ensuring that the EU budget maximizes climate action will require not just increasing the share of climate-related spending in the MFF, but also putting an end to supporting fossil fuel infrastructure and mainstreaming climate goals across all areas of EU investment.[4]

Given a shrinking budget (due to the departure of the United Kingdom), a stricter oversight needs to be applied to ensure that EU taxpayers' money is used purposefully in CEE. Monitoring and control are inevitable for generating a real and well-targeted transition. The European Commission should ensure, through regular monitoring and evaluation, that EU funds contribute to climate objectives, and establish rigorous anti-corruption measures as part of the budget.

Supporting inclusive policymaking processes is essential for speeding up social acceptance, which is key in the transition. The Just Transition Fund and the overall Mechanism could serve as an enabling platform and initiative of change for the affected communities where they can discuss their plans beyond coal. The EU budget can reduce the social impacts resulting from the transition to a green economy, and avoid the transition getting stuck by linking climate ambition to funding. This means that only those countries that present a Paris-compatible phase-out plan for coal or another high-emission technology should be eligible for funding from the Just Transition Fund (see Popp and De Pous 2019).

The role of direct funding for cities and regions is still outstanding. Cities are unquestionably the forerunners of climate policies. Capital cities have a much higher concentration of experts, civil society members and intellectuals, and would thus provide fertile ground for green initiatives. Indeed, V4 capitals are governed by much greener political actors. It is still not too late to consider the possibility of direct financial support to those regions and cities that have put in place sufficiently ambitious programmes to address climate change. Eastern European citizens have just as much of a right to clean air, to climate adaptation plans and to green and efficient energy as Western European citizens.

Member States can play a facilitating role in bringing together renewable energy associations such as the VISEGRAD+ for Renewable Energy (see VISEGRAD+ for Renewable Energy 2019) platform and corporations committed to renewables, such as the RE100 members (see RE100 2020).

Member States that are at more advanced stages of the energy transition can provide their expertise in designing the legal structures for phasing out coal, managing structural change and deploying renewable energy capacities. Cross-border exchange between trade unions on green jobs and unionization can help to ensure the provision of high-quality, climate-friendly jobs.

The current definition of energy security, which focuses on supply source access, needs to be replaced with a definition that incorporates new ways of addressing energy security risks, including energy efficiency, domestic renewables and a smartening of the grid.

Finally, civil society organizations need to be strengthened. This requires increased and coordinated financial support from European and national funding programmes as well as private donors. It is also crucial to build networks that support knowledge transfer and information flows between organizations, Brussels and national capitals.

15.6   COAL CURTAIN OR UNITED UNDER THE EUROPEAN GREEN DEAL

As has been described above, the difficult problems blocking climate-related developments are of a political and institutional nature rather than of an economic or technological nature. This holds even more true for CEE.

A well-managed and fast transition is also in the self-interest of CEE countries. Coal power generation, on which many of these countries still rely, is becoming increasingly unprofitable. At the same time, renewable energy is becoming ever cheaper, a trend that is likely to continue. Embarking on a managed transition away from fossil fuels toward renewable energy systems now is a way to avoid greater disruption in the future.

Thirty years ago, it was the Iron Curtain that divided Europe into East and West. Now, due to the attitude of the CEE governments, we can say that it is the coal curtain. According to the official energy strategies proposed by the Member States to the European Commission, the share of renewable energy will be as high as 50 per cent on the Western side of the coal curtain, while it will stay as low as 20–25 per cent on the Eastern side, leaving room for a high share of fossil fuels and nuclear power. This would be a huge and dividing gap between the two regions. Understanding the factors that lead to this divide will enable us to make the right choices at the European level.

NOTES

1. The Visegrad Group, also known as the Visegrád Four, or V4, is a cultural and political alliance of four Central European countries: the Czech Republic, Hungary, Poland and Slovakia.
2. For details on E3G's Political Economy Mappings for the six CEE countries, see www.e3g.org/showcase/central-and-eastern-europe-in-focus.
3. All Member States must establish ten-year integrated NECPs to show how they will meet the EU's energy and climate targets by 2030. The final plans had to be submitted by 31 December 2019. As they were not yet available when this chapter was written, I rely on the analysis of the draft NECPs available at https://ec.europa.eu/energy/en/topics/energy-strategy/national-energy-climate-plans#related-links-.
4. For in-depth recommendations for the next EU budget, see Pilsner et al. (2018). This report assesses the Commission's sectoral proposals dated March 2018 for the next 2021–2027 MFF. It explores the contribution of several instruments – Cohesion Policy Funds, European Social Fund Plus, InvestEU, Horizon Europe and European Globalisation Adjustment Fund – to the Just Transition agenda, and identifies options for EU policymakers to better align funds with the climate agenda.

REFERENCES

Ámon, A. (2018), 'Mega Infrastructure Projects Win over Clean Energy in Visegrad Four', available at https://www.euractiv.com/section/electricity/opinion/mega-infrastructure-projects-win-over-clean-energy-in-visegrad-four/ (accessed on 14 September 2018).

CEE Bankwatch Network (2019), 'Making the Grade? A Review of Eight National Energy and Climate Plans in Central and Eastern Europe', available at https://www.euki.de/wp-content/uploads/2019/06/BWN-NECP-in-8-CEE-countries-March-2019.pdf (accessed on 30 March 2019).

Emerging Europe (2019), 'Hungary Fined 1.67 Billion Euros for Mismanagement of EU Funds', available at https://emerging-europe.com/news/hungary-fined-1-67-billion-euros-for-mismanagement-of-eu-funds/ (accessed on 15 November 2019).

European Commission (2020), 'Share of Cohesion Policy per Member State to Public Investment', available at https://cohesiondata.ec.europa.eu/Other/Share-of-Cohesion-Policy-per-Member-State-to-publi/drqq-sbh7 (accessed February 2020).

Heilmann, F., R. Popp and A. Ámon (2020), 'The Political Economy of Energy in Central Eastern Europe – Supporting the Net Zero Transition', available at https://www.e3g.org/docs/E3G_2020_Comparative_Analysis_CEE.pdf (accessed on 30 January 2020).

International Energy Agency (2019), 'Renewable Statistics by Country', available at https://www.iea.org/subscribe-to-data-services/renewables-statistics (accessed on 12 December 2019).

IRENA (2017), 'Cost-Competitive Renewable Power Generation: Potential across South East Europe', available at https://www.irena.org/publications/2017/Jan/Cost-competitive-renewable-power-generation-Potential-across-South-East-Europe (accessed on 30 January 2017).

Pilsner, L., P. De Pous, A. Reitzenstein and J. Gaventa (2018), 'Funding the Just Transition to a Net Zero Economy in Europe: Opportunities in the Next EU Budget', available at https://www.e3g.org/library/funding-just-transition-net-zero-economy-in-europe-opportunities-eu-budget (accessed on 30 October 2018).

Popp, R. and P. De Pous (2019), 'The Just Transition Fund: 4 Benchmarks for Success', E3G, available at https://www.e3g.org/docs/9_12_19_E3G_Briefing_Just_Transition_Fund_2019.pdf (accessed on 10 January 2020).

RE100 (2020), 'RE100 Overview', available at http://there100.org/re100 (accessed January 2017).

Reitzenstein, A., S. Schulz, P. De Pous and A. Ámon (2018), 'An EU Budget for Climate Action: Accelerating the Low-Carbon Transition in Central Eastern Europe', available at https://www.e3g.org/library/eu-budget-for-climate-action-accelerating-low-carbon-transition-in-CEE (accessed on 9 May 2018).

Sandbag (2019), 'Playing with Fire: An Assessment of Company Plans to Burn Biomass in EU Coal Power Stations', available at https://sandbag.org.uk/project/playing-with-fire/ (accessed December 2019).

Simon, F. (2019), 'Three EU Countries Bump Up Renewable Energy Goal for 2030', available at https://www.euractiv.com/section/climate-strategy-2050/news/three-eu-countries-bump-up-renewable-energy-goal-for-2030/ (accessed on 24 September 2019).

VISEGRAD+ for Renewable Energy (2019), 'Memorandum of Understanding', available at https://www.e3g.org/docs/Memorandum_Visegrad_for_renewable_energy_PDF.pdf (accessed on 15 May 2019).

16. Demographic change in Central, Eastern and Southeastern Europe: trends, determinants and challenges

Tomáš Sobotka[1] and Alexia Fürnkranz-Prskawetz

The collapse of the state-socialist authoritarian political system in Central and Eastern Europe in 1989–1991 was a watershed moment that put the countries in the region on a completely different economic, social and political trajectory. The region also experienced sweeping changes in its demographic trends and patterns during the last three decades, undergoing a transition towards lower fertility, more diverse families, lower mortality, and high intensity of international migration, especially outmigration. Some of these shifts brought about huge long-term challenges that will last for generations to come: declining populations, especially in the more peripheral countries and areas, accelerated population ageing, shrinking labour force and outmigration of younger, more educated people pose a major challenge for healthcare, social security and pension systems in the region (see IMF 2019). Central and Eastern Europe is the only larger global region with shrinking populations. In many countries, the combination of falling birth rates and outmigration led to massive and long-lasting population declines, which are unparalleled in peacetime. Among 15 countries and territories with the largest population losses globally between 1990 and 2019, 14 were in Central and Eastern Europe and the Caucasus region. Among them, Bosnia and Herzegovina, Latvia, Lithuania and Moldova saw their populations shrinking by more than 20 per cent (see Figure 16.1).

In many respects, countries in Central and Eastern Europe have moved towards the demographic patterns observed earlier in Western and Northern Europe. This is clearly the case for broader fertility and family change (see below). However, two distinct features of the ongoing population trends in Central and Eastern Europe are instability and diversity. Trends in fertility, mortality and migration since the 1990s often showed large fluctuations and reversals, reacting rapidly to changing external conditions. In addition, the region has undergone huge differentiation in its population trends and patterns, especially in mortality and migration. This demographic diversity is

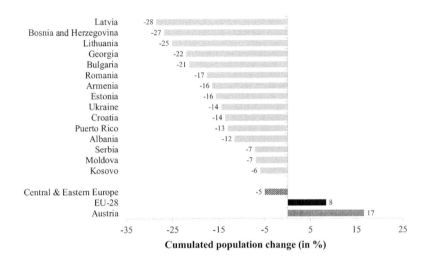

Sources: Data from UN World Population Prospects (UN 2019a) and Eurostat (2020) for Kosovo.

Figure 16.1   *Countries with fastest population decline globally, 1989–2019 compared with population change in Austria, Central and Eastern Europe and the European Union (EU-28)*

an outcome of historical developments and long-rooted differences in culture, religious tradition and family systems, as well as more recent economic, social and policy differences (see, for example, Sobotka 2011).

To some extent, the divergent demographic trends in Central and Eastern Europe reflect disparities in economic and developmental trajectories across the region after 1990. Some countries, especially in Central Europe, have seen a broadly successful transformation process, resulting in sustained economic growth, prosperity and high levels of development. In contrast, countries in Eastern Europe and many countries in Southeastern Europe experienced bumpy and challenging social and economic transitions in the last three decades. As a result, differences in economic and well-being indicators between countries in Central and Eastern Europe are much wider today than the corresponding differences between countries in Western, Northern, and Southern Europe. In 2018 the gross domestic product (GDP) per capita (in current US dollars) of the richest country in Central and Eastern Europe, Slovenia (US$26 124), was eight times higher than in Ukraine (US$3095). This is a much wider gap than that between Greece, the least affluent country in Southern Europe (US$20

324) and Switzerland (US 82 796), the richest country in Europe (besides Luxembourg) (see World Bank 2020). Similarly, countries in Central and Eastern Europe show wide differences in their Human Development Index ranking, ranging from the 24th (Slovenia) to 107th (Moldova) place globally in 2019 (see UN 2019b).

Our chapter aims to provide a broad overview of population changes in Central and Eastern Europe during the last three decades, highlighting the widening demographic divides between countries. We review especially the transformation in fertility patterns and family size, mortality and international migration, and discuss the major challenges stemming from these trends. We look broadly at the whole region encompassing Central, Eastern and Southeastern Europe, denoting the three regions together as 'Central and Eastern Europe' (CEE).[2] We group countries and regions as follows:

- Central Europe: Croatia, Czechia (Czech Republic), Estonia, Hungary, Latvia, Lithuania, Poland, Slovakia, Slovenia.
- Southeastern Europe: Albania, Bosnia and Herzegovina, Bulgaria, Kosovo, North Macedonia, Montenegro, Romania, Serbia.
- Eastern Europe: Belarus, Moldova, Russia, Ukraine.
- Western Europe: Austria, Belgium, France, Germany, Ireland, Luxembourg, Netherlands, Switzerland, United Kingdom.
- Northern Europe (Nordic countries): Denmark, Finland, Iceland, Norway, Sweden.
- Southern Europe: Cyprus, Greece, Italy, Malta, Portugal, Spain.

In addition, parts of our analysis also distinguish the three Baltic countries (Estonia, Latvia and Lithuania), and the three predominantly German-speaking countries (Austria, Germany and Switzerland). We also discuss the former German Democratic Republic (GDR), eastern Germany, as this region witnessed dynamic demographic changes, often moving ahead of the whole CEE region.

Our analysis mostly relies on official data, reports and publications based on statistics, population censuses and selected surveys. However, the quality and reliability of population data and estimates are limited for many countries with substantial outmigration, including Bosnia and Herzegovina, Moldova, Romania and Ukraine, as the official statistics are not able to fully account for emigration. This typically results in inflated estimates of population size, which then lead to distortions in all demographic indicators, including fertility and mortality, as well as other population-related indicators (see, for example, Penina et al. 2015 for Moldova). One partial solution is to provide alternative estimates of population size and structure based on different definitions, as is currently done in Romania (distinguishing between *de jure* population and *de facto* or the usual resident population[3]). In other countries, including Moldova, population data and indicators are subject to large one-time adjustments following population census or expert-based population revisions.

16.1   FERTILITY DECLINES, FAMILY CHANGES AND POLICY RESPONSES

Most of the state-socialist countries in Central and Eastern Europe experienced remarkable convergence in their fertility patterns during the 1950s–1980s. In the 1980s, fertility rates in the region were strongly centred on the two-child family norm, characterized by an early timing of first births, low levels of childlessness, and a close link between marriage and childbearing (see Sobotka 2011). Fertility in many countries was partly propped up by a relatively low use of modern contraception, a high share of unplanned pregnancies and births, but also by pro-natalist policies, preferential distribution of housing to families with children, almost non-existing unemployment and less competitive labour markets (see Sobotka 2016).

The collapse of state socialism in 1989–1991 and the subsequent period of economic transformation, social changes and political turbulences brought about a collapse in fertility across Central and Eastern Europe. Whereas in the late 1980s the region had higher fertility rates than the European Union, around the year 2000 almost all CEE countries recorded very low fertility levels. Fertility in the region fell well below the European Union (EU) average and in many countries also below the persistently low fertility in Austria and Germany (see Figure 16.2; see also Sobotka 2011; Frejka and Gietel-Basten 2016). Period total fertility rate (TFR) in many countries – including Bulgaria, Czechia, Latvia, Russia, Slovakia, Slovenia and Ukraine – tumbled to extremely low levels of 1.1–1.3, down from around 1.8–2.2 in 1989. The sharpest fertility response to rapid societal changes has been observed in eastern Germany (the former GDR), where period TFR plummeted soon after German reunification to extreme low levels, at 0.77–0.78 in 1993–1994 (see Figure 16.2; see Conrad et al. 1996; Goldstein and Kreyenfeld 2011).

In the next decade, during the 2000s, fertility rates recovered across the CEE region, and in some countries this recovery continued also during the 2010s, although at an uneven pace. Some countries recorded a temporary drop in fertility during the period of economic recession around 2010 (for example, Czechia, Hungary, Romania and Poland). By contrast, three Eastern European countries (Belarus, Russia and Ukraine) saw a remarkable fertility upswing that came to an end in 2015–2016, when fertility started falling again (see Figure 16.2).

The recent fertility shifts are part of a broader transformation in fertility and family behaviour across the region. First births and first marriages have

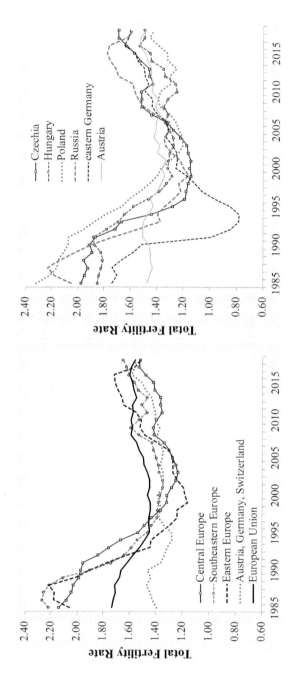

Note: Data for broader regions are computed from country data and weighted by population size of countries in each region.
Sources: Human Fertility Database (2020), Eurostat (2020) and national statistical offices.

Figure 16.2   Period total fertility rate in Central and Eastern Europe compared with the European Union and Austria (1985–2018): broader regions (left panel) and selected countries (right panel)

been postponed to much higher reproductive ages in response to the sweeping social changes, delayed union formation, but also rapid expansion in tertiary education and the spread of more efficient contraception, especially the pill (see Sobotka 2011; Frejka and Gietel-Basten 2016; Billingsley 2010). The mean age at first birth shifted from an average of 22–24 years among women in 1990 to an average of 26–29 years in 2018, and this 'postponement transition' (see Kohler et al. 2002) has been especially fast in Central Europe. As a result, fertility rates at young ages, especially among teenage women, fell sharply.

Families have become more diverse, marriage rates have plummeted and cohabitation and other informal living arrangements have become wide-spread (see Puur et al. 2012). With a few exceptions (especially Estonia, East Germany, Hungary and Slovenia), having children outside wedlock was unusual in the region until the 1990s. Today 40–60 per cent of births in Bulgaria, Czechia, Estonia, Latvia, Hungary and Slovenia take place outside marriage, mostly within cohabiting partnerships (see Perelli-Harris et al. 2012). Many countries have recorded high rates of marriage and union dissolution since the 1970s–1980s (see Härkönen et al. 2020). Together with higher rates of single living and higher childlessness, delayed residential independence, and a more diverse sequencing of family transitions, these wide-reaching family trends are often seen as a sign of a fundamental trans-formation in family relations, the 'second demographic transition' (SDT) (see Lesthaeghe 2010). The SDT trends have evolved unevenly across the region (see Sobotka 2008). Especially in Eastern Europe, there is a strong pushback against non-traditional family behaviour in public discourses. These norma-tive divisions are seen, for instance, in sharp divides in the attitudes towards same-sex relationships, especially same-sex marriage, which are more open in Central Europe and disapproving in Eastern Europe and parts of Southeastern Europe (see Pew Research Center 2018).

The complex changes in fertility and family behaviour have multiple roots. Initially, the breakdown of state socialism brought about a huge increase in economic and policy uncertainty, marked also by a retreat of social policies and falling spending on families in many countries. This was especially the case in the poorer countries in Eastern and Southeastern Europe, which suffered more severe social and economic shocks in the 1990s (see Philipov 2003; Philipov et al. 2006; Perelli-Harris 2005). The privatization of housing and the removal of other policy incentives to early childbearing contributed to delayed family formation. At the same time, new options and opportunities for self-realization emerged, especially for the younger people, who now spend much longer in education than a few decades ago. Tertiary graduation rates went up especially fast among women, strongly contributing to their later marriages and births. Young adults also gained better control over their pregnancies and better access to modern contraception (see Sobotka 2016), with abortion rates and fertility rates at younger ages plummeting. After the turn of the century, when most CEE countries started experiencing sustained economic growth, fertility rates were increasingly affected by similar factors as in other more economically affluent parts of Europe, including economic conditions and broader economic and employment uncertainty among young adults. High costs of housing, especially in larger cities, also contribute to a late pattern of leaving the parental home, delayed union formation and childbearing. Some countries in the region, including Bulgaria, Croatia and Slovakia, now have, together with Southern Europe, the latest pattern of leaving the parental home in Europe (Eurostat 2018).

In addition, fertility and family trends in the last two decades were affected by family policies, which gained prominence on the agenda of many governments concerned about low fertility and population declines. Spending on family policies has been boosted during the last two decades and some governments, including Belarus, Hungary, Poland and Russia, adopted a strongly pro-natalist stance. However, family policies in individual countries have taken different directions (see Frejka and Gietel-Basten 2016; Sobotka et al. 2019). Some governments, especially in Belarus, Poland, Latvia, Russia and Ukraine, expanded cash benefits for families with children. These initiatives include a 'maternal capital' scheme in Russia. Established in 2007, it provides a cashless benefit transferred to mothers having a second, third or later child (since 2020, also to the mothers of a first child), which can be spent on specific purposes, such as housing renovation or purchase, mortgage repayment and education costs (see Pension Fund of the Russian Federation 2020). Governments in Hungary and Lithuania embarked on a more ambitious expansion of family policies. In the case of Hungary, these policies aim to support especially larger families and include a range of initiatives from marriage loans through tax exemptions and financial allowances up to the subsidies for purchasing a larger car. By contrast, Estonia has moved furthest in adopting Nordic-style family policies, with generously subsidized and flexible parental leave coupled with an expansion of public childcare (see Puur and Klesment 2011; Biin 2017; Sobotka et al. 2019). Overall, countries in the CEE region focus mostly on financial benefits for families, and often neglect policies allowing an easier combination of career and family life, such as childcare provision, especially for the parents of small children aged 0–2.

Diverse factors discussed above led to fluctuations in period fertility rates without much affecting the ultimate family size among women born in different years. Women and couples often respond to the changing economic and social conditions by postponing or advancing childbearing. Similarly, new policies can provide an incentive for some people to have their first child earlier in life, or to space their second or third birth more closely to the previous one. As a result, policies often have a stronger short-term influence on period fertility, but appear to have much weaker long-term impact on family size (see Sobotka et al. 2019). Many of the period fertility changes in Central and Eastern Europe since 1990 have been predominantly driven by the shift towards later timing of childbearing and its intensity over time; these time-limited distortions to period demographic indicators are known as the 'tempo effect' (Bongaarts and Feeney 1998).

Cohort (generational) indicators of family size are not affected by period shifts and fluctuations and therefore provide a better picture of the underlying changes in fertility. We compare family size reached by age 40 among women in selected countries born in 1960 and 1976 (see Figure 16.3). The first group mainly represents the fertility pattern during the final years of state socialism. The latter group reached their peak reproductive years in the 2000s, under the new societal and policy conditions.

The analysed CEE countries and regions all experienced a fall in family size: sharpest in Poland and Hungary, and mildest in Czechia. Women born in 1976 in Belarus, Hungary, Poland and in eastern Germany had 1.5–1.6 children by age 40, converging to the smaller family size in Austria. The CEE countries and eastern Germany experienced a move away from the strong two-child family pattern towards a more diverse distribution of family size, with a rising share of women with one child (reaching one-third in Belarus and eastern Germany). The share of women remaining childless, very low during the state-socialist era, jumped fast in all analysed countries, reaching about 20 per cent in Poland and Hungary (similar to Austria, where childlessness has been historically high). The number of women with two children fell across all CEE countries, despite the continuing strong preference for a two-child family across Europe (see Sobotka and Beaujouan 2014). Furthermore, the share of women with three or more children fell to low levels, reaching only 13–15 per cent in Belarus, Czechia, eastern Germany and Poland.

These data hide considerable differences in fertility by social status. Especially in Southeastern and Eastern Europe, women with a higher education degree have very low completed fertility rates. In Bulgaria, Belarus, Croatia, Romania, Russia and Serbia, women with tertiary education born in 1970 had only 1.1–1.4 children on average (see Sobotka et al. 2017). This likely reflects the obstacles that highly educated women in these countries face in juggling their career plans and family obligations in the context of low levels of gender equality. By contrast, low-educated women have much larger family sizes on average. Larger families are also common among economically disadvantaged minorities, especially the Roma ethnic group in Hungary, Slovakia and Romania (see Szabó et al. 2017).

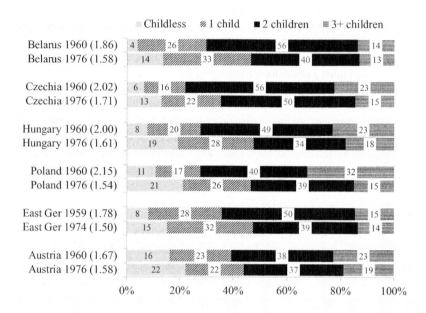

Note: The data for eastern Germany are available only for five-year cohorts. The following cohorts are shown: 1957–1961 for the earlier cohort (labelled 1959) and 1972–1976 for the later cohort (labelled 1974).
Sources: Data from Human Fertility Database (2020), Census 2001 in Austria for women born in 1960 (CFE database 2020) and Microcensus 2016 survey for eastern Germany (Statistisches Bundesamt 2017).

Figure 16.3   *Family size distribution and completed fertility (children per woman, in brackets) at age 40 among women born in 1960 and 1976, selected countries and eastern Germany*

16.2   MORTALITY AND HEALTH: A BUMPY ROAD TO LONGEVITY

Countries in Central and Eastern Europe have a very uneven history of 'stop and go' progress in mortality and public health. Today the region has on average a lower life expectancy, especially among men, than Northern, Western and Southern Europe. At the same time, huge differences between countries in life expectancy and in mortality trends developed over the last three decades. These differences are partly rooted in the long stagnation and setbacks in mortality in Central and Eastern Europe during the 1970s and 1980s, which contrasted with mortality improvements elsewhere in Europe. Between 1970 and 1990, the gap in mortality between the CEE countries and other parts of Europe widened, as illustrated by the comparison of life expectancy among men in Austria and selected CEE countries in Figure 16.4 (see Meslé and Vallin 2002). Countries in the CEE region were unable to effectively reduce mortality from external causes of death and degenerative diseases – including circulatory diseases, cancer, traffic accidents and alcohol abuse – which were stagnating or increasing (see Meslé 2004). In addition, people in Central and Eastern Europe had relatively unhealthy lifestyles and diet, which contributed to their elevated mortality (see Bobak and Marmot 1996; Cockerham 1997).

The divides between countries and regions deepened most during the 1990s (see Meslé and Vallin 2002; Aburto and van Raalte 2018). Several of the more economically developed countries in the region – Czechia, Poland, Slovenia, and also the region of eastern Germany – experienced a turnaround in mortality trends in the early 1990s and since then have followed a pathway of sustained mortality improvements, similar to Western and Southern European countries. The largest improvements in life expectancy stemmed from the progress in the treatment of ischaemic heart disease (see Mackenbach et al. 2015). By contrast, Eastern European countries from the former Soviet Union experienced severe health and mortality crises during the 1990s, when political and economic reforms led to a serious deterioration of public healthcare and welfare provisions, as well as to economic shocks characterized by a surge in economic uncertainty, poverty and unemployment, and declining incomes. Mortality jumped up especially among men, with a large increase in the number of deaths from preventable external causes, including suicides, alcohol consumption and poisoning, and traffic accidents (see Leon et al. 1997; Meslé 2004; Brainerd and Cutler 2005). Because women did not suffer a similar deterioration in mortality, the already large gap in life expectancy between women and men in Russia and other Eastern European countries widened further and reached the highest levels globally in the 1990s. Later on, post-Soviet countries also began experiencing long-term mortality improvements: first in the Baltic countries (Estonia, Latvia and Lithuania) since the late 1990s and then, since about 2005, also in Belarus, Russia and Ukraine. These improvements were mainly attributable to declining mortality from heart disease and falling external, especially alcohol-related, causes of deaths (see, for example, Grigoriev et al. 2014).

Since 2005, mortality rates have been falling across the whole CEE region. However, wide differences between countries have persisted and, with a few exceptions, the ongoing improvements have not eliminated the gap in life expectancy across countries. Only a few countries are unquestionable success stories, with their life expectancy now approaching that in Western Europe (see Figure 16.4): Slovenia has seen a strong mortality convergence, espe-

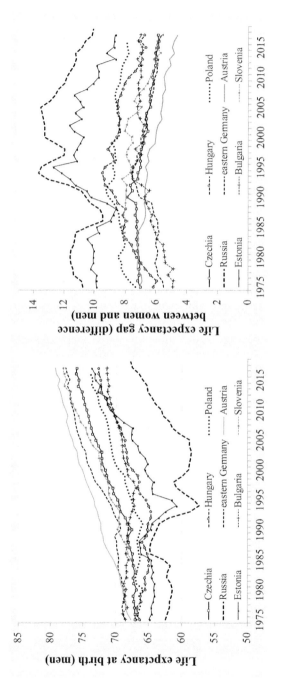

Note: The male–female life expectancy gap depicts the absolute difference in years between the higher life expectancy at birth among women and the lower life expectancy at birth among men.

Sources: Data from Human Mortality Database (2020) and Rosstat (2020).

Figure 16.4   Life expectancy at birth among men and the male–female life expectancy gap (in years) in selected countries and in eastern Germany, 1975–2017

cially among women. The life expectancy gap also narrowed considerably in Czechia. Eastern German mortality has converged to western German mortality after the unification, fuelled in part by the adoption of the West German system of healthcare (Grigoriev and Pechholdová 2017).

Due to uneven mortality developments in the past, countries in Central and Eastern Europe now show much larger differences in their mortality conditions, especially among men, than the countries in other parts in Europe. Among the more developed countries, the ten countries with the lowest life expectancy are all from the CEE region (see IMF 2019). In 2017, male life expectancy in CEE varied by more than ten years, from 67 in Russia and Ukraine to 78 in Slovenia (Human Mortality Database 2020; Eurostat 2020). By contrast, the differences between lowest and highest life expectancy for men across Southern, Western and Northern Europe amounted to three years, ranging from 78.4 in Portugal to 81.6 in Switzerland. Although the male–female gap in life expectancy in Central and Eastern Europe has fallen from its peak in the 1990s, male disadvantage remains much more pronounced compared with other regions in Europe, especially in Eastern Europe and in the Baltic countries, where men are expected to live 9–10 years shorter lives than women, the highest gender gap globally.

What factors account for the persistent mortality rifts across Central and Eastern Europe? It is a similar combination of forces that explained the gap in mortality between the East and the West of Europe in the past, in combination with generally less healthy diets and lifestyles, especially in Eastern Europe. Diseases of the circulatory system have been repeatedly identified as the key factor explaining the differences between countries in the region as well as mortality trends over time (see, for example, Meslé 2004). Standardized death rates from circulatory diseases in all Central European countries except Slovenia still remain much higher than in Austria or the European Union as a whole (see Figure 16.5). They are yet higher in Southeastern Europe and in the Baltic states, especially among men, for whom they surpass the EU average by a factor of two to three. In Bulgaria, standardized male mortality from circulatory system diseases reached 1310 per 100 000 in 2016, three times the EU average of 448. The higher-mortality countries in the region also experience higher mortality from external causes of death among males and diseases associated with an unhealthy lifestyle, including lung cancer (Islami et al. 2015). Some countries, especially Hungary and Czechia, also have high cancer incidence, but this differs widely across the region (Mladovsky et al. 2009). Overall, the CEE region scores high in avoidable mortality; that is, deaths among people below age 75 that could have been prevented through better healthcare and public health interventions (see Eurostat 2019). Avoidable mortality among the EU countries is highest – and with wide gender gaps showing

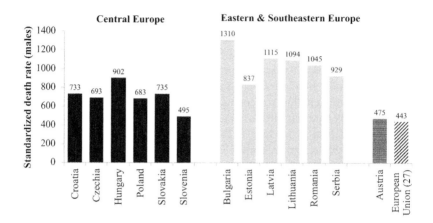

Note: Diseases of the circulatory system include all diseases included in Chapter IX of the WHO International classification of diseases (codes 100 to 199); these include especially cardiovascular and cerebrovascular diseases.
Source: Data from Eurostat (2020, Causes of death statistics, Table hlth_cd_asdr2).

Figure 16.5   Standardized death rate (per 100 000) from diseases of the circulatory system among men in 2016; CEE countries compared with Austria and the European Union

male disadvantage – in the three Baltic countries, Romania, Bulgaria, Hungary and Slovakia (Eurostat 2019).

16.3   INTERNATIONAL MIGRATION AND POPULATION DECLINE SINCE THE 1990s

Migration is the least stable, least predictable and, in terms of data quality and reliability, the most uncertain component of population change. Yet it is of paramount importance. International migration has become the key differentiating demographic factor across Europe, reflecting the geopolitical division of Europe until 1989. Most countries in Central and Eastern Europe have experienced sizeable outmigration since 1990. By contrast, most countries in Southern, Western and Northern Europe have recorded relatively large immigration, including from many countries in Central and Eastern Europe. Migration has become the key factor in the overall population dynamics. Austria, Switzerland, Spain, and some other Western and Southern European countries, saw relatively robust population growth in the last three decades despite having persistently low fertility rates. At the same time, parts of Central and Eastern Europe have been rapidly 'losing' people due to emigration to the more affluent parts of the continent. Population growth in the rich countries in Western Europe was in part made possible by the 'population drain' in the poorer countries in the East.

The East–West migration divide is illustrated in Figure 16.6, which shows that in some CEE countries – including Latvia, Lithuania, Bosnia and Herzegovina, and Moldova – between 16 per cent and 26 per cent of their 1990 population left for good between 1990 and 2017. Another staggering statistic, based on United Nations (UN) estimates, shows that the ratio of population living outside of their country of birth to the number of people in their country of origin reaches very high levels of 22–50 per cent in eight countries from Southeastern and Eastern Europe: Bosnia and Herzegovina, Albania, Kosovo, North Macedonia, Moldova, Lithuania, Croatia and Bulgaria. In some countries, including Albania, this share increased from very low levels in 1990. In the extreme case of Bosnia and Herzegovina, the ratio of 50 per cent implies that among the people born in the country and alive today, every third person actually moved out and lives abroad (see Figure 16.7).

However, the CEE region is also widely differentiated with respect to international migration (see King and Okólski 2019). In particular, Central European countries, including Czechia, Hungary, Poland and Slovenia, show a more positive migration balance and much lower estimated ratios (7–9 per cent) of their population living in other countries. Russia, the largest country in the region, has attracted substantial immigration, especially from the former Soviet Union, which has outpaced the rate of outmigration (see Figure 16.7).

The available data underestimate the full extent of outmigration, as most CEE countries do not have registration systems that would allow them to properly track outmigration of their citizens. As a result, much of the outmigration remains unreported in the countries of origin, leading to occasional adjustments in population and migration data. The gaps in international migration data can be illustrated by comparing the official statistics on outmigration produced by a sending country with comparable data from the receiving countries.[4]

Even these incomplete data give a hint of the huge impact of outmigration. For instance, the cumulated net migration and statistical adjustments of population statistics – usually performed to correct for underreported outmigration – show that the CEE region without Russia lost 11 million people due to emigration from 1990 to 2017. Another dataset, compiled by the UN, showed that the number of migrants from the CEE countries (excluding Russia) who were living abroad increased by 11.6 million between 1990 and 2019, out of the total CEE population of around 200 million in 1990 (see UN 2019c). The demographic and economic impact of outmigration is aggravated by the young age structure of migrants, with migration usually peaking among people in their twenties (see Eurostat 2020). This means that outmigration makes the

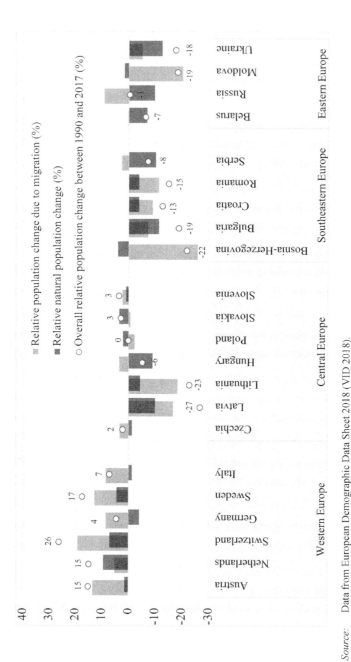

Source: Data from European Demographic Data Sheet 2018 (VID 2018).

Figure 16.6   *Components of population change in selected countries in Europe between 1990 and 2017: natural population growth and estimated net migration (% of the 1990 population)*

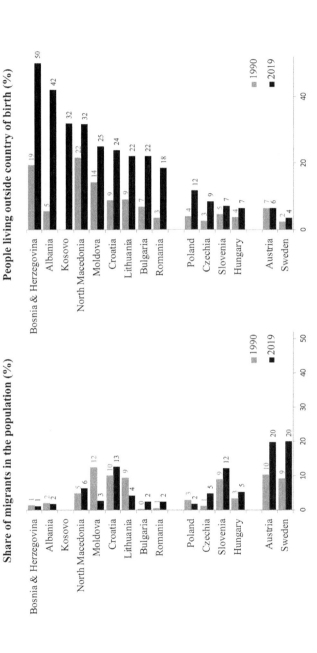

Source: Own computations based on UN International Migrant Stock Data (UN 2019b). Data for Kosovo, unavailable from the UN database, were estimated from Eurostat data on the number of migrants from Kosovo living in the EU countries.

Figure 16.7 *The share of migrants in the population and estimated share of people living outside their country of birth (relative to the country's population); selected CEE countries, Austria and Sweden, 1990 and 2019*

biggest dent in the population structure at peak productive and reproductive ages, contributing to the falling numbers of births as women leaving the country give birth to their children in their new countries of residence.

Why are many CEE countries facing such population slumps due to outmigration? A combination of three broad factors is at play. The first one is the opportunity to leave and work abroad, which had been absent in most countries in the region prior to 1990, with freedom of movement severely curtailed (see King and Okólski 2019). Citizens of countries joining the European Union in several waves of enlargement between 2004 and 2013 gained access to the EU-wide labour market soon thereafter. Citizens of many other CEE countries enjoy visa-free travel to the EU and, in some cases, access to the labour market of some of the Member States. Persistent economic disparities are the second, and arguably the most important, driver of migration from the CEE region (see IMF 2019). This is depicted in Figure 16.8, which shows a close link between GDP level and long-term population change due to migration. A number of countries in Southeastern Europe, as well as Ukraine and Moldova, display a problematic mixture of low economic performance, low wages and unstable employment conditions, but also persistent social and political instability and corruption. As a result, younger generations often feel that there is no long-term future for them in the country (see Lavrič et al. 2019). Violent conflicts and upheavals constitute the third broad force, pushing many people to leave their countries of origin: this happened on a large scale during the wars and conflicts following the break-up of Yugoslavia in 1991, as well as during the more localized conflicts and military interventions pertaining to disputed territories, often linked to specific ethnic groups; for example, in Ukraine (Crimea and elsewhere), Moldova (Transnistria) and Kosovo. Some countries also saw an intensive outmigration of ethnic groups facing long-term discrimination, including the disadvantaged Roma minority, and the mass outmigration of the 'Bulgarian Turks' from Bulgaria to Turkey in the late 1980s.

As the economic gaps between CEE countries remain colossal, large-scale outmigration is likely to continue from the poorer countries in the region. This is also revealed in different surveys on migration intentions and desires. These data reveal that the countries with the most intensive outmigration in the last decades also have the highest share of people who would like to move in the future (Lavrič et al. 2019; Raggl 2019). Gallup's (2019) Potential Net Migration Index indicates that Bosnia and Herzegovina, North Macedonia, Kosovo, Albania and Moldova would potentially lose 30 per cent or more of their current population if the reported desires to emigrate were realized. Not surprisingly, this balance is even worse for the young people aged 15–29, with potential losses amounting to about a half of this population in Bosnia and Herzegovina, North Macedonia, Kosovo and Moldova, and about 40 per cent in Lithuania and Romania (Figure 16.9). The OeNB Euro Survey conducted

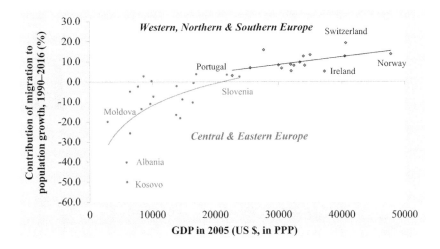

Sources: Estimated net migration: data from European Demographic Data Sheet 2018 (VID 2018); GDP: data from World Bank (2020).

Figure 16.8   *Estimated population growth due to migration in 1990–2016 (% of the 1990 population) and GDP per capita in 2005 (current US dollars, in purchasing power parity) in European countries*

in ten countries in Central and Southeastern Europe shows that an intention to move abroad within the next year is not closely linked to education or skills, but is elevated at young ages (especially below age 30) and among men (see Raggl 2019). More than 10 per cent of respondents aged 25–39 in all but two surveyed countries (Czechia and Poland) intended to migrate in the next year (see Raggl 2019, online appendix, Table 1).

The migration prospects are different in the more affluent Central European countries, which experience a slower outmigration and increasing rates of immigration, especially from the poorer countries in the region, including Ukraine, Moldova, Serbia and Romania (see King and Okólski 2019). Central European countries have experienced rising economic prosperity, higher wages, low unemployment and labour force shortages during the last decade, with immigrants increasingly filling some of the gaps in their labour markets. The most prominent movement was migration from Ukraine to Poland, Czechia and Hungary, which amounted to 350 000–400 000 legal migrants in 2015–2018.[5] In the longer term, Croatia, Czechia, Hungary and Slovenia, and more recently also Poland, have experienced increases in the share of their foreign-born population (see Figure 16.7). However, this trend may be affected

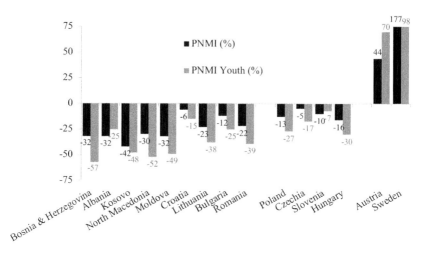

Note: Potential Net Migration Index (PNMI) denotes potential change to the adult population through out- and in-migration, based on expressed desire to move in or out of a given country. PNMI for the youth population denotes potential change for the population aged 15–29. For instance, if all adults in Poland who expressed a desire to leave the country left, and all people in other countries who expressed a desire to move to Poland moved in, the adult Polish population would shrink by 13 per cent and its youth population would contract by 27 per cent.
Source: Data from Gallup (2019).

Figure 16.9   Potential Net Migration Index and Potential Youth Net Migration Index, selected CEE countries, Austria and Sweden, 2015–2017

by the widespread negative public attitudes to immigration and immigrants, especially from the more distant and culturally different countries. A 2019 survey found that in Poland, Hungary and Romania, people worried that both outmigration rates from their country and immigration flows into their country were 'too high' (see Rice-Oxley and Rankin 2019).

16.4   DISCUSSION AND FUTURE OUTLOOK: POPULATION AGEING AND POLICY CHALLENGES

Mass emigration of East German citizens in 1989 was one of the pivotal events marking the fall of the Iron Curtain that divided Europe into two broad political blocs. East Germans were attempting to find alternative ways to move to Western Germany, as their options for legal travel to the 'West' were severely restricted by the government of the German Democratic Republic. In autumn 1989 thousands of East German citizens scaled the wall of the West German Embassy in Prague, and in early October about 13 000 were allowed to travel by train to Western Germany. Within a few months, the walls and barriers that were put up to prevent an escape of the citizens of Central and Eastern European countries from their socialist 'paradise' were crumbling, and the travel restrictions were being lifted fast. The events in autumn 1989 and the new freedom of movement also marked the beginning of a defining demographic trend in the region during the last three decades: the movement of millions of people from the poorer to the richer parts in Europe, contributing to population losses in most countries in Central and Eastern Europe.

Many observers see mass outmigration as the main challenge and an 'existential problem' for the region (see Krastev 2020). In terms of population change, Europe now seems to be split into the 'shrinking East' and the 'growing West', and this split cuts largely along the boundary of the former Iron Curtain. In an ironic twist of history, the former geopolitical division in Europe is now reproduced in the map of population decline across the continent. This cleavage is even visible within Germany, where the geography of long-term population decline still follows the division between East and West Germany between the 1950s and 1990.

Countries in Central and Eastern Europe are especially susceptible to population ageing. The combination of persistent low fertility rates and outmigration among younger people multiplies the demographic challenges for the future, as it dents the number of births, shrinks the population at peak productive and reproductive ages, and accelerates the pace of population ageing. Old-age dependency ratios (OADRs; relating the share of population aged 65+ to that of productive ages, 20–64) were growing fast in the region during the 2010s, catching-up or surpassing the OADRs in Western European countries. Other indicators of ageing and healthy life expectancy also show that the region is lagging behind Western and Northern Europe. The shrinking numbers of births and of people in their twenties and thirties generate a long-term population momentum which implies that even future increases in fertility, or huge falls in outmigration, may not reverse the demographic decline in the near future.

A comprehensive International Monetary Fund (IMF) report (IMF 2019) documents multiple long-term challenges posed by the demographic headwinds that are picking up pace across the region. Interrelated trends foster a vicious cycle of demographic, social and economic decline, with governments unable to sustain the existing welfare arrangements. An ageing population puts pressure on health and social spending that has outpaced the GDP growth. This also means that governments may not have sufficient resources to support younger generations and boost spending on education, families and infrastructure. At the same time, shrinking numbers of people at productive ages are eroding the tax base and government income. Efforts to address this trend by raising taxes may stifle investment and economic growth. In addition, high-skilled emigration leads to serious skills and labour shortages, further reducing economic growth, but also weakening governance. The IMF report suggests that in most countries, even bold reforms would ultimately be 'overwhelmed by population changes'.

Our chapter documents the enormous – and often growing – demographic diversity across the CEE countries. The description of dramatic demographic challenges best fits the poorer and more peripheral countries with weak infrastructure, and in some cases also long-lasting territorial conflicts, where the root causes of demographic problems lie with weak governance and dysfunctional institutions. These include Bosnia and Herzegovina, Kosovo, Moldova and Ukraine. In these countries, possible future turnaround in outmigration is conditioned by deep and sustained social and political reforms and the solutions of regional conflicts. A large share, and at times a majority, of young people in these countries desire to move to another country, suggesting a long-term continuation of migration pressure in the future. By contrast, Central European countries, especially Czechia, Poland and Slovenia, and to a smaller extent Estonia, Hungary and Slovakia, create a very different picture. These countries are the 'winners' of economic and social transformation in the CEE region. They have shared dynamic economic growth and relative prosperity in the last decade; low, but not extreme low, fertility rates; rapidly improving longevity; and relatively low or slowing outmigration. Also, immigration is on the rise, often from the poorer countries in the CEE region, despite the anti-migrant rhetoric adopted by some of the governments. Immigration is fuelled by rising wages, very low unemployment, and the resulting shortages of both skilled and unskilled labour.

If these trends continue, Central European countries are likely to see a long-term shift towards becoming immigration countries, comparable with the more affluent countries in Western, Northern and Southern Europe. With a lag of three to four decades, Central European countries may follow in the footsteps of Southern European countries, which experienced a transformation from being countries of emigration to becoming important immigration destinations in the 1980s–1990s (see King 2000). This would help Central European countries to escape the trap of demographic and economic downturn outlined above. These divergent population outlooks in Central and Eastern Europe are also reflected in population projections (see Figure 16.10). The JRC/CEPAM scenarios envision a continuation of rapid population shrinking in Bosnia and Herzegovina, Bulgaria and Romania; more moderate population declines in Czechia and Hungary; and a stable population in Slovenia. As the scenarios with zero migration show, migration plays an important role in these projected trends. If more countries experience a reversal towards larger

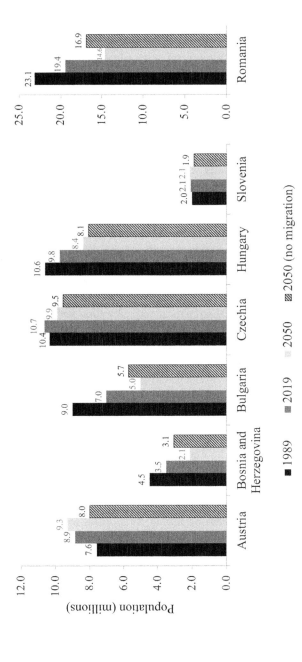

Source: Population in 1990 and 2019: data from Eurostat (2020). Projected population in 2050: data from Joint Research Centre (European Commission) / CEPAM 2019. The main projection for 2050 is based on CEPAM SSP2 Medium scenario; the zero migration projection is based on CEPAM SSP2 Zero Migration scenario.

Figure 16.10   *Observed (1990 and 2019) and projected (2050) population (millions) in selected countries in Central and Eastern Europe and in Austria*

immigration in the future, the expected population declines may be moderated or even reversed.

However, reversing migration trends alone will not be sufficient to address the many challenges that CEE countries will face in the coming decades. Family policies, which have been at the forefront of government attention during the last decade, should focus more on supporting a combination of motherhood and paid employment, including childcare provision for children below age 3 (see Sobotka et al. 2019). As many more women than in the past complete tertiary education, the group of highly educated women with stronger career aspirations will drive the future fertility trends, and family policies should better address their needs and expectations. Countries need to develop effective migration policies supporting return migration, housing provision and employment of returning migrants, as well as attracting new migrants with appropriate skills and education (see IMF 2019). Governments should improve conditions for younger and better-qualified people which would motivate them to stay and thrive in the country. Numerous adjustments need to be enacted with respect to employment and labour market policies. There is huge untapped labour market potential in women and elderly workers. Lutz et al. (2019) show that adjustments in labour force participation have a strong potential to slow down or even ameliorate the impact of population ageing on labour force size. Finally, the shrinking numbers of young people create an opportunity to improve their access to high-quality education and training, nurturing the human capital of future generations, and providing a lasting boost to productivity and economic performance. As highly educated women and men have the highest labour force participation of all groups, the shift towards a more-educated population will also strengthen the labour force (see Lutz et al. 2019).

NOTES

1. This chapter is based on research by Tomáš Sobotka. The main input for this chapter is also by Tomáš Sobotka.
2. Often, the term 'Central, Eastern and Southeastern Europe' (CESEE) is used for the same group of countries.
3. In Romania, the estimate of the 'usually resident population' was 19.6 million in 2017, whereas the 'permanent resident population' in 2018 was by 2.6 million higher, at 22.2 million, as it included all Romanian citizens who have retained resident status in the country despite actually living abroad (NIS 2019).
4. For instance, an analysis of the data for the receiving countries found that in 2012–2015 at least 100 000 Hungarian citizens were moving to other European countries each year, whereas the official data by the Hungarian Central Statistical Office showed only 13 000 to 33 000 citizens outmigrating annually (Gödri 2019).
5. According to Eurostat data, in 2015–2018 the flow of immigrants born in Ukraine reached 43 000 to Czechia and 35 000 to Hungary. The migration from

Ukraine to Poland reached 188 000 in 2015–2017 according to the Organisation for Economic Co-operation and Development (OECD) International Migration Database (OECD 2020), with the 2018 data likely to be yet higher, as also suggested by the high numbers of work permits for Ukrainian workers in Poland (Jaroszewicz 2018).

REFERENCES

Aburto, J.M. and A. van Raalte (2018), 'Lifespan Dispersion in Times of Life Expectancy Fluctuation: The Case of Central and Eastern Europe', *Demography* 55 (6), 2071–2096.

Biin, H. (2017), 'Estonia: Reform of the Parental Leave and Benefit System to Better Reconcile Work and Family Life. European Commission', *ESPN Flash Report* 2017/62, July.

Billingsley, S. (2010), 'The Post-Communist Fertility Puzzle', *Population Research and Policy Review* 29 (2), 193–231.

Bobak, M. and M. Marmot (1996), 'East–West Mortality Divide and its Potential Explanations: Proposed Research Agenda', *BMJ* 312 (7028), 421–425.

Bongaarts, J. and G. Feeney (1998), 'On the Quantum and Tempo of Fertility', *Population and Development Review* 24 (2), 271–291.

Brainerd, E. and D.M. Cutler (2005), 'Autopsy on an Empire: Understanding Mortality in Russia and the Former Soviet Union', *Journal of Economic Perspectives* 19, 107–130.

CFE database (2020), Cohort Fertility and Education database, available at www.cfe -database.org (accessed on 24 February 2020).

Cockerham, W.C. (1997), 'The Social Determinants of the Decline of Life Expectancy in Russia and Eastern Europe: A Lifestyle Explanation', *Journal of Health and Social Behavior* 38 (2), 117–130.

Conrad, C., M. Lechner and W. Werner (1996), 'East German Fertility after Unification: Crisis or Adaptation?', *Population and Development Review* 22 (2), 331–358.

Eurostat (2018), 'Bye Bye Parents: When do Young Europeans Flee the Nest?', available at https://ec.europa.eu/eurostat/web/products-eurostat-news/-/EDN-20180515-1 (accessed February 2020).

Eurostat (2019), 'Preventable and Treatable Mortality Statistics. Online Publication', available at https://ec.europa.eu/eurostat/statistics-explained/index.php/Preventable _and_treatable_mortality_statistics#Leading_causes_of_avoidable_deaths (data from July 2019, accessed February 2020).

Eurostat (2020), 'Data on Births, Fertility Rates, Mortality, Life Expectancy, Causes of Deaths, and Migration Accessed', available at https://ec.europa.eu/eurostat/data/ database (accessed February 2020).

Frejka, T. and S. Gietel-Basten (2016), 'Fertility and Family Policies in Central and Eastern Europe after 1990', *Comparative Population Studies* 41 (1), 3–56.

Gallup (2019), 'Potential Net Migration Index', Gallup, available at https://news.gallup .com/migration/interactive.aspx.

Gödri, I. (2019), 'International Migration', in J. Monostori, P. Őri and Z. Spéder (eds), *Demographic Portrait of Hungary 2018*, Budapest: Hungarian Demographic Research Institute, 237–272.

Goldstein, J.R. and M. Kreyenfeld (2011), 'Has East Germany Overtaken West Germany? Recent Trends in Order-Specific Fertility', *Population and Development Review* 37 (3), 453–472.

Grigoriev, P., F. Meslé, V.M. Shkolnikov, E. Andreev, A. Fihel, M. Pechholdová and J. Vallin (2014), 'The Recent Mortality Decline in Russia: Beginning of the Cardiovascular Revolution?', *Population and Development Review* 40 (1), 107–129.

Grigoriev, P. and M. Pechholdová (2017), 'Health Convergence between East and West Germany as Reflected in Long-Term Cause-Specific Mortality Trends: To What Extent was it Due to Reunification?', *European Journal of Population* 33 (5), 701–731.

Härkönen, J., S. Billingsley and M. Hornung (2020), 'Divorce Trends in Seven Countries over the Long Transition from State Socialism: 1981–2004', in D. Mortelmans (ed.), *Divorce in Europe*, Cham: Springer, 63–89.

Human Fertility Database (2020), Max Planck Institute for Demographic Research (Germany) and Vienna Institute of Demography (Austria), available at www.humanfertility.org (accessed in February 2020).

Human Mortality Database (2020), 'Data on Life Expectancy at Birth', University of California, Berkeley (USA), and Max Planck Institute for Demographic Research (Germany), available at www.mortality.org (accessed on 24 February 2020).

IMF (2019), 'Demographic Headwinds in Central and Eastern Europe', Washington, DC: International Monetary Fund, European Departmental Paper Series No. 19.

Islami, F., L.A. Torre and A. Jemal (2015), 'Global Trends of Lung Cancer Mortality and Smoking Prevalence', *Translational Lung Cancer Research* 4 (4), 327.

Jaroszewicz, M. (2018), 'Migration from Ukraine to Poland: The Trend Stabilizes', OSW Centre for eastern Studies Report 2018-10-17, available at https://www.osw.waw.pl/en/publikacje/osw-report/2018-10-17/migration-ukraine-to-poland.

King, R. (2000), 'Southern Europe in the Changing Global Map of Migration. In Eldorado or Fortress?', in R. King, G. Lazaridis and C. Tsardanidis (eds), *Migration in Southern Europe*, London: Palgrave Macmillan, 3–26.

King, R. and M. Okólski (2019), 'Diverse, Fragile and Fragmented: The New Map of European Migration', *Central and Eastern European Migration Review* 8 (1), 9–32.

Kohler, H.-P., F.C. Billari and J.A. Ortega (2002), 'The Emergence of Lowest-Low Fertility in Europe during the 1990s', *Population and Development Review* 28 (4), 641–680.

Krastev, I. (2020), 'Depopulation is Eastern Europe's Biggest Problem', *Financial Times*, 27 January 2020, available at https://www.ft.com/content/c5d3e0ae-36eb-11ea-ac3c-f68c10993b04.

Lavrič, M., S. Tomanović and S. Jusić (2019), 'Youth Study Southeast Europe 2018/2019', Berlin: Friedrich-Ebert-Stiftung.

Leon, D.A., L. Chenet, V.M. Shkolnikov, S. Zakharov, J. Shapiro, G. Rakhmanova, et al. (1997), 'Huge Variation in Russian Mortality Rates 1984–94: Artefact, Alcohol, or What?', *Lancet* 350 (9075), 383–388.

Lesthaeghe, R. (2010), 'The Unfolding Story of the Second Demographic Transition', *Population and Development Review* 36 (2), 211–251.

Lutz, W., G. Amran, A. Bélanger, A. Conte, N. Gailey, D. Ghio, et al. (2019), 'Demographic Scenarios for the EU – Migration, Population and Education', Luxembourg: European Commission Publications Office.

Mackenbach, J.P., M. Karanikolos, J. Lopez Bernal and M. Mckee (2015), 'Why did Life Expectancy in Central and Eastern Europe Suddenly Improve in the 1990s?

An Analysis by Cause of Death', *Scandinavian Journal of Public Health* 43 (8), 796–801.

Meslé, F. (2004), 'Mortality in Central and Eastern Europe: Long-Term Trends and Recent Upturns', *Demographic Research* 2, 45–70.

Meslé, F. and J. Vallin (2002), 'Mortality in Europe: The Divergence between East and West', *Population* 57 (1), 157–197.

Mladovsky, P., S. Allin and C. Masseria (2009), 'Health in the European Union: Trends and Analysis', WHO Regional Office Europe, Observatory Study Series No. 19.

NIS (2019), *Romanian Statistical Yearbook 2019*, Bucharest: National Institute of Statistics.

OECD (2020), 'International Migration Database. Inflows of Foreign Nationals by Nationality', Paris: OECD, available at https://stats.oecd.org/Index.aspx ?DataSetCode=MIG.

Penina, O., D. Jdanov and P. Grigoriev (2015), 'Producing Reliable Mortality Estimates in the Context of Distorted Population Statistics: The Case of Moldova', MPIDR Working Paper WP-2015-011, 35.

Pension Fund of the Russian Federation (2020), 'Maternity (Family) Capital. Summary Information', available at http://www.pfrf.ru/en/matcap (accessed February 2020).

Perelli-Harris, B. (2005), 'The Path to Lowest-Low Fertility in Ukraine', *Population Studies* 59 (1), 55–70.

Perelli-Harris, B., M. Kreyenfeld, W. Sigle-Rushton, R. Keizer, T. Lappegård, A. Jasilioniene, et al. (2012), 'Changes in Union Status during the Transition to Parenthood in Eleven European Countries, 1970s to early 2000s', *Population Studies* 66 (2), 167–182.

Pew Research Center (2018), 'Eastern and Western Europeans Differ on Importance of Religion, Views of Minorities, and Key Social Issues', Pew Research Center, 29 October, available at https://www.pewforum.org/2018/10/29/eastern-and-western -europeans-differ-on-importance-of-religion-views-of-minorities-and-key-social -issues/.

Philipov, D. (2003), 'Fertility in Times of Discontinuous Societal Change', in I. Kotowska and J. Jóźwiak (eds), *Population of Central and Eastern Europe: Challenges and Opportunities*, Warsaw: Statistical Publishing Establishment, 665–689.

Philipov, D., Z. Spéder and F.C. Billari (2006), 'Soon, Later, or Ever? The Impact of Anomie and Social Capital on Fertility Intentions in Bulgaria (2002) and Hungary (2001)', *Population Studies*, 60 (3), 289–308.

Puur, A. and M. Klesment (2011), 'Signs of a Stable or Provisional Increase in Fertility? Reflections on Developments in Estonia', *Demográfia, English Edition*, 54 (5), 31–55.

Puur, A., L. Rahnu, A. Maslauskaite, V. Stankuniene and S. Zakharov (2012), 'Transformation of Partnership Formation in Eastern Europe: The Legacy of the Past Demographic Divide', *Journal of Comparative Family Studies* 43 (3), 389–417.

Raggl, A.K. (2019), 'Migration Intentions in CESEE: Sociodemographic Profiles of Prospective Emigrants and their Motives for Moving', *Focus on European Economic Integration* Q1/19, 49–67.

Rice-Oxley, M. and J. Rankin (2019), 'Europe's South and East Worry More about Emigration than Immigration – Poll', *Guardian*, 1 April, available at https://www .theguardian.com/world/2019/apr/01/europe-south-and-east-worry-more-about -emigration-than-immigration-poll.

Rosstat (2020), 'Data on Life Expectancy at Birth in Russia, 2014–2018', Russian Federal State Statistics Service, available at https://gks.ru/folder/12781 (accessed on 23 February 2020).

Sobotka, T. (2008), 'The Diverse Faces of the Second Demographic Transition in Europe', *Demographic Research*, Special Collection 7, 19 (8), 171–224.

Sobotka, T. (2011), 'Fertility in Central and Eastern Europe after 1989: Collapse and Gradual Recovery', *Historical Social Research* 36 (2), 246–296.

Sobotka, T. (2016), 'Birth Control, Reproduction, and Family under State Socialism in Central and Eastern Europe', in L. Niethammer and S. Satjukow (eds), *Gender Relations and Birth Control in the Age of the 'Pill'*, Göttingen: Wallstein Verlag, 87–116.

Sobotka, T. and É. Beaujouan (2014), 'Two is Best? The Persistence of a Two-Child Family Ideal in Europe', *Population and Development Review* 40 (3), 391–419.

Sobotka, T., É. Beaujouan and Z. Brzozowska (2017), 'Reversals, Diminishing Differentials, or Stable Patterns? Long-Term Trends in Educational Gradients in Fertility across the Developed Countries', Paper presented at XVIII IUSSP International Population Conference, Cape Town, 31 October.

Sobotka, T., A. Matysiak and Z. Brzozowska (2019), 'Policy Responses to Low Fertility: How Effective Are They?', New York: UNFPA, Working Paper No. 1, May, Technical Division Working Paper Series, Population & Development Branch, available at www.unfpa.org/publications/policy-responses-low-fertility-how-effective-are-they.

Statistisches Bundesamt (2017),'Kinderlosigkeit, Geburten und Familien. Ergebnisse des Mikrozensus 2016', Wiesbaden: Statistisches Bundesamt (Destatis).

Szabó, L., I. Kiss, L. Šprocha and Z. Spéder (2017), 'Fertility of Minorities in Eastern and Central European Countries: Similarities or Dissimilarities?', Paper presented at the conference on 'The Fertility of Migrants and Minorities', Hannover, 6–8 February.

UN (2019a), 'World Population Prospects 2019', New York: United Nations, Department of Economic and Social Affairs Population Dynamics, available at https://population.un.org/wpp/.

UN (2019b), 'Human Development Reports 2019', Table 1: Human Development Index and its Components, United Nations Development Programme, available at http://hdr.undp.org/en/content/table-1-human-development-index-and-its-components-1.

UN (2019c), 'International Migrant Stock 2019' (United Nations database, POP/DB/MIG/Stock/Rev.2019), United Nations, Department of Economic and Social Affairs, Population Division, available at https://www.un.org/en/development/desa/population/migration/data/estimates2/estimates19.asp.

VID (2018), 'European Demographic Datasheet 2018', Vienna Institute of Demography (VID) and International Institute for Applied Systems Analysis (IIASA), Wittgenstein Centre (IIASA, VID/OEAW, WU), Vienna, available at www.populationeurope.org.

World Bank (2020), 'International Comparison Program Database', available at https://data.worldbank.org/indicator/NY.GDP.PCAP.PP.CD and https://data.worldbank.org/indicator/NY.GDP.PCAP.CD.

17. The demographic challenge of Eastern Europe and potential policy options

Mario Holzner

Eastern Europe's economic convergence toward the West has come at a high cost. Outward migration to Western Europe was a key driver, and negative demographic trends are increasingly becoming a major socio-economic challenge. Population projections foresee a drop in the number of inhabitants of Eastern European countries of about 5–15 per cent over the next three decades. The available policy options to counter these demographic trends include: increasing productivity, scaling up immigration, raising activity rates or elevating fertility rates. However, the room for more female employment is rather limited in the region; the level of labour-saving robotization is still quite low, when compared to Western Europe; and most countries in the region are not well prepared for the digital economy. Successfully implementing new policies to counter adverse demographic trends also depends on the functioning of institutions. Unfortunately, recent years have seen a rise of authoritarianism and state capture in Eastern Europe, with an anti-immigration stance and negative implications for institutional quality.

17.1 WHAT HAS HAPPENED SO FAR

In 2019, the world celebrated the 30-year anniversary of the fall of the Berlin Wall. Eastern Europe has changed dramatically since 1989. While in many ways it has been a change for the better, the path of transition has been hard and some of the outcomes are less positive (see Grieveson et al. 2019a). The initial phase of the 1990s was marked by an unprecedented and often prolonged breakdown of the economy in the wake of so-called 'shock therapy'. For most countries it was a lost decade, and only in the following boom years of the early 2000s did they regain the level of the (already low) 1989 economic activity. Strong economic growth came to an end with the outbreak of the global financial crisis, and from 2009 on, the catch-up process was much less impressive. Nevertheless, convergence has continued in recent years.

Against the benchmark of the European technology leader, Eastern European economies managed to catch up by an equivalent of about a quarter of the

German gross domestic product (GDP) per capita at purchasing power parities between 1991 and 2018 (see wiiw Annual Database n.d.). As of 2018, the average GDP level in the region was at about half that of Germany. Czechia (the Czech Republic) and Slovenia have almost reached three-quarters of the German level. At the opposite end of the scale, Ukraine, Moldova and Kosovo have not yet reached one-quarter of the German level of economic activity. As the only country of the region, Ukraine has even regressed by 11 percentage points over the whole period versus Germany. Thus, a certain (South-)East–(North-)West gap can be found within Eastern Europe.

However, most countries' economic convergence toward the West has come at a high cost. According to United Nations (UN) data, between 1989 and 2019 the population figures in the Baltics and the Balkans fell by 15–30 per cent. Outward migration to Western Europe was a key driver. In some cases, this was also due to wars. A more general trend throughout Eastern Europe was a sharp decline in birth rates after 1989, reflecting a sharp rise in economic insecurity. Throughout the region, a counteracting trend was the increased life expectancy at birth (World Bank data) over the last three decades. Although, during the same period, global advances in life expectancy were much more impressive, Eastern Europe is among the most rapidly ageing regions of the world. Demographic trends are increasingly becoming a major socio-economic challenge.

17.2   THE DEMOGRAPHIC CHALLENGE

Following a history of mass emigration, particularly of young families, and declining fertility, heavy population losses are forecast for the decades to come. The UN population projections (in their medium fertility variant) foresee a drop in the number of inhabitants of Eastern European countries of about 5–15 per cent (see Figure 17.1) over the next three decades. Bulgaria and Latvia might lose even more than 20 per cent. By comparison, in Turkey and Kazakhstan the population is expected to grow by around a quarter during the same period. If one were to look at the working-age population, the decline in numbers would be even stronger in Eastern Europe.

If the trend of shrinking (working-age) populations and population ageing continues, the functioning of the labour market is at risk as labour shortages are increasingly more likely to emerge, which might be an obstacle to further economic growth and thus catching-up. Simulation exercises by Leitner and Stehrer (2019a) demonstrate that in many European Union (EU) Member States in Eastern Europe, labour supply-side constraints would materialize in the mid-2020s, when labour demand is estimated to equal labour supply (see Figure 17.2). For Czechia, Lithuania and Poland, the estimates even indicate

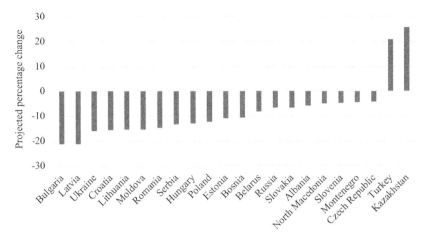

Note: Medium fertility variant.
Source: United Nations.

Figure 17.1   *United Nations population projections between 2015 and*
                  2045

full employment in 2021. Bulgaria, Slovenia, Estonia, Hungary and Slovakia
are expected to follow suit over the next few years.

17.3   POTENTIAL POLICY OPTIONS

Grieveson et al. (2019b) conclude that demographic trends are an enormous
challenge for the region's policymakers, and will become even more so in the
future. The available policy options to counter these trends include: increasing productivity, scaling-up immigration, raising activity rates or elevating
fertility rates. However, even if all of these policies are pursued successfully,
it is questionable whether they will be able to fundamentally alter the picture.
Moreover, many of these options are difficult to implement.

For instance, apart from the Balkans, the room for more female employment
is rather limited in the region. Most Eastern European societies are close to or
far above the average EU female employment rate of around 48 per cent (see
Figure 17.3). Elevating fertility rates is extremely difficult and might only
show a positive effect after decades. Also, (non-European) immigration is,
at least currently, not a politically feasible option in most of Eastern Europe.
Thus, productivity-increasing measures might be the most realistic option for
tackling the demographic challenge.

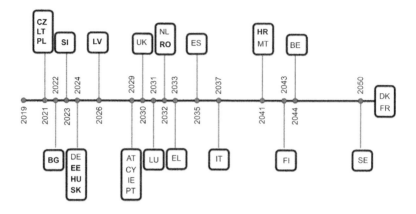

Note: Country codes: AT = Austria, BE = Belgium, BG = Bulgaria, CZ = Czechia, CY = Cyprus, DE = Germany, DK = Denmark, EE = Estonia, EL = Greece, ES = Spain, FI = Finland, FR = France, HR = Croatia, HU = Hungary, IE = Ireland, IT = Italy, LT = Lithuania, LU = Luxembourg, LV = Latvia, MT = Malta, NL = Netherlands, PL = Poland, PT = Portugal, RO = Romania, SE = Sweden, SI = Slovenia, SK = Slovakia, UK = United Kingdom.
Source: Grieveson et al. (2019b).

Figure 17.2   *Estimated year in which labour demand will become equal to supply*

Leitner and Stehrer (2019b) show that the hypothetical increase of labour productivity growth which would be required to keep real GDP growth in the EU at its current level, despite the projected reduction in the workforce, is about one percentage point higher than the actual growth rates. This implies that the current labour productivity growth rate in the EU needs to more than double. Though robots have been exhibiting a positive impact on labour productivity growth, their impact is not strong enough to close the gap.

Intensified robotization would be a strategy to strengthen productivity growth in Eastern Europe as well. Recent dynamics, in fact, show a strong increase in the use of industrial robots, particularly in the important automotive sector, in the eastern parts of the EU (see Figure 17.4). However, the levels of robots per employed persons are still quite low when compared to Western Europe. Among the countries in the region only Slovenia has similar levels to those of Austria or Germany, of about 1100 industrial robots per 10 000 persons employed in the automotive industry.

It is important to note that most of the export-oriented industry in Eastern Europe, such as the automotive industry, was established as foreign direct

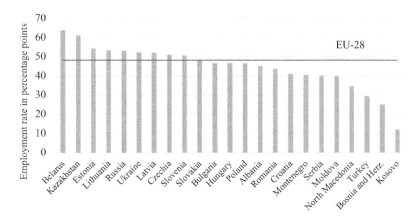

Note: Belarus age: 15–74; Kosovo age: 15–64.
Source: Eurostat, wiiw and World Bank SEE Jobs Gateway Database.

*Figure 17.3   Employment rate (Labour Force Survey) of women aged 15
years and above, 2018*

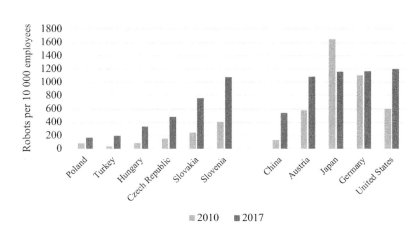

Source: International Federation of Robotics.

*Figure 17.4   Estimated number of multipurpose industrial robots per
10 000 persons employed in the automotive industry*

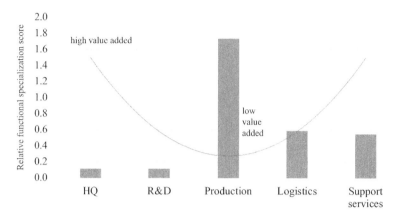

Relative functional specialization score

Notes: A relative functional specialization of above 1 in any value chain function indicates that a particular country is more often used as the greenfield FDI location for that value chain function than the world average would suggest. HQ = headquarters; R&D = research and development.
Source: fDi Markets database, wiiw calculations.

Figure 17.5   Relative functional specialization of Serbian greenfield FDI projects, average over 2003–2015

investment (FDI) by multinational enterprises. These typically outsourced the lower value added production functions (see, for instance, the relative functional specialization of greenfield FDI in Serbia in Figure 17.5). Here, robotization might be a threat to the main source of FDI-related value added, even if it is only value added in the lower part of the value chain's so-called 'smile curve'. Also, re-sourcing of fabrication back to high-income countries is increasingly an issue and a potential threat for Eastern Europe.

Clearly, policies that aim at attracting investment in higher value added segments of the global value chains would also be helpful in countering further emigration from Eastern Europe. However, it is fairly difficult to supply the type of (public) infrastructure necessary to attract investment related to, for example, headquarters or research and development functions. Thus, alternatively, the digital economy might be an area of specialization and an opportunity for catch-up for Eastern Europe, given the long tradition of good schooling in science, technology, engineering and mathematics (STEM) disciplines.

However, overall, the countries are prepared for the digital economy to varying degrees. The World Economic Forum's Networked Readiness Index (see Figure 17.6) is an attempt to capture the multitude of factors important for

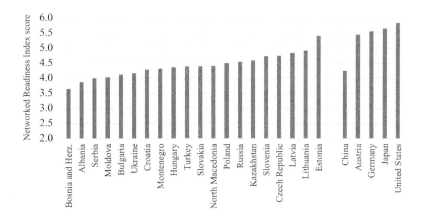

Note: The index assesses countries' indicators including the legal framework around ICT, ICT use by government and firms, availability of latest technologies and venture capital, tax rate on profits, ease of starting a business, education level, electricity, mobile and broadband coverage, innovation capacity, and knowledge-intensive jobs as share of workforce.
Source: World Economic Forum.

Figure 17.6   Networked Readiness Index, 2016

the digital world. It measures how well an economy is using information and communications technologies (ICT) to boost competitiveness and well-being.

Among the countries in Eastern Europe, Estonia is the only one that is prepared for the digital economy in a way comparable with the technological leaders, such as the United States, Japan or Germany. Others from the region clearly lag behind, but variation in networked readiness is vast and some countries might be able to implement policies that will help them to catch up and use the potential opportunities of the digital economy.

However, successfully implementing new policies also depends on the functioning of institutions. Unfortunately, recent years have seen a rise of authoritarianism and state capture in Eastern Europe, with negative implications for institutional quality. The Varieties of Democracy's (V-Dem) Electoral Democracy Index (see Figure 17.7) captures the electoral, liberal, participatory, deliberative and egalitarian principles of democracy; and while these mostly improved throughout Eastern Europe during the 1990s and early 2000s, the situation deteriorated after the outbreak of the global financial crisis everywhere in the region.

In this respect it is interesting to note that it is believed that the process of ageing, declining birth rates and massive outmigration have further contributed

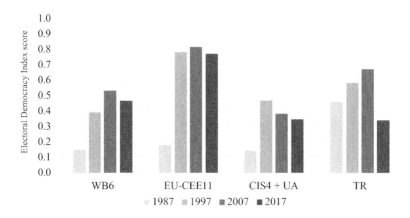

Note: Five high-level principles of democracy: electoral, liberal, participatory, deliberative and egalitarian principles are measured. WB6 = Western Balkans, that is Albania, Bosnia and Herzegovina, Kosovo, Montenegro, North Macedonia and Serbia; EU-CEE11 = EU Member States from Central and Eastern Europe (CEE), namely Bulgaria, Croatia, Czechia, Estonia, Hungary, Latvia, Lithuania, Poland, Romania, Slovakia and Slovenia; CIS4+UA = four geographically (at least partly) European Commonwealth of Independent States (CIS) countries and Ukraine, specifically Belarus, Kazakhstan, Moldova, Russia and Ukraine; TR = Turkey.
Source: Varieties of Democracy (V-Dem).

Figure 17.7   V-Dem Electoral Democracy Index, overall score over time

to illiberalism in the region (see Krastev and Holmes 2018). Accordingly, this largely unspoken preoccupation with demographic collapse manifests itself as a fear that the arrival of unassimilable foreigners might dilute national identities and weaken national cohesion. However, anecdotal evidence suggests that Hungary, for instance, after first allowing immigration of a Ukrainian and Serbian workforce, has more recently started to organize the arrival of workers from as far away as Mongolia and Vietnam. The contradiction between the government's anti-immigration stance and the growing number of permits granted to immigrants reveals the dilemma that large parts of Eastern Europe find themselves in.

17.4   CONCLUSIONS

Eastern Europe has changed dramatically since the fall of the Berlin Wall. While in many ways it has been a change for the better, the path of transition has been hard, and some of the outcomes are less positive. Most countries' economic convergence toward the West has come at a high cost. Outward migration to Western Europe has been a key driver, and negative demographic trends are increasingly becoming a major socio-economic challenge. The UN population projections (in their medium fertility variant) foresee a drop in the number of inhabitants of Eastern European countries of about 5–15 per cent over the next three decades. In many EU Member States in Eastern Europe, labour supply-side constraints are expected to materialize in the mid-2020s, when labour demand is estimated to equal labour supply.

The available policy options to counter these demographic trends include: increasing productivity, scaling up immigration, raising activity rates or elevating fertility rates. However, even if all of these policies are pursued successfully, it is questionable whether they will be able to fundamentally alter the picture. Moreover, many of these options are difficult to implement. The room for more female employment is rather limited in the region; most Eastern European societies are close to or far above the average EU female employment rate. Intensified robotization would be a labour-saving strategy to strengthen productivity growth in Eastern Europe. Recent dynamics show a strong increase in the use of industrial robots, particularly in the important automotive sector, in the Eastern parts of the EU. However, the levels of robots per employed persons are still quite low when compared to Western Europe.

Policies that aim at attracting investment in higher value added segments of the global value chains would also be helpful in countering further emigration from Eastern Europe. The digital economy might be another area of specialization and an opportunity for Eastern Europe to catch up. Among the countries in Eastern Europe, Estonia is currently the only one that is prepared for the digital economy in a way comparable with the global technological leaders. Others from the region clearly lag behind, but might be able to implement policies that help them to catch up and use the potential opportunities of the digital economy. However, successfully implementing new policies also depends on the functioning of institutions. Unfortunately, recent years have seen a rise of authoritarianism and state capture in Eastern Europe, with negative implications for institutional quality. This process may itself have been triggered by the decades of outward migration. In this respect it is interesting to note that recently we have seen a reversal of migration flows in the western parts of Eastern Europe.

REFERENCES

Grieveson, R., V. Gligorov, P. Havlik, G. Hunya, O. Pindyuk, L. Podkaminer, et al. (2019a), 'Looking Back, Looking Forward: Central and Eastern Europe 30 Years After the Fall of the Berlin Wall', wiiw Essays and Occasional Papers No. 4, November.

Grieveson, R., S. Leitner and R. Stehrer (2019b), 'EU Faces a Tough Demographic Reckoning', wiiw Policy Note/Policy Report No. 30, June.

Krastev, I. and S. Holmes (2018), 'Explaining Eastern Europe: Imitation and Its Discontents', *Journal of Democracy*, 29 (3), 117–128.
Leitner, S. and R. Stehrer (2019a), 'Demographic Challenges for Labour Supply and Growth', wiiw Research Report No. 439, March.
Leitner, S. and R. Stehrer (2019b), 'The Automatisation Challenge Meets the Demographic Challenge: In Need of Higher Productivity Growth', wiiw Working Paper No. 171, October.
wiiw Annual Database (n.d.), available at https://data.wiiw.ac.at/annual-database.html (accessed on 27 October 2019).

Index